D0428672

THE WEALTH OF OCEANS

The Wealth

of Oceans

MICHAEL WEBER

AND

JUDITH GRADWOHL

W·W·NORTON & COMPANY
New York   London

The text of this book is composed in Sabon
with the display set in Sabon italic.
Composition and manufacturing by The Maple-Vail Book Manufacturing
Group.
Book design by Jacques Chazaud.

Library of Congress Cataloging-in-Publication Data

Weber, Michael (Michael L.)
The wealth of oceans / Michael Weber and Judith Gradwohl.
p.   cm.
Includes bibliographical references and index.
1. Marine resources.   I. Gradwohl, Judith.   II. Title.
GC1015.2.W43   1995
333.71'64—dc20   94-35997

ISBN 0-393-03764-9

W.W. Norton & Company, Inc. 500 Fifth Avenue, New York, N.Y. 10110
W.W. Norton & Company Ltd., 10 Coptic Street, London WC1A 1PU

1 2 3 4 5 6 7 8 9 0

We dedicate this book to
our parents

KATHLEEN and LEO
DORIE and AL

Contents

Preface

≈≈≈≈≈

This book is as much about people as it is about the oceans and their myriad forms of life. It is difficult to say which is more complex and fascinating—people or the oceans. Or which will have the greater influence on the future of the other.

Certainly, the oceans as a body of water will persist well beyond the passing of human civilization. And many fishes and shellfishes, plants and animals of all sorts will avoid extinction at human hands. That is not our chief concern.

Life is rough and brutish for more and more people every day, partly because every day there are more and more people, and partly because we consume more and more. Those of us who live in industrialized societies take some pity on those who don't have it so good as we. The irony is that we don't have it as good as we did or we could.

Compared with the billions and billions of dollars to be made from mining the land or arming the skies or generating riches from riches, the oceans offer relatively little in the way of wealth that conventional accounting can measure. The same was said of tropical forests not so long ago. Now, conservation of tropical forests has become a mainstream objective. We hope that this book will generate the same kind of interest in the oceans. There certainly is no part of the planet where people and earth engage so intensely in so many ways.

The idea for this book arose from discussions that Judy began with friends and associates regarding a follow-up to the very successful Tropical Rainforest exhibition that the Smithsonian Institution had mounted in 1988. Mike had been promoting marine conservation, most recently as Special Assistant to the Director of the National Marine Fisheries Service. Meeting in the underground offices of the Smithsonian's S. Dillon Ripley Center in Washington, D.C., in 1989 and 1990, we and others hatched a plan for elevating concern for the oceans, just as Judy and others had done for tropical rainforests.

In November 1991, the ocean initiative was launched with the National Forum on Ocean Conservation, which was held at the Smithsonian's Museum of Natural History. The 400 participants heard more than 50 speakers describe the challenges and opportunities for ocean conservation in the coming decades. The forum also provided Judy and her staff with material for the "Ocean Planet" traveling exhibition that the Smithsonian Institution opens in April 1995.

Although the Smithsonian's Office of Environmental Awareness published a summary of the discussions at the Ocean Forum, we were convinced that we had to reach a much broader audience with a broader view of the oceans than we had found in our review of the literature. Our goal was to write a book that involved readers in exploring the ways that people view and use the seas. Like many others, we believe that the seas and sea life will take care of themselves if allowed to do so. It is people that concern us first and foremost.

With so many concerns pressing upon people, advocates for this or that conservation issue often have had to generate interest by focusing attention on endangerment of wild places and wild species. As Aldo Leopold said many years ago, the first step in intelligent tinkering is keeping all the parts. We agree. But focusing on keeping all the parts, on preventing extinction and total loss, also has diverted from another legitimate, pressing goal: to restore the abundance that the seas produced not so long ago. We need more than survivors in the seas, for their sake and our own.

Focusing on specific wildlife or habitat or pollution issues also has dissolved the very linkages between land and sea, between economics and exploitation that our daily lives reinforce. We have made a special effort in this book to draw these linkages. For instance, the demand for shrimp in affluent countries has indirectly encouraged the conversion of thousands of square miles of mangrove forests into shrimp ponds in developing countries. In many parts of the world, growing numbers of people are moving to the coast as the economic vitality of inland areas declines.

The greatest opportunity for progress, we believe, lies in ocean conservationists expanding their vision to embrace broader environmental and social concerns. The oceans do not exist apart from land, air, or the aspirations of people. Ocean conservationists can gain an enormous advantage, we believe, by becoming as knowledgeable and concerned about social trends as about the status of fisheries or the effects of sewage on sea-grass beds. Continued isolation from broader conservation and social concerns will unnecessarily reinforce the position of marine conservation at the margin.

This broader view underlies the structure and content of this book. Rather than focusing on the biology or oceanography of the seas, or upon coastal development or pollution, we have sought to explore the linkages among different perspectives on the oceans. If we emphasize anything, it is the relationship between human behavior and the life of the oceans.

ACKNOWLEDGMENTS

In the long course of researching and writing about the oceans, we have benefited greatly from the encouragement and advice of old and new friends, colleagues, and those who have so patiently and resolutely filled in our picture of the oceans over the years. To all of these, we express our gratitude.

As part of a larger initiative on the oceans that the Smithsonian Institution has been pursuing for the last several years, the book has benefited from research in support of the 1991 National Forum on Ocean Conservation and the "Ocean Planet" exhibition. Generous funding from a number of benefactors made the National Forum possible; these include the Smithsonian Institution, the National Oceanic and Atmospheric Administration, the David and Lucile Packard Foundation, SEA (Swim Environmental Awareness Foundation), the W. Alton Jones Foundation, the Stroud Foundation, and the National Fish and Wildlife Foundation. Additional research was enabled by grants from the Geraldine R. Dodge Foundation and National Science Foundation under Grant No. ESI-9254703.

At a critical point, the Curtis and Edith Munson Foundation provided a generous grant that enabled Mike to devote more time to preparation of the manuscript. The Manomet Observatory kindly managed this grant.

We were fortunate in being able to rely upon the scholarship and good sense of many colleagues in providing background research and reviewing drafts of the manuscript. Taking up so wide a range of topics and disciplines has exposed us to making the errors of newcomers. The following people certianly reduced such errors in the final manuscript: Trevor Bain, Susan Boa, Jim Broadus, William M. Eichbaum, John Everett, Don Hinrichsen, Matthew LaMourie, Elizabeth McCance, Leslie Dawson, Kent Mountford, Elliott A. Norse, Lili Sheeline, Patricia Waak, Peter Weber, and John P. Wise. Both Burr Heneman and Mary Paden meticulously reviewed the entire manuscript. Mike benefited from Jon Goldstein's patient tutoring regarding economics.

Although both of us had collected considerable amounts of material for the book before launching into its composition, our research was considerably enriched by information graciously volunteered by colleagues, some of whom no doubt wondered whether the materials they sent would plunge into a black hole or become part of the skein of the book. There are no black holes here. There is a book. Among the many who shared information with us are the following: Jodi Asarch, George Balazs, Rich Batiuk, Blair Bower, Jim Chambers, Richard Condrey, David Cottingham, Robert Costanza, Clif Curtis, Helen Dizikes, Katherine L. Dixon, Ryan Dwight, John Farrington, Christine Gault, Debra Goldstein, Fred Grassle, Greg Stone, Bob Higgins, Maureen Hinkle, John Knauss, Jon Kohl, David Korten, Susan J. Leet, Jim Mead, Beth Milleman, Madeline Nagy, Beth Nalker, Doyle Rice, Clyde Roper, Melissa Sagun, Manoj Shivlani, John R. Twiss, Jr., Usha Varanasi, Ray Visel, Kathleen Weber, Edward Wenk, Jr., Dean Wilkinson, Eric Wing, and George Woodwell. We give our thanks as well to the participants at the National Forum on Ocean Conservation, whose presentations broadened everyone's view of the future. We are grateful to Lucinda Leach for skillful and rapid photo research.

Mike owes a special debt of gratitude to two dedicated public servants, William W. Fox, Jr., and Nancy Foster at the National Marine Fisheries Service. Besides encouragement, they provided inspiring examples of how important thoughtful and experienced people are to government and to conservation.

Since first conceiving the general outlines of this book, we have received encouragement and support from several people, who deserve special mention: Francine Berkowitz, Lester Brown, Paul Ehrlich, C. Wolcott Henry III, Robert S. Hoffmann, Catherine Porter, Scott Robinson, and Jim Wilson gave us critical early support and advice.

From the beginning, we have felt blessed with our publishers. Besides the distinction that a book by Norton carries, we have enjoyed and benefited greatly from the patient guidance and encouragement of Iva Ashner, Hilary Hinzmann, and Daniel Conaway.

Our families have learned once again the risks of living with writers. Besides patiently bearing with recurring cases of writer's block, Mike's wife Frances Spivy-Weber read and commented upon every page of the manuscript at least once. The hours of discussion on the front couch have influenced nearly every page of the book.

Judy's husband Russ Greenberg provided valuable encouragement, advice, and review. He and Cresing Caballero generously took care of matters at home, freeing up writing time. Finally, Judy's son Jeremy did not provide any assistance, but he was a great source of comic relief.

THE WEALTH OF OCEANS

1

*Great Shellfish Bay:
A Parable*

For all at last returns to the sea—to Oceanus,
the ocean river, like the everflowing stream of
time, the beginning and the end.

RACHEL CARSON,
The Sea Around Us

Otsego Lake near Cooperstown, New York, is one of hundreds of
beginnings for the Chesapeake Bay. There, with a spill of water
from Clinton Dam, the Susquehanna River begins a 444-mile
course through the Appalachian Mountains and the rolling hills
of southern Pennsylvania, gathering water from thousands of
streams that branch through the river's 27,000-square-mile watershed. Just above Havre de Grace, Maryland, the solid rock of the
Piedmont gives way to soft deposits of soil and plant debris that
the Susquehanna has deposited over millennia, and the Susquehanna meets the first hints of salty water that enters the bay from
the Atlantic Ocean 200 miles away.

In the upper bay, the Susquehanna's freshwater flood, which
accounts for nearly half the fresh water flowing into the bay, over-
whelms the Atlantic's salt water, even when the river has been
starved by drought. Rains from hurricanes like Agnes in 1972 or
floods from snowmelt and rain as in 1993 can expand the Susquehanna's influence the length of the bay and into the Atlantic
Ocean. Between the extremes of drought and flood, between

Havre de Grace at the head of the bay and Cape Charles at its mouth, fresh water and salt water mix and struggle, creating extraordinarily productive, changeable, and stressful conditions for life in hundreds of forms.

Measured by geologic time, the Chesapeake Bay is a recent, ephemeral form of the lower Susquehanna River valley. Beginning about one million years ago, the valley of the Susquehanna River was alternately submerged and exposed as massive glaciers advanced and retreated across large parts of North America and stored or released water, lowering and raising sea level by hundreds of feet. Twenty thousand years ago, when average temperatures were 20 degrees colder and the sea level was more than 300 feet lower, the Susquehanna River flowed through a high valley of meadows, forests, and freshwater marshes for hundreds of miles more than its present length before reaching the sea. Most of the 19 major rivers and 400 creeks that now flow into the Chesapeake Bay flowed instead into the Susquehanna River. Some rivers, such as the James River, flowed separately to the sea.

As the climate began to warm about 18,000 years ago, the enormous sheets of ice that had moved as far south as the latitude of New York City in the most recent Ice Age began to melt, feeding a rise in sea level that gradually lifted the Pleistocene oceans from their basins. Between 15,000 and 5,000 years ago, the ancient oceans rose about three feet each century and flowed over the shelf of land that extended from the continents, reaching the current mouth of the Chesapeake Bay about 10,000 years ago. About the same time that Egyptians were building the first dikes and canals for irrigation 5,000 years ago, the rate of rise in sea level began slowing and gradually reached an equilibrium with the flow of sediment into the Chesapeake Bay. About 1000 B.C., when the bay ceased growing, its surface covered about 2,200 square miles—twice that if the tidal sections of its rivers are included. The surrounding 64,000 square miles of watershed were almost completely covered by forests. The waters of its rivers flowed cool, clear, and steady.

Life in the bay is greatly influenced by the minerals and other materials that rainfall and snowmelt wash from land and air into the bay's creeks, streams, and rivers. In the tidal parts of the bay's rivers and in fresher waters of the upper bay, phosphorus especially feeds the growth of plants, from microscopic algae that bloom in spring and summer to bottom-growing sea grasses that can form enormous submerged meadows. In saltier waters, nitrogen becomes more important to the growth of the plants that form the basis for life in the bay.

Forests, wetlands, sea-grass beds, striped bass, shad, menhaden, eel, bait fish, oysters, and crab all helped keep the bay's productivity in balance. Besides absorbing some of the nutrients released in the decay of plants, wetlands and forests also stored storm waters, releasing them later and more gradually. The meadows of sea grasses, which once covered the bay's bottom over hundreds of square miles, absorbed nutrients as well, especially during the spring floods, when the land gave up more nutrients than at other times of the year. As the sea grasses died back and decomposed in the fall, they released the nutrients they had stored, leveling the amount of nutrients during the year. By slowing the flow of water, they also captured sediment and debris that would otherwise muddy the water.

The enormous clouds of floating algae that bloomed with pulses of nutrients produced by spring and summer rains were themselves held in check by masses of consumers such as crab larvae and oyster larvae, menhaden come to spawn in the bay, and bait fish such as bay anchovy. Pumping as much as two gallons of water an hour individually, oysters built upon oysters until they formed extensive reefs that taken together could filter a volume of water as large as the entire bay in the space of a few days. As they did so, oysters cleared algae and other plant material from the water and made nutrients available to other bottom dwellers. Fishes such as menhaden grazed in enormous schools and themselves became food for striped bass and other fishes.

MINING THE LAND

The European settlement of the bay's watershed in the 17th century began a long, accelerating process of dissolving linkages and disrupting the productive balance of the bay. Long before overfishing or the discharge of wastes from towns and industries had much effect on the waters and life in the bay, clearing the land for agriculture profoundly altered the relationship between land and water and undermined the ability of the bay to recover from other threats.

As elsewhere on the mid-Atlantic seaboard, tobacco was the first agent of change on the land. Soon after the future husband of Pocahontas, John Rolfe, brought back tobacco seed from the Caribbean and introduced it to the colonists at Jamestown in 1611, settlers began converting forest and marsh into fields of tobacco in Virginia and Maryland. Taking advantage of the Chesapeake Bay's many navigable rivers, tobacco planters exported their crop to a growing market in Europe.

Within a century of its introduction to North America, tobacco began to take its toll on the bay's lands and water. In the late 17th century, visitors to the Chesapeake Bay noted the muddiness of its rivers. By the early 18th century, formerly important ports such as Annapolis found their harbors rendered useless by sediment washed from surrounding tobacco fields. By the mid-19th century, eroded soil filled navigation channels and closed major tobacco ports in Virginia and Maryland. Once begun, the erosion of soil continued after the decline of tobacco. At Joppa Town, one former tobacco port in Maryland, seagoing sailing ships once secured their lines to mooring posts that now are hidden by brush two miles from navigable water.

As economic activities changed in the bay, so too did land uses. After World War II especially, agriculture ceased being the principal agent of change. Instead, as industrial and residential development accelerated in the watershed, farmland and forest gave way increasingly to industrial parks and suburban subdivisions. Between 1950 and 1980, twice as much land was converted to urban and suburban asphalt and concrete as in the previous 340 years. Of the 41 million acres of land in the watershed, 95 percent were forested at the time of European settlement, and much of the balance was coastal or freshwater wetland. Now, forests cover only 60 percent of the watershed, and wetlands have been reduced by half.

Like forests, wetlands are productive regulators between what happens on land and what happens in the bay, absorbing nutrients, capturing sediments, storing storm water, and producing food and shelter. Draining marshes for agriculture, mosquito control, marinas, highway construction, and residential and commercial development has reduced tidal wetlands in Virginia by 42 percent and in Maryland by 73 percent in the last 100 years. As dredging and filling reduced the area of wetlands that could be altered and states began regulating wetland uses, the rate of coastal wetlands loss declined from more than 1,000 acres per year in the 1960s to net losses of less than 100 acres.

The phenomenal economic growth that this transformation of the watershed brought has fundamentally altered the relation between the bay and its watershed. Before agriculture and urban development, peak flows of water from rivers into the bay were 25 to 30 percent less than they are today, and rivers ran 10 to 15 percent higher during drought. Deforested areas now release at least twice as much nitrogen and at least ten times as much phosphorus into rivers, and eventually into the bay.

One cannot understand what has happened to the waters of the Chesapeake Bay without understanding what has happened to its lands.

What Is Water For?

In 1914, the state of Virginia cited health reasons for prohibiting S.J. Watson from selling oysters from the beds in Hampton Creek that he leased from the state. Watson sued, successfully at first. But the state Supreme Court of Appeals reversed Watson's early victory. Its opinion illustrates a widespread view of the time and an unacknowledged principle of everyday life even now:

> The sea is the natural outlet for all the impurities flowing from the land, and the public health demands that our large and rapidly growing seacoast cities should not be obstructed in their use of this outlet, except in the public interest. One great natural office of the sea and of all running waters is to carry off and dissipate, by their perpetual motion and currents, the impurities and offscourings of the land.

In the view of the court, the legislature was the proper place for determining which use of Virginia's waters should take precedence. By not requiring nearby cities to treat their sewage before discharging it, the state legislature had decided to favor use of the waters near Hampton Roads for diluting pollution over their use for producing oysters.

Soon after settlement, the state of Maryland had also encouraged discharge of human and industrial wastes into the bay's rivers, marshes, and the bay itself. As population and industry swelled, however, sewage contaminated sources for drinking water and created a legendary stench that helped travelers determine when they were approaching the bay's principal port at Baltimore. In response to public protests, commissions were convened, hearings were held, and reports were issued, to little effect.

Near the end of the 19th century, a threat to Maryland's oyster fishery raised the pressure on the city of Baltimore to treat its sewage. The threat had little to do with the abundance of oysters. Rather, it had to do with a collapse in the market for oysters that was provoked by the deaths of several Wesleyan University students, who had contracted typhoid fever in October 1893 after eating Maryland oysters.

Another decade passed before the city did anything more than reject recommendations by two more commissions to discharge sewage into the bay. However, in 1904, a fire that devastated much of the city provided an opportunity to install a modern sewer system and, later, to build the first sewage treatment plant for a major U.S. city. When completed in 1912, the facility was the most advanced of its day. Its discharge into Back River stirred little opposition. Gradually, other cities and towns in Maryland, Virginia, and Pennsylvania developed sewer systems that collected domestic and industrial waste before discharging it into the bay's rivers and bays. More often than not, however, the sewage was discharged untreated.

Even as the technology for reducing health risks through sewage treatment advanced in response to the Clean Water Act in the 1970s, other problems associated with sewage became apparent. Human waste is rich in phosphorus and nitrogen, and conventional sewage treatment did little to remove these nutrients. As a result, the more human waste that sewage treatment plants processed, the more nutrients were discharged into the bay. This unwitting but widespread fertilization fed massive growths of floating algae that prevented sunlight from reaching sea-grass beds and then robbed water of oxygen as the algae decomposed. When Hurricane Agnes in 1972 dumped even more organic matter into the bay's waters, submerged plants were completely overwhelmed and died off in most of the bay.

As difficult and expensive as it was, sewage treatment addressed only one source of the pollution pouring into the bay. By the early 1990s, runoff from lands that had been converted to farms, cities, and suburban development accounted for nearly half of the nitrogen entering the bay. Another 11 percent was first released in the exhaust of power plants and automobiles and then fell on the bay as particles or as rain.

Agriculture now contributes nearly half of the phosphorus entering the bay, compared with one-third from sewage treatment plants. Although farm acreage has declined by nearly one-third in the last several decades, the amount of nutrients in runoff from agricultural fields has doubled or tripled in many areas. These enormous increases reflect increasingly intensive farming of animals that produce mountains of manure, as well as the continued high use of chemical fertilizers. The number of milk cows on Pennsylvania farms increased four and one-half times between 1954 and 1987. During the same period, the density of hogs increased from 11 per farm to 140 per farm. Pennsylvania farms raised 100 times more chickens in 1987 than in 1954.

By the time federal and state governments began concerted efforts to manage the bay as an integrated whole in the late 1970s, the demands upon bay waters to absorb the "offscourings of the land" were growing even as the capacity of sea-grass beds, wetlands, forests, oysters, shad, and other natural parts of the bay ecosystem to do so had been crippled. As a result, the principal consumers of the bay's productivity were no longer oysters, striped bass, or dabbling ducks but bacteria that consumed oxygen in consuming the surfeit of algae.

EXHAUSTING THE RESOURCES OF THE CHESAPEAKE

To survive in the stressful conditions of the Chesapeake Bay, plants and animals must be tough, able to tolerate rapid changes in water temperature, oxygen, nutrients, and food. No animal in the bay better characterizes this toughness than the American oyster. So successful was the American oyster that Algonquin Indians referred to the bay as "Chesepioc" or "Great Shellfish Bay."

Early European settlers also marveled at the oyster's abundance, and as long as they relied on methods of oystering taught them by local Indians, harvesting remained well within bounds of sustainability. But the Chesapeake Bay's oysters did not remain protected by isolation and traditional technology for long. In the early 19th century, oystermen who had exhausted oyster beds in New England began raiding the Chesapeake's oyster reefs, selling the oysters to markets in New York City and Philadelphia and sending seed oysters home to restock their depleted reefs. Legislation prohibiting nonresidents from fishing for oysters in the bay did not deter New England oyster interests, who turned to financing some of the largest harvesting, processing, and shipping operations in the bay fishery. Nor did the legislation prevent the depletion of oyster beds by local fishermen.

The opening of new markets by railways, together with the introduction of new fishing and processing technology, such as deepwater dredges and canning, provoked a rush to mine the waters of the Chesapeake Bay and turn its oyster reefs into cash, much of which left the area for investment elsewhere. The yield from landings of oysters soared after 1860 and reached a peak of 115 million pounds in 1880. With their new-found wealth and presence in a majority of legislative districts, watermen in Maryland effectively blocked any efforts to slow the fishery.

As the fishery declined, sewage contamination became a useful scapegoat and vehicle for raising concerns about water quality. But the principal cause of the decline, harvesting and consuming oysters with no regard for the future, was as well known as it was studiously ignored by watermen, bankers, processors, coastal communities, and politicians alike. After 1931, fishermen never again landed more than 40 million pounds of oysters in any year; after 1962, annual landings had fallen to less than 15 million pounds. Still, the fishery continued with little restriction by the watermen themselves or government agencies.

By 1993, many of the oysters sold as "Fresh Maryland Oysters" or "Virginia Selects" actually had been imported from native oyster beds in the Gulf of Mexico and from oyster beds on the West Coast, where private leaseholders farm the Japanese oyster.

Like oysters, American shad offered convenient material for generating cash for investment in endeavors more immediately profitable than sustainable fisheries. Near Harrisburg, Pennsylvania, fishermen-farmers landed as much as 400,000 pounds of shad a year at the turn of the century. In the upper bay, enormous nets were strung across the path of migrating shad and, when filled, took two days or more to unload. Entire railway cars filled with shad left the watershed every evening in shad season for consumers in New York City and Boston, who were taken with the fish's distinctive flavor and tenderness. Soon the poor, who had depended upon shad as a cheap source of protein, were priced out of the market.

At the turn of the century, fishermen in the whole area of the bay landed more than 17 million pounds of shad in a single year. But within two decades, overfishing and the proliferation of mill-dams and culverts that blocked shad migrations up their spawning streams had reduced landings to less than 4 million pounds. By 1929, when the 110-foot high Conowingo Dam was completed on the Susquehanna River just 12 miles from the Chesapeake Bay, dams had blocked American shad from ancient spawning grounds in hundreds of miles of streams throughout the Chesapeake Bay watershed. By 1985, shad landings fetched fishermen just $170,000, compared with the $6 million that the 1900 harvest of 17 million pounds would have fetched.

Within half a century, then, people had reduced oysters and shad to remnants of their former abundance. Those fishermen who remained on the water turned to other species, only to repeat the story. Within decades, the enormous population of striped bass that spawn in the bay collapsed as unlimited access attracted unlimited fishing effort. Only a moratorium on fishing in 1985 prevented the decimation of a particularly large generation of young fish spawned in 1982. Five years later, the moratorium, which had been bitterly opposed by recreational and commercial fishermen, started to pay off with record numbers of fish being counted in the bay.

If the pattern of mining the bay's fisheries is broken at last, the 1982 generation of striped bass will continue paying off into the next century.

RESTORING THE BAY

In 1983, representatives of the federal government, Maryland, Pennsylvania, Virginia, the District of Columbia, and the Chesapeake Bay Commission signed the first of three Chesapeake Bay agreements and launched an ambitious experiment—to collaborate in the restoration of the Chesapeake Bay. Six years of environmental studies sponsored by the Environmental Protection Agency had documented what citizen organizations and previous government studies had concluded long before: The Chesapeake Bay was breaking down. In signing the agreement, the partners committed themselves to developing and implementing coordinated plans to improve and protect the water quality and living resources of the bay.

As state and local governments turned to reducing nutrient discharges from sewage treatment plants and to curbing development in sensitive areas near the bay shoreline, scientific understanding of the bay continued to evolve. A monitoring program begun in 1984 collected information on water quality at nearly 50 sites in the main bay and twice that many in the bay's tributaries. With this information, scientists began constructing computerized models of the bay and the flow of pollutants from the watershed through the bay. By 1987, the models suggested that areas of oxygen-starved water in the bay would continue expanding unless the extravagant growth of algae were curbed by reducing the amount of nutrients entering from the land. In December, the parties to the 1983 agreement adopted 29 new commitments, including reducing levels of nitrogen and phosphorus in the bay by 40 percent below 1985 levels by the year 2000.

By the time the partners reviewed their agreement in 1992, it had become clear that many of the problems they had identified would be more difficult to solve than they had suspected in 1983. A ban on phosphate detergent and improvements in sewage treatment had reduced the discharge of phosphorus from pipes by 41 percent and had reduced the level of phosphorus in the bay by 16 percent. But bay states had managed only to prevent nitrogen levels from rising.

Recognizing that additional measures were needed to meet the target of 40 percent reduction in nutrients by the year 2000, the partners directed the states to develop strategies for reducing nutrients by specific amounts in individual tributaries. By moving upstream, the bay restoration effort now is directly affecting how farmers, suburban developers, highway departments, and others use land.

From the beginning, the goal of the Chesapeake Bay agreements has been the restoration of the living resources of the bay. A modest reduction in nutrient levels in the bay and some of its tributaries already has contributed to a reversal in the decline of submerged plants. By 1992, submerged grasses covered 75 percent more bay bottom than in 1984. By 1994, the bay's population of shad appeared to be recovering, and more than 300 miles of river had been opened to shad and other migrating fish. Reversing centuries of laissez-faire management of fisheries, the bay states had adopted more than a dozen baywide fishery management plans. Furthermore, the partners began developing a management plan to protect species of fish that are ecologically valuable, although they may not be commercially or recreationally valuable. Many of these species, such as bay anchovy, not only provide food for harvested species such as striped bass, but they graze on floating algae that would otherwise die and decompose, depleting surrounding waters of oxygen.

THE FUTURE

In the next 25 years, more people will be asking more from the bay than ever before. The number of people living in the Pennsylvania, Maryland, and Virginia parts of the watershed alone will grow by 19 percent, to 16.2 million people, between 1990 and 2020. Not only will there be more people in the watershed, but on average, they will be using more land if current patterns hold. From 1950 to 1980, forest and farm land was converted to commercial and residential development at a rate three and one-half times greater than population growth. Already, each additional person in the Chesapeake Bay watershed uses three times as much land as 40 years ago.

The problems with sprawl are not simply esthetic. A 1988 evaluation of growth patterns and their consequences in the bay area found that such unmanaged new growth "has the potential to erase any progress made in [all other] bay improvements, overwhelming past and current efforts." Among other things, the study found that suburban sprawl requires twice as much roadway as more compact development, doubling driving time and energy use for commuting. In the last decade alone, the number of miles driven by residents in Virginia and Maryland has increased by 41 percent and 31 percent respectively. The amount of air pollution generated by automobiles in the bay area increased five times faster than population, and now accounts for more than one-third of the nitrogen that enters the bay from the atmosphere. If nitrogen entering the bay from air pollution is not greatly reduced, achieving the target of 40 percent reduction from other sources will yield only a 16 percent reduction of nitrogen in the bay, and efforts to restore the quality of the bay's waters will be undermined if not completely undone.

Although fully informed about this more crowded future in 1988, the government members of the Chesapeake Bay agreements have taken only tentative steps toward managing the growth and development that will continue transforming the bay and its watershed to the year 2020 and beyond. Political leaders may only be reflecting a kind of schizophrenia among their constituents regarding pollution of the bay and its causes. In a 1994 survey of public attitudes, 85 percent of watershed residents who were interviewed expressed concern about the pollution of the bay, but very few saw any connection between their own activities and the state of the bay. Instead, sewage treatment plants and industry continued to be targeted as the chief culprits, despite significant reductions in their discharges and the well-documented and advertised problems of suburban sprawl.

Constituents themselves were reflecting the double message that government seemed to be sending about restoring the bay. On the one hand, federal and state governments had committed to reducing pollution by conducting studies and spending millions of dollars on reducing pollution from sewage treatment plants and other sources. On the other hand, these same governments were subsidizing the kind of suburban sprawl that their studies had shown was compromising pollution control efforts.

As in many other similar situations, citizens have disregarded the government's research and educational messages and responded to the economic incentives it offered. For instance, by exempting from taxes most of the value of free parking provided by government agencies and private employers, the federal government effectively has reduced the cost of commuting by private automobile. Largely because such tax subsidies reduced the price of commuting to downtown Washington, D.C., in a private automobile to a level well below the cost of using public transit, the number of automobiles entering downtown Washington, every work day increased by more than 11,000 just between 1990 and 1993.

UNDERVALUED SEAS

The history of use, enjoyment, and transformation of the Chesapeake Bay after European settlement matches the history of other coastal areas around the world. Generating wealth by mining rich fisheries, lands, and waters continues to fuel economic growth while undermining the productive capacity and diversity of coastal ecosystems. These losses compromise the future of coastal communities and the biological richness that marks coastal waters and lands.

This pattern seems to come to us naturally. Indeed, economic theory tells us that people not only favor shifting costs onto other people but also assume that if something becomes scarce, someone will find a substitute. Shifting costs is particularly common when it comes to coastal fisheries or water quality, which no one person owns. Using streams, rivers, bays, and the ocean for disposing of wastes, whether human sewage, agricultural runoff, or trash, makes sense to most people, because they bear only the cost of getting the waste into the water. The cost of degraded water and unhealthy seafood is borne by society or mitigated by the government. If we fish out the salmon in a stream, we assume we can find another stream with salmon, or we begin fishing for another species or start raising salmon in pens.

Since conventional accounting tallied the income from the sale of Chesapeake Bay oysters, shad, timber, and wetlands, but did not record the future income foregone by the destruction of their productive capacity, businesses and government agencies had little reason to suspect that continued exploitation did not make sense—economically or ecologically. Whatever cash was generated by their exploitation was easily enough put to productive use elsewhere. In general terms, it seemed to matter little that instead of being able to make a living from fishing, people were becoming wealthy through manufacturing or farming.

The resulting decline in fisheries, water quality, beaches, wetlands, and other ocean resources, together with conflicts among competing groups for their use, eventually brought on greater intervention by government agencies. But, for a variety of reasons, government has only a limited capacity for promoting prudence and long-term thinking where they do not already exist. First, government funding for doing so generally falls far short of the need. Among other things, limited funding for activities such as monitoring compromise our ability to anticipate problems. As a result, government generally is reacting to situations after they have reached crisis, or it is beset with so many problems, such as thousands upon thousands of untested chemicals, that it can only pick and choose and hope to make an intelligent, correct decision.

Second, government can do only what it is permitted to do. Although general agreements about problems and solutions may be reached, the application of the solutions to specific situations often triggers strong opposition from affected people and interests. The decline of Chesapeake Bay oysters has been closely observed and openly acknowledged for many years; yet, efforts to reduce harvesting have been successfully stymied by watermen and other beneficiaries of continued exploitation. The human mind is extraordinarily inventive in devising means of ignoring the most obvious signs of impending loss.

Third, government sometimes works at cross-purposes with itself because of the influence of narrow interests upon different agencies who share fragmented authority over a resource or an area. For instance, tax subsidies for parking that encourage long-distance commuting promote the very suburban sprawl that generates air and water pollution addressed by government agencies and taxpayer funding. Similarly, even as many taxpayers decry high taxes, they insist upon government funding for restoring communities and private homes built in hazardous areas and destroyed by recurring storms.

Like the prevailing principle of freedom of the seas, which was first articulated in a time of great natural abundance, many of the economic principles by which we measure economic welfare come from times and societies whose view of the world was shaped by riches pouring in from the Americas. As long as abundance was the rule, these principles were sensible, if not prudent.

Now, the limitations of conventional accounting and of the free-for-all produced by freedom of the seas are being more broadly discussed, even if they are not being corrected quite yet. Conservative institutions such as the World Bank and the United Nations are embracing the notion that conventional accounting misrepresents the wealth of a country by ignoring the lost economic potential of depleted fisheries or deforested countryside. Instead of immediately assuming that the price paid for a wetland on the open market fairly represents its value to society, economists are expanding the valuation to include the many goods and services that such areas produce, from storm protection and cleansing of waters to serving as nursery grounds for most fish and shellfish caught by fishermen around the world.

For the time being, short-term exploitation of coastal and ocean resources will likely remain the rule, and government agencies will be the principal protectors of the future. As long as people can shift costs to other people or society at large, it will appear rational to overexploit, pollute, and degrade productive habitats.

A Larger Context

Like the Chesapeake Bay, ocean and coastal waters around the world are greatly affected by apparently irrelevant trends, such as population growth and movement, patterns of economic growth, global environmental change, and the development and use of technology, as well as activities taking place hundreds of miles from the shoreline. The relevance of these trends and activities to marine conservation generally has received little attention. Besides being breathtakingly broad, factors like population growth force sticky questions of how much control society will exert over the decisions of individuals.

Even in countries such as the United States, where population growth rates are much lower than elsewhere in the world, population movement becomes a central concern for coastal conservation. Many of the most polluted and fished-out marine areas in the world are near coastal cities. Villages and suburban developments that hug the coast also have damaged small bays.

Distant markets also greatly influence coastal and ocean resources. Just as thousands of acres of forest in Maryland and Virginia were cleared to grow tobacco for markets in Europe three centuries ago, so too are mangrove forests in Indonesia, the Philippines, Ecuador, and many other countries now being cleared to grow shrimp for consumers in the United States, Japan, and Europe.

However unobtrusive its role may be, technological development has triggered changes in the use of ocean and coastal resources. Rather than fully evaluate the economic and ecological effects of introducing new technology so that long-term rather than short-term benefits might be assured, new fishing, processing, marketing, or manufacturing technology is commonly embraced with uncritical enthusiasm. Too often, the failure to analyze how technology might increase the risk of depleting a fishery, for instance, sparks increased levels of exploitation, rather than more efficiency. In the mid-19th century, the introduction of deepwater dredges greatly increased the speed of oyster harvesting, with predictably destructive results. Similar failures to evaluate industrial and agricultural chemicals repeatedly have led to environmental damage, from fish kills to the near extinction of osprey and bald eagles.

The fluid, transporting nature of water and the atmosphere links distant areas more intimately than we generally recognize. Most of us assume that the way a farmer manages manure in upstate Pennsylvania has little effect on water quality in the Chesapeake Bay. Likewise, we do not connect commuter traffic jams outside Washington, D.C., with the rain of nitrogen that contributes to overenrichment of Chesapeake Bay waters. As long as concern was focused on the pollution that poured from sewage treatment plants or manufacturing facilities, these links were obscured. But as pollution from the more easily identified sources has been curbed, the problems of pollution carried in water or air from diffuse sources have become inescapable.

Similarly, the migrations of fish and other wildlife for spawning and feeding connect distant areas in many ways that confound political jurisdictions. Erecting dams on the Susquehanna River in Pennsylvania contributed to the near demise of the fishery for American shad in the waters of Maryland and Virginia. For many species, early life is spent as an egg or larva floating on currents over hundreds of miles. Pollution that harms or kills fish and shellfish in these early stages can affect fisheries or hamper the recolonization of damaged coral reefs in distant areas.

The anticipated global warming caused by the accumulation of so-called greenhouse gases in the atmosphere will have even more wide-ranging effects than regional air pollution or land use. Both marine waters and coastal habitats, from Indonesian coral reefs to Chesapeake Bay wetlands, will be profoundly affected by changes in currents and sea level. The sources of greenhouse gases, such as fossil fuels and methane, span the globe as well. Continued high levels of gasoline consumption in the United States will be matched by growing levels of coal consumption in countries such as China and India, which are seeking to develop their own economies much as the United States did just a century ago.

WATERSHEDS

The earth's most productive areas are coastal. By coastal, we do not mean simply the narrow strip of land and water along the shoreline. Since understanding and protecting the coasts requires acknowledging the links that air and water fashion, the fundamental unit of the coasts is the watershed and adjacent coastal waters. That is why conservationists speak as passionately about the 64,000 square miles of watershed surrounding the Chesapeake Bay as the 2,200 square miles of the bay itself.

Falling within watershed boundaries marked sometimes by a mountain ridge and at others by a nearly imperceptible hump of ground, rainwater and snowfall gradually collect or dissolve the minerals and chemicals that lie on or near the surface. Simply by studying the chemistry of the water in a stream, one often can determine whether a watershed is covered by forests or pavement. The waters that course down streams to rivers eventually reach the coast and carry with them the good and the bad from the land above.

As in the Chesapeake Bay, so in many other coastal areas of the world—settling and working the land along the coasts has fundamentally altered the relation between land and sea. In many watersheds, we first disrupt the mosaic of forest, wetland, and meadow that capture, confine, and store storm waters, nutrients, and soil. Then, with our communities flooded and streams polluted, we seek to recover those critical functions with expensive engineering works that often offer only partial solutions. Working with the land would be less expensive and better for coastal waters especially. Conservation of the sea cannot be secured apart from conservation of the land.

The coastal zone also is a hotspot for life in many forms. Tropical waters in many areas host some of the most diverse and productive ecosystems in the world, including coral reefs and mangrove forests. Coastal fisheries account for most of the world's fish catch. Increasingly, it is the coasts where growing numbers of people are settling. Already, more than one-half of the U.S. population lives within 50 miles of the shoreline, a band that accounts for less than ten percent of the land area of the United States. By the middle of the next century, some people predict, more than six billion people (three-quarters of the world's population) will live within 90 miles of a coastline.

As modern telecommunications make the consumer culture of the industrialized democracies a worldwide standard, the resulting additional demand for economic growth will heighten the impact of so many people being concentrated near coastal waters. Already in the United States, one-third of all economic activity takes place in the counties of the coastal zone. The near total loss of wetlands, good water quality, healthy fisheries, beaches, and other coastal amenities near cities around the world gives some indication of what the future will be like, if we continue with business as usual. The change will occur most rapidly, and disastrously perhaps, in developing countries that are seeking to improve the lot of their people by selling natural resources with as little regard for the income foregone by spending the principal as the industrialized countries had in the last century.

NATURE AND HUMAN INSTITUTIONS

Scientific study has been slowly filling in our incomplete picture of the oceans and their limits. The difficulty and expense of studying even relatively small areas of marine waters, such as the Chesapeake Bay, often has delayed their description and assessment and contributed to unwise practices. Furthermore, the dynamics of fish populations and the behavior of pollutants in water, for instance, are so variable as to make it very difficult to show an unequivocal link between a certain level of fishing or discharge of pollutants on the one hand, and some effect on the abundance or health of seafood or on the risks of swimming in coastal waters, on the other hand.

The link between deadly diseases and the consumption of oysters contaminated by human sewage was drawn only a century ago, when it led to renewed discussion of the need to end the discharge of sewage into Baltimore Harbor. Even then, however, some political and business leaders could still argue that the bay was the proper place to discharge sewage, if the discharge pipe were simply extended. Debate dominated public policy for years into the 20th century, before any meaningful action was taken to reduce the hazards of discharging raw sewage into oyster beds.

Now, the debate over sewage seems foolish, but one can only wonder what current debates over toxic chemicals will sound like a decade from now. It is clear that we are engaged in a massive chemistry experiment. Poorly known quantities of poorly evaluated chemicals enter the Chesapeake Bay and other coastal waters every day. Although less and less chemical residue is intentionally discharged by industry, we are now coming to appreciate how much washes off streets and fields in rainstorms or snowmelt. Unless massive fish kills occur, we are largely unable to detect damage to fish, shellfish, or people, partly because techniques for detecting sublethal effects are still being developed and are expensive to use. If there is a problem, we will likely find out about it only after it has happened.

Responding to marine conservation problems often brings additional sources of delay. However widely accepted a problem and solution might appear to be, those that will be most affected may be the last to admit that specific changes are needed. Often there is outrage, even surprise, at this resistance, as those responsible for applying the solution are either persuaded or forced to do something about the problem. The level of effort that must be devoted to resolving these kinds of conflicts over responses often reflects a failure to study people's behavior and the incentives that encourage it. Instead, fact-finding and analysis generally are confined to learning about biological or oceanographic processes.

While we are studying problems and trying to fashion and adopt what we think are solutions, the processes that power ocean currents and produce life in such profusion continue. In some cases, these processes will work in our favor. Given a rest from exploitation, fish populations like Chesapeake Bay striped bass have recovered. With an end to the discharge of raw sewage, good water quality and fisheries are returning to many rivers such as the Chesapeake's Potomac and the Patuxent Rivers.

The business of restoring the abundance and health of ocean waters in many areas will require that people overcome traditional ways of thinking and behaving and make restoration and the future at least as important and valued as consumption and the present.

TRANSFORMATION

In 1946, American whalers ceased commercial hunting of California gray whales. For a century, whalers had pursued gray whales as they migrated along the west coast of North America to feeding areas in the Bering Sea and breeding lagoons in Baja California. As explosive harpoons were introduced and steam power replaced sails, catches increased to several hundred gray whales each year. By the time the International Convention for the Regulation of Whaling ended commercial whaling for gray whales after the end of World War II, the population had been reduced to a small fraction of its former abundance.

Unlike other species of great whales that have enjoyed protection from whaling, gray whales have rebounded spectacularly. Now, scientists estimate that more than 21,000 gray whales migrate along the west coast of North America, delighting tens of thousands of whalewatchers perched on the bows of boats or seated on limestone cliffs. Now, the challenge is to insure that, as we crowd upon the coast with our homes and businesses, we do not jeopardize the waters through which gray whales have migrated for eons.

There is more at stake than the whales themselves or the businesses that profit by their accessibility. In 1980, a small nonprofit organization in Oakland, California, by the name of the Whale Center arranged a whale-watching trip for a group of troubled teenagers from the California Conservation Corps. When they boarded the boat at eight in the morning in Half Moon Bay, the teenagers were exuberant enough to cause some concern among the trip leaders. But once the vessel left the protection of the breakwater, encountering heavy seas, the youngsters lost their high spirits.

After an hour and a half of bouncing about with no whale in sight, two blows shot into the air about a mile away. Within minutes, the boat was floating, its engine at full stop, just 100 feet from a pair of courting gray whales. As the boat rocked in the waves, the graceful and awesome play of the whales captivated the young people, and for the next 45 minutes, silence and awe reigned on board, except for the occasional rush of excited conversation. The trip leaders, who had seen hundreds of whales before, were as caught up in the magic of the moment as the teenagers.

As the earth becomes a more and more crowded and compromised place, we will need every chance to capture such magic. There are some things for which we can never find substitutes.

2

$\approx\approx\approx$

Exploration

The most beautiful thing we can experience is
the mysterious. It is the source of all true art
and science.

ALBERT EINSTEIN,
What I Believe

In the fall of 1893, the Norwegian explorer Fridtjof Nansen sailed
his three-masted schooner, the *Fram,* into the pack ice of the Arctic Sea off the coast of Siberia. As far as Nansen and his crew
knew, no one had ever drifted with the Arctic pack ice and survived. But Nansen had convinced the Norwegian Parliament and
private benefactors that only by risking the crush of ice could he
learn about the currents of the Arctic Sea and their influence on
the Norwegian and Greenland Seas.

Over the next three years, Arctic ice carried the *Fram* more than
1,500 miles westward. By the time the *Fram* emerged from the ice
near Spitzbergen Island in the fall of 1896, it had completed one
of the boldest and most productive of all oceanographic expedi-
tions. Among other things, the expedition disproved a popular
view of the Arctic Sea as a shallow body of water driven by strong
currents. By drifting with the pack ice, Nansen and his crew were
able to take repeated measurements of water salinity and temperature that revealed several distinct layers of water. Working from
data on the course of the *Fram,* the great Swedish oceanographer
Vagn Walfrid Ekman first described the effect of the earth's rotation on wind-driven currents.

Even a century after the voyage of the *Fram,* the age of ocean discovery seems to have only begun. Theory after theory has fallen before the careful analysis of data, often collected with sampling instruments that have hampered as much as they have helped. Scientists still must contend with enormous difficulties in collecting information about the features and inhabitants of the enormous, corrosive, and opaque oceans. The explosion of information generated by satellite sensors and remotely operated vehicles as well as an increasing understanding of links among the atmosphere, land, and the oceans now feed complex models that overwhelm even the most powerful computers.

At the same time, environmental problems large and small impose greater demands for environmental information and insight, generating tension between the rigors of the scientific method and the pressing need to make decisions in the face of uncertainty. From global warming to the healthfulness of seafood, the marine sciences are facing greater challenges in many ways than those faced by early oceanographers.

This chapter can only sample the enormous range of disciplines that comprise the modern study of the oceans.

A MOST DIFFICULT SUBJECT OF STUDY

Sometimes violent and unforgiving, crushing and buoyant at the same time, dark for the most part, the dominant feature of an entire planet—the oceans present a prodigious challenge for their students. For most of the short history of oceanography, scientists have had to rely on scanty evidence from nets, bottles, dredges, fragile thermometers, and corers to piece together a sensible picture of the 99 percent of the earth's living space that is ocean.

Even the commonest tasks, such as maintaining a fixed position, have presented tremendous challenges. Just over a century ago, Naval Lieutenant John Elliot Pillsbury launched an extraordinary series of voyages aboard the steamer *Balke.* Pillsbury's goal was to measure the strength of the Gulf Stream, which Benjamin Franklin had first mapped in the 1770s. Using a combination of engineering innovation, good seamanship, and scientific imagination, Pillsbury constructed a contraption of spars, booms, wire rope, and anchors that could hold the *Balke* in a given place amid the surging waters of the Gulf Stream. For the first time in history, an oceanographic vessel was able to measure the speed of currents at a fixed position in the ocean. With data from 164 anchorages between Cape Hatteras and the Netherlands Antilles, Pillsbury showed that the Gulf Stream was not a fixed feature, but an ocean phenomenon that was constantly changing position, speed, temperature, and direction.

If Lieutenant Pillsbury's technological breakthrough revealed features of the Gulf Stream, the limits of scientific technology in the 19th century obscured other features of ocean waters and reinforced theories that appear incredible in hindsight. Believing that salt water like fresh water is its densest at a temperature of 4 degrees Centigrade, scientists assumed that the depths of the ocean never moved, and so never received the nutrients that life needs. This belief was so entrenched that the repeated recovery of worms, sea stars, and other animals from abyssal depths was regularly dismissed with some other explanation.

Holding to prevailing beliefs, Sir James Clark Ross sailed for the Southern Ocean in 1839, taking dredge samples of the sea floor and temperature readings in his course. As anticipated, the thermometers lowered from the *Erebus* and *Terror* into the south polar waters returned with readings consistently at 4 degrees Centigrade. Unknown at the time, the readings of these thermometers were distorted by increasing water pressure: For every degree of decrease in temperature that was caused by greater depth, the increasing water pressure raised the temperature in the unprotected thermometers by one degree. Thus, for example, waters that were actually 36 degrees Fahrenheit continued to register as 39 degrees Fahrenheit on the expedition's thermometers. Until the 1868 cruise of the *Lightning,* a paddleboat steamer built and operated by the British Post Office, the mistaken thermometer readings of Ross's expedition to the Southern Ocean seemed to confirm the theory that the depths of the oceans were of unvarying temperature and so must be a lifeless, inert mass of cold water.

In 1860, just one year after Charles Darwin's *On the Origin of Species by Means of Natural Selection* was published, the theory of lifeless depths dissolved when a cable was recovered from waters off Sardinia. Previously, sceptics had been able to argue that organisms found clinging to recovered cables had simply

attached themselves as the cables were being pulled through surface waters. However, the organisms on the cable recovered off
Sardinia were not simply attached, but were thickly encrusted. At
a meeting of the French Academy of Sciences, the belief in lifeless
regions of the oceans was given last rites.

Among naturalists and oceanographers, disbelief gave way to
excitement at what was yet to be discovered in the enormous
realm of the deep ocean. Some naturalists sought to apply Darwin's revolutionary theory of evolution by looking for living fos-
sils in the depths, where comparatively changeless conditions
would presumably have slowed the rapid pace of evolution found
on land. Scientists earnestly hoped that deep waters would yield
some of the links missing from the chain of evolution.

One of Charles Darwin's most effective defenders, Thomas
Henry Huxley, was also one of the most persistent advocates of
the theory that the deep oceans were a great reservoir of evolutionary history long since entombed in geological strata on land.
In 1868, while reexamining bottles of sediments collected by the
Cyclops expedition of 1857, Huxley found support for the theory
in a slime that had formed on the surface of the preserved sediments. Huxley hypothesized that this slime coated the depths of
the ocean, providing a source of food for the creatures of the deep.
What is more, it was just the kind of amorphous substance that
seemed to beg for evolution. Accordingly, it was dubbed *Bathybius* or "life of the deep." Huxley's theory ruled for more than a
decade. As Susan Schlee remarks in *The Edge of an Unfamiliar
World,* "[N]aturalists expected that they would soon be able to
trace the branches of the evolutionary tree upward . . . from abyssal *Bathybius* to the naturalist himself."

Exposure of *Bathybius* as only the most recent imposter from
the deep had to await results from the explorations of the HMS
Challenger. On December 21, 1872, the *Challenger* and its crew
of 240 men began a cruise of nearly four years and 69,000 miles
around the world. Under the direction of C. Wyville Thomson,
the four naturalists and one chemist aboard the ship collected
13,000 species of plants and animals and 1,441 water samples,
made countless measurements of temperature and salinity, and
obtained hundreds of sea-floor sediment samples. By the time the
fiftieth volume of the expedition's report was published in 1895,

the *Challenger* had set the standards for future oceanographic exploration.

Although it could not completely refute the belief in lifeless areas of the seas, the *Challenger*'s sampling did confirm that some areas of the sea floor could be rich with life. Some sediment grabs pulled up little more than an ooze of plankton debris, but others recovered a profusion of life. One of the richest grabs, in 3,600 feet of water off Argentina, recovered 500 individual specimens of fish and invertebrates, representing 127 different species. Of these, 103 species were entirely new to science.

Still, the myth of lifeless regions persisted by being banished to mid-water areas, where uncertainty still reigned. There, the capture of organisms in standard nets fell prey to the same criticism as the capture of organisms clinging to submarine cables recovered in past years: Held open by a rigid frame, a net might well capture creatures in shallow waters as it was being drawn up from the depths. Another decade passed before nets that would open and close only at the desired depth finally established that life occurred throughout the oceans, from sea floor through mid-waters to the very surface.

Finally, it was John Young Buchanan who unmasked the green slime *Bathybius*. In two years of examining muds taken freshly from the ocean's floor, the *Challenger*'s scientific team had not encountered the kind of living slime that Huxley had first identified in 1868. Buchanan did find a green slime on sediments collected early in the voyage of the *Challenger* and preserved in alcohol, but none on sediments collected later and preserved in seawater. With further testing, Buchanan became convinced that the slime was produced by mixing alcohol with seawater. Rather than *Bathybius*, the slime was revealed to be calcium sulphate. Informed of Buchanan's findings, Huxley wrote to the British journal *Nature* and graciously withdrew his theory.

INTERNATIONAL COLLABORATION

In the 1890s, convinced that expanded surveys would reveal the complexities of currents in the North Atlantic, the oceanographer Otto Pettersson persuaded the newly created Swedish Hydrographic Commission to sponsor an international conference on the chemical, physical, and biological dynamics of the North Atlantic. Encouraged by King Oscar II of Sweden, representatives from Great Britain, Norway, Denmark, Germany, Ireland, the Netherlands, and Russia met in Stockholm in 1899 to discuss collaborative vessel surveys aimed at collecting the kind of information that Pettersson believed would elucidate the reasons for fluctuations in fish populations in the North Sea.

Like their former colonies, which had created the U.S. Fish Commission thirty years before, the British were eager to refer a growing conflict between fishermen to a group of scientists. As in the United States, steam had replaced sails in many British fishing fleets in the last two decades of the 19th century. Fishermen who still fished from 25-foot dories with long lines of hooks accused the steam trawlers of depleting fish stocks by catching anything and everything that entered the maw of their nets. Trawlermen claimed that the decline in fish had more to do with changes in the Gulf Stream and with the great storms of the North Atlantic.

There was little agreement on how to design the studies. The physical oceanographers, who wanted to detail the changeable course of water bodies in the North Atlantic, never completely agreed with the biological oceanographers, who wanted to tag fish or count rings on fish scales or earbones. Physical oceanographers held the view that fish were cosmopolitan in their tastes and swam where their wishes took them. Biological oceanographers argued that changes in the temperature and salinity of surrounding waters influenced the movement of fish.

In the end, there was enough agreement between competing theories to launch an extraordinary series of research cruises into the North Atlantic that did combine physical and biological oceanography. With maiden voyages in 1902, in which each nation's vessels were assigned particular survey tracks and stations, the International Council for the Exploration of the Sea (ICES) was born.

Within a few years, huge amounts of data on water temperature and salinity as well as the distribution of fishes in the North Sea had been collected in atlases. Some scientists had expected a pattern to emerge from the data that would link the abundance of fish with a particular physical factor, such as salinity or temperature. But daunting problems in basic fish biology confronted ICES

investigators. Were all the herring in the North Sea one population or did they represent several populations? Were they all of
the same age? If not, how old were they? Not only did scientists
lack answers to these questions, but at first they did not have the
tools to get any answers.

In Germany, Dr. Friedrich Heincke developed one tool by
applying methods used in physical anthropology to distinguish
among human populations. With calipers in hand, Dr. Heincke
began taking measurements of herring caught in different parts of
the northeast Atlantic Ocean. After measuring the eyes, heads,
tails, and other features of hundreds of herring, Dr. Heincke
found that herring from different parts of the North Sea did
exhibit significant differences in the relation among measurements. Thus, Icelandic herring had large eyes, a short skull, and a
long tail compared with Norwegian herring. Instead of one enormous population of herring, whose movements about the northeast Atlantic caused the rise and fall of commercial fisheries, Dr.
Heincke found dozens of smaller populations whose fluctuations
were difficult to explain except as the result of overfishing.

But doubts remained. Presumably, overfishing would have eliminated all but the youngest fish from a population, whereas a fish
population that was not affected by fishing would be made up of
fish of several ages. As long as scientists could not determine the
age of fish, however, this theory could not be tested. With the
publication of "Fluctuations in the Great Fisheries of Northern
Europe" in 1914, Norway's Johan Hjort showed that he had
removed this obstacle by carefully examining scales of individual
fish and by analyzing the resulting data with recently developed
statistical methods.

Although Hjort's microscopic inspection of thousands of fish
scales must have been mind-numbing, the technique provided
extraordinarily revealing information. For instance, Hjort found
that the age of herring in a single catch could range from two to
twenty years. Furthermore, the mix of ages varied from year to
year. With detailed analysis of herring catches from 1907 to 1910,
Hjort formulated a basic concept in the study of fish population
dynamics—year classes. Hjort had found that the catch of spring
herring in 1907 included some three-year-olds—fish born in
1904—but mostly older fish. In 1908, however, herring from the

1904 year class made up more than one-third of the catch. In 1909, fish from the 1904 year class, which were then five years old, made up 43 percent of the catch, and by 1910 the 1904 year class made up 77 percent of the catch. Clearly, many more herring eggs had hatched and survived in 1904 than in most other years.

Hjort theorized that abundant year classes resulted from a fortunate coincidence: If the eggs of herring hatched when food was plentiful, more hatchlings would grow to maturity and later be caught by fishermen. Exploring this theory required exploring the relationship between physical and biological oceanography still further and greatly increasing the use of quantitative methods in marine biology.

For decades already, oceanographers had been trying to measure the productivity of ocean areas, but were confronted with the task of estimating the abundance of minuscule forms of life at the base of marine food webs: the drifting plant and animal life known as plankton. In the 1880s, a German physiologist by the name of Victor Hensen introduced quantitative methods to marine biology and set out to develop techniques for counting the plankton in the seas. Although many scientists found fault with Hensen's techniques, few were able to counter his conclusion that temperate waters were far more productive than tropical waters— not the reverse, as current theory had it.

More puzzling was the seasonality of growth in temperate waters: The times of greatest abundance of plankton were not the long days of summer but the shorter and cooler days of spring and fall. Relying on investigations by chemists and plant physiologists more than 50 years before, Karl Brandt determined that more important than light and warmth was the presence of key nutrients, especially nitrate and phosphate. These nutrients were more plentiful when waters were well mixed, as during the fall and spring in the North Atlantic.

Although the methodical investigations of ICES had elucidated many of the factors in the dynamics of fish populations, the role of fishing could not be discounted. World War I provided the kind of experimental evidence about fishing that ICES could never have obtained on its own. With the onset of war, submarines and other military vessels incidentally enforced a moratorium on commercial fishing in the North Atlantic for the length of the war. By the time the war ended, fish stocks in the North Atlantic had rebounded to levels unseen in many years—and were as swiftly depressed with peace and the resumption of fishing.

SCIENCE FOR WHOM?

Science and government are uneasy, fickle allies. Government bureaucrats and politicians sometimes recast difficult political issues as technical issues and refer them to scientists, who are eager to receive funds to study the question but often are unable to provide the kind of unequivocal answers that government officials believe they have paid for. Science that does not meet some clear and present social need has received little support. Linking their research to practical applications, as government funding generally demands, has required scientists sometimes to pursue second or third priorities in order to receive any funding at all.

In the early years of the United States, opponents of funding for oceanography raised doubts whether the Constitution authorized any federal funding of science. Convinced that charting coastal waters would assist navigation and commerce, in 1832 Congress provided financial support for physical oceanographic work off the coasts of the United States and for developing the Navy's navigational capabilities on the high seas. In 1838, a constituency of whalers, sealers, and other business interests persuaded Congress to fund a circumnavigation of the globe. This show of national prowess ended in congressional bitterness about "this thing called Science" when much of the expedition's collection of specimens and records was carelessly lost or destroyed upon return. Nonetheless, dozens of laborious soundings with a lead weight attached to a line had produced clear evidence that the sea floor was not flat and featureless as the prevailing view of the time had it, but was in places even more mountainous than the land.

World Wars I and II fundamentally changed the nature of oceanographic research as well as the relationship between the oceanographic community and the federal government. During World War I, development of sonar for detecting submarines convinced the U.S. Navy that oceanographic research could further military purposes. The scientific community saw benefit as well in associating with the military. In 1922, the USS *Stewart* used the sonic depth finder, developed for the Navy, to take soundings in its voyage across the Atlantic from Rhode Island to Gibraltar. In nine days, the *Stewart* collected 900 depth soundings, three times as many as the HMS *Challenger* had collected in its voyage of three and a half years.

After World War I, federal funding of oceanographic research declined again, but with the growing threat of war in the late 1930s, the federal government dramatically increased funding for oceanographic research. By the time the United States entered World War II in 1941, the Woods Hole Oceanographic Institution's staff alone, which normally reached a peak of 60 in the summer, had swelled to 335 scientists.

Many researchers refocused their investigations to address military objectives. Once again, both the military and scientific communities seemed to benefit. For instance, newly developed echo-ranging equipment failed to detect submarines when signals were sent at angles other than vertical through upper waters—a significant limit on the usefulness of the new devices. Investigators later found that the signals were being bent as they encountered boundaries between layers of water of different temperatures. Learning the location of such a boundary, called a thermocline, would benefit submariners, who could hide in its shadow. In theory, submarine chasers could adjust an echo-sounding signal to compensate for bending by the thermocline. But the charts of ocean water then available were too sketchy to help locate the thermocline on any particular day.

A breakthrough in locating the thermocline came with improvements in a device first developed in the 1930s by Athelstan Spilhaus and others: the bathythermograph. Deployed from a surface vessel or a submarine, a bathythermograph recorded water temperature and depth on a glass slide. Besides enabling submariners and sub-chasers to determine the exact location of the thermocline, the glass slides from bathythermographs provided oceanographers with their first data on the temperature structure of upper waters. During the war, 60,000 slides were collected from the North Atlantic alone.

The needs to detect and hide submarines led to other advances in both physical and biological oceanography. Because sound does not reflect so much as it ricochets off hard surfaces, locating rocky reef areas would help submarines hide from sonar of surface ships. Under contract to the U.S. Navy, the University of California's Division of War Research was given the task of compiling hundreds of thousands of notations about the nature of the sea floor that had been written on charts and in the notebooks of research cruises by various countries. Notations from Japanese cruises were particularly copious and useful, since they were based on the traditional instrument for taking depth soundings: a lead weight, which incidentally recovered sediments from the bottom. Besides meeting the Navy's need to know the location of rocky and sandy areas of the sea floor, the resulting maps refuted a prevailing theory that the nearshore sea floor was composed of coarse sediments, whereas the offshore sea floor was largely mud flat.

Even as the end of World War II reduced federal funding for civilian research, Cold War tensions spurred the spending of billions of dollars on research for military purposes as well as on development of more sophisticated systems for collecting information about the movement of Soviet military forces. For instance, in the mid-1950s, the U.S. Navy deployed an elaborate network of listening devices on the sea floor for detecting and tracking Soviet submarines. Capable of discriminating among sounds from different types of submarines, surface ships, and hundreds of sources in the deep, the hydrophones in the Navy's Sound Surveillance System (SOSUS) collected acoustic signals and relayed them to land stations in Maine and Oregon, where specialists analyzed computer-enhanced images in tracking the movement of vessels.

As the end of the Cold War reduced the need for such ambitious data gathering, the civilian scientific community and members of Congress, including then-Senator Al Gore, pressed for converting these systems to civilian use rather than allowing the enormous investment to waste away. Spurred on by a Congressional mandate, the Navy recently has been collaborating with the civilian scientific community in exploring ways in which its intelligence-gathering capabilities can assist in understanding the oceans.

The early results of this collaboration have been tantalizing. For instance, in a project called Whales '93, biologists used SOSUS to survey deep waters that would have been prohibitively expensive to survey with conventional techniques. In just three months, scientists gathered more "sightings" of blue, minke, and fin whales than had been gathered by all previous studies. Earlier, SOSUS enabled geologists investigating seismic activity in the northeast Pacific Ocean to detect 20 times the number of seismic events that they could with land-based listening devices.

The relaxation of restrictions on military information and technology presents great opportunities and difficult choices. SOSUS and other systems such as over-the-horizon radar make it possible, as never before, to study large areas of ocean over long periods of time. This capability can permit detecting the kinds of changes in ocean currents and temperatures that may signal global warming. But maintenance and operation of these information-gathering systems as well as storage and analysis of the gathered data are expensive. Exploiting these new sources of information will mean abandoning other investigations that may be only slightly less promising or valuable.

OCEANS AS SEEN FROM BEYOND THE EARTH

In the fall of 1987, fishermen and residents along the coast of North Carolina began complaining of teary eyes and congested lungs. Over the next four months, a massive red tide settled upon the bay and coastal waters of North Carolina, causing $24 million in economic losses. Tourist restaurants along the Outer Banks had to import oysters from the Chesapeake Bay when 570 square miles of shellfishing beds in Pamlico and Albemarle Sounds were closed. As early as November, scientists identified the culprit as a tiny plant called *Gymnodinium breve,* but could not say how this resident of the Gulf of Mexico had traveled nearly 500 miles farther north than it had before.

The answer came from the heavens. Perched on a satellite orbiting at an altitude of about 540 miles, a device with the inscrutable label of an Advanced Very High-Resolution Radiometer had recorded the intensity of electromagnetic radiation emitted by the waters off North Carolina. Color-coding the data from the satellite, computers made visible a swirl of water temperatures. A pool of warm water, appearing on the charts as bright yellow and orange, had broken from the Gulf Stream and floated onto the continental shelf off Cape Lookout in mid-October. Besides unseasonably high water temperatures, the meandering pool of water brought a bloom of *Gymnodinium breve* that it had picked up in the Straits of Florida a month before.

This finding was small consolation for the residents of coastal North Carolina, perhaps. But it did confirm the extraordinary influence that oceanic currents can have on our lives and demonstrated the unprecedented perspective on the earth that remote sensing from satellites has provided to oceanographers in the last 20 years.

Since 1957, when the Soviet Union launched its first *Sputnik,* thousands of satellites have been launched by a handful of countries. Taking advantage of the broader perspective on land and ocean areas that space offers, dozens of satellites now record radiation from the invisible portion of the electromagnetic spectrum— much larger than the band represented by visible light. Such radiation has proved to be a rich source of information. Whether it is water vapor or carbon dioxide in the atmosphere, chlorophyll in plants, a parking lot on land, or an iceberg at sea, matter radiates a portrait of itself in a palette composed of different wavelengths, frequencies, and intensities of radiation—from gamma rays, with a wavelength of one ten-billionth of a yard, to cloud-piercing microwaves, with wavelengths up to nearly a foot. Sensitive instruments aboard satellites, such as radiometers and sounders, focus and convert the different wavelengths emitted by areas on earth or in the atmosphere into a digital format that can be transmitted to receiving stations and converted into images.

Some satellite instruments passively collect electromagnetic radiation from the earth and its atmosphere. From 1978 to 1984, for instance, the Nimbus-7 satellite carried a Coastal Zone Color Scanner that collected information on the density of phytoplankton in surface waters by recording electromagnetic radiation from chlorophyll pigments. Other devices measured sources of distortion, such as water vapor and sediments, in order to insure that the radiation recorded by the scanner was close to what was actually emitted from the phytoplankton.

LANDSAT

Among the longest-running series of remote-sensing satellites are the Landsat satellites, the first of which was launched in 1972. With sensors that detect electromagnetic radiation from the visible to the near infrared, Landsat satellites compose scenes covering 13,000 square miles at a time with a resolution that can distinguish between objects 90 feet or larger. If clouds do not interfere, Landsat can gather information on plant productivity over large areas of ocean, and can chart marshlands, rivers, shoals, turbidity, and water pollution, as well as various kinds of land cover, from forests to shopping malls. If distortion by the atmosphere and water can be accounted for and adequate surveys on the surface can be conducted, Landsat can aid in mapping submerged reefs, sandbars, and sea-grass beds.

From agronomists and geologists to hydrologists and urban planners, a wide audience has been able to draw on the historical record of images that Landsat has compiled over the last two decades. Using new geographic information system technology that makes possible the graphic representation of a wide range of information, from population density to vegetative cover, coastal zone managers in the United States have been able to use historical Landsat data to analyze change in the uses of coastal land.

In the most ambitious of these projects, scientists at the National Oceanic and Atmospheric Administration laboratory in Beaufort, North Carolina, have prepared maps showing change in ground cover in the watersheds surrounding the Chesapeake Bay. The project has required processing tremendous amounts of data from Landsat records as well as from field surveys, which are essential for insuring a close relation between the image produced from Landsat data and what is actually on the ground. The analysis made possible by historical Landsat records is giving government decision makers and citizens an unprecedented overview of change in the Chesapeake Bay watershed.

Where money is scarce, Landsat and other remote-sensing programs can provide an important edge in mapping and protecting remote areas in particular. By 1979, conservation agencies in the Philippines had begun to take steps to address the conversion of mangrove forests into shrimp ponds. However, they did not possess detailed information on where or how much mangrove forest had been destroyed, nor did they have the capability to survey all 11,000 miles of coastline. Rather than generating entirely new data, Philippine scientists turned to the data that Landsat had been collecting for a decade. On master maps of the Philippines coastal zone, scientists color-coded the Landsat data. The resulting maps allowed conservation agencies to focus further efforts on areas where mangrove forests were still extensive enough to support nearshore fisheries. They then flew aerial surveys of these areas, taking photographs with a hand-held camera. All of this information was combined to illustrate current land use and cover and to identify areas for preservation.

Like many other data-gathering activities, however, the Landsat effort is flawed by a poor system for storage of historical images and by erratic coverage. Generally, the private company that now manages Landsat—EOSAT—captures images only when there is a known or potential customer. As a result, there are large parts of the earth for which EOSAT does not regularly capture and store images. Furthermore, older images are stored on magnetic tapes that can deteriorate or in formats that cannot be read by existing equipment.

OTHER SATELLITES

Other types of satellite instruments both emit and receive electromagnetic signals. The most common of these sends a pulse of microwaves, much as radar does, and receives the signal reflected back by clouds, ice, forests, or the sea surface. When pulses are sent directly beneath a satellite, the time taken by the pulse to return to the antenna accurately measures the distance between the satellite and the reflecting object. In this way, satellites can generate information on the topography of land and sea alike.

In 1982, satellite altimeters detected the three-foot-high swell of water that moved from an area off Australia to the coastal waters of Peru, launching a catastrophic El Niño event. More recently, the joint French-U.S. satellite called *Topex/Poseidon*, launched in September 1992, has begun measuring the height of the ocean with an accuracy of an inch. As a result, scientists are gaining unparalleled views of the risings and fallings in the ocean's surface caused by currents and, quite possibly, the rise in sea level expected from the warming of the earth's atmosphere.

Taking advantage of the different degrees to which smooth and rough surfaces reflect microwaves, another radar device called a scatterometer can perceive even finer detail about the surface of areas at sea or on land. Using these differences, sophisticated scatterometers can discriminate between forests composed of different species of trees or between choppy and calm seas. The technology has advanced so that a satellite hundreds of miles above the earth can determine the speed and direction of winds blowing over the sea surface. Over shallower waters, scatterometers may locate submerged banks and reefs by detecting the swell of waves above them.

Other capabilities of satellite sensors will play crucial roles in better understanding the earth as a system of land, water, and air entering a period of enormous change. Besides collecting truly global temperature readings to complement those taken at thousands of stations on the ground, satellites also detect changes in cloud cover and in the mix of gases in the atmosphere that influence global climate.

The unprecedented amounts of information that satellite sensors will be sending earthward in the coming decades will be a mixed blessing unless we can develop the technology to channel and analyze it. Equally important will be the burden of discriminating between meaningful and meaningless information, between information that is worth spending money on and information that is not.

MONITORING AND MANAGEMENT SCIENCE

A decade ago, the detection of a hole in the stratospheric ozone layer, which protects life on earth from ultraviolet radiation, prompted the nations of the world to halt the production of ozone-destroying chlorofluorocarbons (CFCs). Although the launch of the Nimbus satellites in the 1970s had enabled scientists to map ozone concentrations in the atmosphere, the thinning of the ozone layer was first detected by Antarctic ground sensors designed in the 1920s. The satellites had recorded the hole only incidentally, because the scientists analyzing data from the Nimbus satellites had been tracking ozone levels in order to study atmospheric circulation, not the thickness of the ozone layer itself.

We were lucky with the ozone layer. Although scientists long anticipated that the release of CFCs would destroy ozone, the task of monitoring the status of the ozone layer went begging. And monitoring the ozone layer is not alone in this neglect. The scientific community, industry, and government have forsaken most kinds of monitoring and pursued conventional research instead. The United Nations Environmental Programme, the only agency specifically responsible for acquiring global environmental data, must rely on other agencies to supplement its annual monitoring budget of $5 million. As a result, we possess very little national, regional, or international information on status and trends in coastal water quality, sources and levels of pollutants entering coastal waters, changes in land use, withdrawal of fresh water from rivers for irrigation, soil erosion, or production and transport of toxic chemicals.

Even in this age of massive environmental change, monitoring remains the Rodney Dangerfield of environmental sciences, partly because few people believe that funding for monitoring has yielded a fair return for the investment. Lack of coordination among agencies on what is sampled and how it is analyzed as well as a common failure to publish results in any form, much less a form that decision makers can use, all contribute to this dissatisfaction. The near impossibility of predicting that a particular change in water quality will lead to a particular change in fish populations at a particular time or place frustrates developers, industrialists, fishermen, and government officials. For their part, scientists chafe at the politicization of monitoring programs, which often are launched in order to avoid a difficult political decision. Unfortunately, it is also true that designing and running effective monitoring programs does not lead to advancement in the scientific community.

Now, most funding and effort is directed at monitoring compliance with water quality laws or with measures protecting vulnerable populations of marine wildlife, including commercially valuable fish, sea turtles, and marine mammals. Compliance monitoring seldom yields much information of lasting value for assessing trends in water quality, for example. In the waters off southern California, industry spends $17 million each year monitoring individual discharges in order to comply with clean water legislation. Doubts have arisen over the wisdom of investing so much money in data that is virtually useless in assessing water quality trends in the Southern California Bight as a whole.

The potential for chaos in information about the marine environment increases as well when each monitoring program adopts its own protocol for taking and analyzing samples and employs different standards for assuring the quality of the process. In its 1990 report on the health of the oceans, the United Nations Group of Experts on the Scientific Aspects of Marine Pollution despaired over the lack of international standards that would help insure comparability of information collected by monitoring programs. The UN group concluded that many of the measurements taken in the previous decade were of little use in assessing trends in marine pollution because of uncertainties over quality control.

Whether the concern is water quality or the status of coral reefs, choices must be made about what will be monitored and what will not be monitored. If the overall health of a coral reef area is being measured, will repeated surveys of coral cover yield meaningful measures of coral reef health? Or should monitoring focus on the abundance of certain fishes that depend upon healthy reef ecosystems? Or would it make more sense to monitor the metabolic processes of representative reef areas by measuring the production of oxygen and rates of calcification in corals? Can we confidently link a change in the variable we have selected to a change in the status of the reef?

Because many factors, only some of which can be monitored at any time or at all, contribute to change in ecosystems, identifying change due to human activities can be a difficult task. In the case of the Southern California Bight, for instance, water quality is affected by more than the discharges of pollutants or treated sewage. Runoff from city streets and sewer overflows from storms, not to mention heavy metals and other pollutants from air pollution, all contribute to the water quality of the bay.

Lack of information about baseline conditions also is a common weakness of monitoring programs. Sometimes this lack is caused by a disagreement over what to measure and how to measure it. Now, different agencies in the United States use different methods for measuring the coastline, wetlands, and the coastal zone. As a result, estimates of coastal habitat losses vary, as do estimates of coastal population growth. Furthermore, conflicting rules over land ownership and development undermine any attempt to assess how much coastal land is private and how much is publicly owned.

Even when well designed, monitoring programs often do not quickly produce the kind of dramatic and unequivocal findings that attract continued funding over a long period of time. Yet, a break in collection of environmental information can prevent the detection of trends amidst natural variations. For instance, the number of loggerhead sea turtles nesting in the southeastern United States varies greatly from year to year. Because of the biology of this species, trends are unlikely to emerge in less than eight or nine years.

Unlike most other beaches in the area, where monitoring of turtle nesting has been a recent and sporadic matter, monitoring on Little Cumberland Island by Dr. Jim Richardson and his associates has continued for more than 20 years, often with little or no funding. The result is one of the most valuable sets of data on sea turtle nesting anywhere in the world, and a clear record of a declining nesting population. Detecting other environmental trends, from global warming to changes in fish populations, will continue to depend upon such long-term commitments.

The value of a monitoring program is greatly undermined if the information is not directed at testing a clearly articulated hypothesis about how a particular habitat or animal and plant community functions or responds to a human activity. Inevitably, seeking agreement on such matters forces choices not simply about monitoring one thing rather than another, but also about the relative importance of different environmental values. Often, monitoring programs emphasize scientific understanding of what is important and ignore what decision makers, including private citizens, think is important. If those with a stake in a monitoring program do not explicitly agree on the priority questions, monitoring information simply becomes another focus for disagreement and disillusionment among scientists, managers, and the public.

One way of insuring that assumptions and standards are made explicit is through the development of a model that tries to predict how a marine ecosystem will respond to human activities. Information from a monitoring program allows continuing refinement of the model, making for more useful information for decision makers as well as advancing scientific understanding.

In 1990, the National Research Council of the National Academy of Sciences published a review of existing programs for monitoring marine environments. Given the pervasive lack of coordination in testing protocols and a continuing inability to generate credible assessments of trends in the status of marine environmental quality, this review offered a program for designing monitoring programs that can produce scientifically sound information that considers the needs and perceptions of decision makers and the general public. The most difficult part of the National Research Council's proposal has more to do with communication among people with very different languages and points of view than with the technical difficulties of capturing information.

BENEATH THE ARCTIC ICE

On August 11, 1993, a group of civilian scientists boarded the U.S. Navy's nuclear powered research submarine the USS *Pargo* in Groton, Connecticut, after weeks of unprecedented collaborative planning. A century after Fridtjof Nansen had wedged the *Fram* into the Arctic pack ice as a drifting research station, the scientists aboard the *Pargo* planned to take many of the same types of measurements as did Nansen and his crew, but to do so from beneath the Arctic ice. Many of these measurements, and others that Nansen could hardly have imagined, were aimed at learning about the movement of water into the Arctic from freshwater rivers and from the Atlantic Ocean.

Since the first sub-Arctic cruise of the nuclear powered USS *Nautilus* in 1958, the U.S. Navy had used submarines to collect enormous amounts of information about the bathymetry, chemistry, currents, and ice of the Arctic Sea. Under congressional pressure, the Navy agreed to release information on ice cover, but that was all. The *Pargo* expedition marked an entirely new, more open relationship between the military and a civilian scientific community that, for decades, had watched helplessly as the civilian research fleet declined and valuable oceanographic and environmental information flowed only into the Pentagon, not out of it.

Capable of remaining submerged for months at a time beneath Arctic ice or howling storm, the *Pargo* offered scientists an extraordinary platform for research that would contribute to understanding how the ocean currents distribute pollutants and to detecting early signs of global warming. During the cruise, scientists collected 1,500 water samples, 46 of them through the submarine's seawater system. By testing these samples for pollutants such as CFCs and radioactive cesium-137, analysts will be able to map the movement of water into and around the Arctic Sea. Upward-looking sonar sounders and video cameras also gathered information that may help in detecting changes in the thickness of Arctic ice. Finally, at two locations in the ice pack, scientists and the Navy crew installed buoys from which sensors hang at six depths to nearly 1,000 feet. For the next three years, information on water salinity and temperature collected by these sensors will be relayed to ground stations via Argos satellites.

Since the fall of the Soviet Union, the world has moved from an era dominated by international ideological tension to one in which global warming, pollution, resource declines, and population growth are redefining national security. The voyage of the *Pargo* suggests some of the benefits to be gained from redirecting the tremendous resources of the military toward the challenge of understanding the oceans and of monitoring the health and abundance of marine life. Failure to complete this transition will carry a high ecological and human cost.

3

~~~

Global Change

There is a river in the ocean: in the severest
droughts it never fails, and in the mightiest
floods it never overflows. . . . There is in the
world no other such majestic flow of waters.

MATTHEW FONTAINE MAURY,
*The Physical Geography of the Sea
and Its Meteorology*

The Sneaker Society started in the spring of 1991, in Shirley Tar-
nasky's backyard in Rockaway Beach, Oregon. Shirley, friends,
and neighbors gathered on a Sunday afternoon to swap Nike
sneakers that had been washing up on the Oregon coast in great
numbers. The purpose of the Sneaker Society was to exchange
and match shoes in good condition so that people could assemble
pairs of the normally high priced sneakers. However, members
also contributed to our knowledge of the North Pacific gyre, a
major ocean current that travels clockwise around the Pacific.

One year earlier, on May 27, 1990, the *Hansa Carrier,* a
freighter en route from Korea to Seattle, encountered a violent
storm. About 500 miles southeast of the Alaskan peninsula, four
boxcar-sized containers of sneakers broke open and 60,000 shoes
spilled into the North Pacific Ocean. The shoes floated east and
began to hit land in Washington State by the following winter.
Additional shoes were later found by beachcombers in British
Columbia and Oregon. By early 1993, some of the golf shoes,

hiking boots, and running and basketball shoes had washed up on beaches in Hawaii.

Although the shoes were a small financial windfall for the residents of coastal Canada, Oregon, and Washington, oceanographers found them to be a valuable source of information. The Nike shoe spill was the largest release of human-made drift objects ever, and therefore the largest experiment for charting the ocean surface currents.

"It's a fascinating piece of detective work, and I'm hoping the trail will lead to a better understanding of the ocean," said physical oceanographer Curtis Ebbesmeyer, who studied the paths of the drifting shoes. Knowledge of ocean currents helps oceanographers predict what will happen to small spills of oil, sewage, and even bodies lost at sea.

Currents keep ocean water in constant movement around the planet. The complicated patterns of currents are affected by the rotation of the earth, the energy of the sun, wind, and the salt content and temperature of the ocean. They both affect and are affected by climate.

Water moves in three dimensions—it can travel horizontally in two dimensions at the surface, sea floor, and mid-ocean, and it can rise to the surface as well as sink to the bottom. Regional movement of water has effects on climate as far inland as the centers of continents. Waters driven by ocean currents also distribute nutrients that support life throughout the oceans. The study of currents helps scientists understand the complex relationships between oceans and climate, and may provide a better understanding of the processes affecting global climatic change.

THE GLOBAL CONVEYOR BELT

The largest circulation pattern of ocean waters moves like a global conveyor belt. The circuit begins with cool, dense water that sinks near the poles, circulates throughout the deep oceans, surfaces again in the Indian, Atlantic, or Pacific Oceans, and travels along the surface toward the poles, where it sinks once again. If a single drop of water were to travel the entire journey, it could take 1,000 years to return to its starting point. In moving huge volumes of ocean water, the conveyor belt moves massive amounts of heat around the planet.

Near the equator, ocean waters pick up heat and move toward the poles. In the North Atlantic, the surface water, warmed by the sun, travels north in the Gulf Stream and meets cold air from Canada. The collision causes the ocean water to lose much of its heat to the atmosphere, and the water cools considerably by the time it reaches the northern polar region. As surface water cools and becomes denser and heavier, it sinks to the ocean floor. The water flows south again along the sea floor in the western North Atlantic.

For scientists studying deepwater formation, nuclear bomb tests from the late 1950s and early 1960s are the equivalent of the Nike shoe tracers. Just before the nuclear test ban treaty was signed in 1962, many nuclear bombs were detonated, releasing radioactive compounds high above the atmosphere. Twenty years of water sampling revealed the path of the radioactive tracers as they entered the water and followed the North Atlantic deepwater formation. By 1964 radioactive tritium was found in the surface waters of the North Atlantic. It had taken about ten years for this water to sink to the sea floor, and after another ten years, the same tritium was found in deep water off the coast of Florida. Over a period of 20 years, the water had traveled around 3,000 miles at an approximate speed of 150 miles per year—about 90 feet per day.

North Atlantic deep water travels south until it meets up with a similar current flowing from the Wedell Sea in Antarctica. The joining of these two big currents drives deep, cool water into the rest of the world's ocean basins, where it rises up again when it hits the western edges of continents. Most of the upwelling occurs around Antarctica, although water also moves slowly to the surface through diffusion in the Atlantic, Indian, and Pacific Oceans.

The conveyor belt's movement of water and heat around the planet has profound and wide-reaching consequences for life on earth. It influences the weather on the coasts and far inland. For example, the great release of heat in the North Atlantic is picked up by winds blowing west to east, making the climate mild in western Europe. Both Paris and Boston are at the same latitude, but winters are much less harsh in Paris because of the winds blowing Caribbean heat off the Atlantic Ocean.

Cold deep waters hold greater amounts of oxygen and essential nutrients than warmer surface waters, and the conveyor belt helps distribute this wealth. Where deep water rises to the surface through upwelling, it brings oxygen and nutrients to the sunlit zone. Such upwelling currents are of particular importance to ocean life and human economic gain. Because most surface waters are poorer in nutrients than deep water, but plants need sunlight to flourish, upwellings create localized areas with ideal growing conditions for marine life. The world's richest fishing grounds are in areas along the western edges of continents, where the cold water rises in upwellings. Although upwellings account for one-tenth of one percent of the sea surface, half of the world's fish catch occurs in these areas. The greatest numbers of seabirds off the California coast are found around upwellings, and many species have breeding seasons that coincide with peak upwelling periods. Many types of animals, from sperm whales and fur seals to tidepool invertebrates such as sea urchins, take advantage of extra nutrients and food to breed during upwelling peaks.

CLIMATE CHANGE

Nearly 100 years have passed since Swedish chemist Svante Arrhenius first predicted that the burning of fossil fuels would cause carbon dioxide to accumulate and trap heat in the earth's atmosphere. This early description of the potential for chemicals in the earth's atmosphere to trap heat by acting like the glass on a greenhouse prompted later scientists to coin the term "greenhouse effect."

The heat-trapping capacities of carbon dioxide and other three-atom molecules in the earth's atmosphere make life possible on the planet. Without these heat-trapping gases floating in the atmosphere, the average temperature of the surface of the earth would be around 0 degrees Fahrenheit. "Greenhouse gases" make up a surprisingly small proportion of the earth's atmosphere. Over 99 percent of the atmosphere is composed of two-atom molecules: oxygen and nitrogen gas. The trace quantities of three-atom "greenhouse gases"—carbon dioxide, methane, chloroflourocarbons (freons), and water vapor—form an effective blanket to trap heat radiating from the surface of the earth.

Ironically, the scientific community discounted Arrhenius's theory about the potential for excess carbon dioxide to bring on global climatic change because of the oceans' capacity for absorbing atmospheric carbon dioxide. Scientists assumed that the oceans, with their tremendous capacity for processing atmospheric carbon, would assimilate and store any excess carbon generated by humans. It wasn't until 1958 that scientists Hans Suess and Roger Revelle calculated that the upper oceans would not absorb carbon dioxide as rapidly as was previously assumed. More recent studies estimate that the oceans absorb between 30 and 50 percent of the carbon dioxide generated by human activities. Today, the role of the oceans in absorbing and storing carbon dioxide remains one of the largest unknown variables in the models climatologists use to predict the extent and effects of climate change.

Levels of carbon dioxide in the atmosphere have been rising steadily since systematic monitoring began in 1958, when David Keeling, of the Scripps Institution of Oceanography, started his measurements at the Mauna Loa Observatory in Hawaii. The now-famous "Keeling curve" shows seasonal variations in the amount of carbon dioxide, with a steady rise since 1958. Other studies, which have analyzed air bubbles trapped in glacial ice, indicate that carbon dioxide levels have been rising slowly since 1850, and are now 25 percent higher than the earliest measurements.

Scientists are stumped by an incredibly complex system of feedbacks that affect each other and influence climate. Climate is shaped by the sun, the oceans, the atmosphere, and the influence of continental areas. Water vapor, clouds, reflectivity of the earth's surfaces, changes in the earth's orbit, and biological and human activities also exert major influences.

Several qualities of the oceans make them important players in shaping climate. Water itself has the capacity to store, move, and release heat. The oceans can absorb and buffer carbon dioxide, the major greenhouse gas. Ice caps can also have a number of effects. Large ice caps serve as barriers preventing heat and carbon dioxide from passing between the atmosphere and the oceans. The white color of ice caps is a cooling influence because the light-colored surfaces reflect solar radiation. The great conveyor belt of ocean circulation, together with the smaller currents, influences climate as it moves heat, salt, carbon dioxide, and other elements around the globe.

CARBON AND THE OCEANS

The plants and animals that inhabit the oceans also play a role in shaping the earth's climate by processing and storing planetary carbon. As one of the building blocks of life, carbon is ubiquitous on earth. Forest trees, soil microorganisms, insects, and humans all are storehouses of carbon. Of all of the biological systems on earth, the oceans house the largest reservoir of carbon—roughly 75 to 80 percent of the carbon on earth—and the yearly exchange of carbon between the atmosphere and oceans is far greater than the exchange between atmosphere and land.

Photosynthesizing algae and corals are major players in the carbon cycle. During photosynthesis, chemical processes turn atmospheric carbon dioxide into elemental carbon, which is incorporated into the bodies of marine organisms and leaked into the seawater. Because of this capacity, and its significance in global warming scenarios, the life and death of the tiny marine algae called phytoplankton are objects of intense scientific scrutiny. In a process scientists call the "biological pump," phytoplankton take in atmospheric carbon dioxide and convert it to organic carbon.

Elemental carbon passes through food webs in the oceans when animals eat phytoplankton or capture free-floating carbon. When phytoplankton and other forms of marine life die, their bodies begin a descent to the abyss, carrying carbon in the form of body tissue toward the ocean floor. Scavengers and decomposing bacteria strip most of the nutritional value out of the descending material in the uppermost 3,000 feet. However, decay continues slowly until the organic matter arrives at the sea floor, where it is buried under falling sediment. Buried carbon generally remains at the bottom of the oceans unless geologic processes lift the sea floor above the surface, where weathering causes erosion.

The biological pump is more efficient in some areas than in others. Scientists working in the Southern Ocean around Antarctica have described one "leak" in the pump. Around one-fifth to one-quarter of the carbon absorbed into the Antarctic Southern Ocean each year by phytoplankton may be released back into the atmosphere through respiration by enormous numbers of plankton-eaters and predators, such as whales, penguins, and other birds and mammals. The importance of the leak in the Antarctic biological pump may be exaggerated, because most of this respiration takes place during the short austral summer season. However, we should not discount the potential for animals in other areas of the oceans to siphon off and reduce the amount of carbon that is ultimately stored.

The biological pump is only one of the means by which the oceans absorb atmospheric carbon dioxide. Airborne particles also carry carbon to the seas when they fall. The physics of mixing causes atmospheric carbon dioxide to be dissolved into the surface of the oceans. Once in the oceans, carbon dioxide is moved around through ocean water mixing and by the enormous conveyor belt of currents.

Sophisticated models run on supercomputers are the only tools available for climatologists to run "experiments" on the climate. Called general circulation models, these complex computer programs allow scientists to alter one or more factors, such as the amount of carbon dioxide or the sea surface temperature, and see the effects on climate. However, given the possibilities for feedbacks among ocean currents, clouds, and the lives and deaths of marine organisms in a warming climate, predicting the outcome defies the capabilities of even the most powerful supercomputer.

Although scientists generally agree that the oceans play a central role in absorbing atmospheric carbon dioxide, the role of oceans in storing carbon is a point of critical debate among students of global warming. Uncertainty about how oceans take in carbon and how long they store it, as well as how these processes might be affected by a warming climate, hampers efforts to determine just how large a role the oceans may play in absorbing increasing amounts of carbon dioxide generated by human activities.

PAST CLIMATIC CHANGE

The field of paleoclimatology offers a means of closely examining shifts in climate that occurred thousands to millions of years ago. Much of our ability to understand global climate change and predict its effects on the oceans and marine ecosystems comes from a look back into the geological record.

Sea floor sediment often contains the remains of tiny but abundant animals called foraminifera or forams, which provide an enlightening record of past climatic conditions. In areas called foram oozes, the calcium carbonate shells of these minute single-celled organisms make up almost a third of the sediment on the sea floor. Studies of the shapes and composition of foram shells yield insight into past ocean water temperature, the extent of polar ice caps, distribution of carbon dioxide, and the amount of nutrients in sea water. Forams in tropical waters have larger, more porous shells than those in colder waters. The surface-dwelling forams sport more delicate shells than those that live on the bottom.

Just as foram shells differ in shape depending upon these factors, their chemical composition depends upon the exact chemical makeup of the waters where they grew. Forams fashion their shells using oxygen, carbon, and other elements from surrounding seawater. Each element can have several isotopes, that is, forms of different weight. For example, most oxygen atoms weigh 16 times as much as hydrogen atoms, but a few rare others weigh 18 times as much as hydrogen. Lighter oxygen evaporates more readily than heavier.

Ordinarily, seawater contains a stable ratio of lighter to heavier oxygen, because the oxygen that evaporates returns to the oceans in rainfall. However, during past ice ages, much of the water that evaporated returned to the poles as snow, leaving the seawater with a higher than usual amount of heavier oxygen. This change was dutifully recorded in the calcium carbonate shells of forams. Additionally, in cores of ice-age ice from the poles, containing tiny amounts of ancient atmosphere trapped in air bubbles, paleontologists have found a surplus of lighter oxygen.

Studies of the different isotopes of carbon in foram shells have also revealed the distribution of carbon dioxide in ancient seawater. Finally, when the oceans contain an abundance of cadmium they also contain an abundance of nutrients, primarily phosphates and nitrogen. Since forams tend to mistake cadmium for calcium and absorb it into their shells, the amount of cadmium in their shells is an indication of the amount of nutrients in the water. Thus, in nutrient-rich conditions, forams have shells replete with cadmium.

Nestled in the sediment along with forams are indicators of the earth's magnetic field, which can be used to date the layers. It appears that the earth experienced a number of ice ages, perhaps triggered by small changes in the amount of sunlight that reached the planet. These fluctuations occurred in a rhythmic pattern, corresponding to changes in the earth's rotation and orbit around the sun.

Although the diminution of sunlight may have triggered the ice ages, this factor alone could not cause climate change of ice-age proportions. Fortunately, cores of ancient sea floor and ice caps have yielded other clues about conditions during the cold spells. Studies of air bubbles trapped in ancient ice, and layered like the sea floor sediments, reveal a corresponding drop in atmospheric carbon dioxide during the ice ages. Furthermore, comparisons of cadmium in foraminifera shells from the last ice age indicate that nutrients were dispersed equally through the all of the planet's bottom waters.

Dr. Wallace Broecker of Columbia University pieced these clues together. He proposed that the great conveyor belt of ocean circulation slowed or halted during the ice ages. Dr. Broecker showed how ocean circulation and the exchange of carbon dioxide between oceans and atmosphere could force climate changes on the scale of global ice ages. Some researchers agree that it is possible to understand major climatic changes over the past 180 million years in terms of changes in ocean circulation.

The North Atlantic conveyor may play a key role in climate change. When the conveyor operates normally, the cold salty water that sinks in the North Atlantic flows south, around Africa, across the Indian Ocean, and into the Pacific. When the current resurfaces in the Pacific, it carries carbon dioxide from the depths, some of which is released into the atmosphere. If the conveyor were to stop, carbon dioxide would build up on the ocean floor and shallow waters would have less carbon dioxide. The drop in surface-water carbon dioxide would cause more carbon dioxide to be drawn into the seawater from the atmosphere, causing the climate to cool. Possibly the conveyor could be stopped and started by changes in ocean salinity, which could in turn be brought about by melting or freezing large areas of ice.

This explanation does not consider the potential for other factors, such as changing reflectivity, other greenhouse gases, and cloud cover, to influence climate, but it does provide a basis for several generalizations about oceans and climate. If the North Atlantic conveyor plays a major role in influencing climate, climatic change on a global scale might not be gradual, but could be sudden and drastic. Although it remains unclear what would cause the current to cease flowing, the world as we know it will never be the same if that should happen.

In fact, the paleontological record shows several abrupt switches in climate over the past 20,000 years. Scientists studying pollen grains from land around the North Atlantic found indications of temperature changes over hundreds or thousands of years—a virtual snap of the fingers in geologic time.

Several periods of warmer climate can be seen in the geologic record. If we look back one hundred million years ago, to the Cretaceous period, when dinosaurs were common and flowering plants abundant and widespread, we find a warmer world. Known as the "dawn of modern times," the Cretaceous hosted plants that looked much like today's flora, and the ancestors of today's marine life were ensconced in the seas. The Cretaceous was also a period of ice-free conditions on the earth. The world's continents were still drifting apart, and were partially flooded with shallow seas, 300 to 600 feet deep. Ocean circulation patterns were most likely quite different from what they are today.

There is evidence of rapid global warming more recently, around 57 million years ago, at the end of the Paleocene period. It, too, implies that the oceans and climate can be knocked out of equilibrium, causing rapid and drastic changes. Studies conducted on ocean sediment cores from Antarctica reveal that surface water temperatures warmed from 55–57 degrees Fahrenheit to around 70 degrees, and the bottom waters increased from 50 degrees to around the same temperature as the surface. A warm, humid climate prevailed on Antarctica, and subtropical species of plankton moved into the warm surface waters. The changes in the deep waters caused cataclysmic extinctions of deep-sea organisms, as the normally near-freezing, oxygen-rich seawater was replaced with warm, salty, oxygen-poor water.

In fact, the warming provoked the greatest spate of extinctions of bottom-dwelling animals of the past 90 million years. In the space of 2,000 years—a twinkling for the fossil record—40 percent of the bottom-dwelling foraminifera went extinct, while the surface forams were virtually unaffected. Up to half of the foraminifera that occurred below 300 feet in Antarctica became extinct in less than 3,000 years. Cores from other areas during this period revealed corresponding extinctions in deep-sea bottom-dwelling foraminifera around Trinidad, Austria, and northern Italy. Cores from continental shelf areas showed little loss of species. The Antarctic system apparently recovered its cool, oxygen-rich waters around 100,000 years after the warming began, but the massive extinctions changed the character of the Antarctic bottom-dwelling fauna.

EL NIÑO / SOUTHERN OSCILLATION

More recent changes in ocean currents demonstrate the ocean's influence on the climate and ecosystems of the planet. On an early spring day in 1992, sport fishermen set out from San Francisco Bay to pursue prized rockfish. Much to their surprise, the anglers landed barracuda and bonito—species usually found much farther south, in warmer waters. During that same month, farther south in the waters off Catalina Island, divers studying giant kelp noticed that the plants had begun to decompose at their tops, from the surface to six or seven feet below. Commercial fishermen chasing the Pacific whiting also reported strange occurrences in April. The fish had moved from the California–Oregon border north to waters off Oregon and Washington. These phenomena and others, such as high sea levels in San Diego, were the hallmarks of what climatologists and oceanographers call an El Niño / Southern Oscillation, or ENSO.

For much of the year, the Peru Current and upwellings of deep water bring nutrients to the surface off Peru and Ecuador, feeding

algal blooms that support one of the most productive marine communities in the world. Toward the austral summer, however, the
Peru Current weakens and warm equatorial water flows into the
area, blocking the upwelling of the nutrient-rich waters. Since this
phenomenon occurs near Christmastime each year, fishermen
dubbed the phenomenon El Niño, Spanish for "the Child."

In most years, the El Niño phenomenon is transitory and weak.
But in some years, a much stronger, long-lasting El Niño triggers
a catastrophic change not only in the productivity of the waters
as far north as British Columbia, but in weather patterns as far
away as Indonesia and Africa. These catastrophic El Niños, which
generate headlines and widespread devastation, occur every two
to seven years. The El Niño of 1982–83 was especially intense.

The reason for the variability in the intensity of El Niños
escaped oceanographers for many years, until careful study of cli-
matological and oceanographic records revealed that strong El
Niños were associated with changes in dominant atmospheric systems on the other side of the world. In most years, an enormous
high pressure system sits over the South Pacific, while a giant low
pressure system sits over the Indian Ocean. In years of strong El
Niños, however, the South Pacific high weakens and the Indian
Ocean low strengthens. This southern oscillation, as it is called,
causes the trade winds that generally blow westward to weaken
or even reverse direction. Water that the winds and air pressure
have piled up in the western Pacific then flows eastward until it
encounters the South American continent, which diverts it north
and south. During an El Niño, sea levels off Peru are unusually
high as the thick blanket of warm water floats above the colder
sea water.

The most recent severe El Niño or ENSO began in 1982. Characteristically, there were record rainfalls and unusually warm seawater. The temperature of the surface water off Peru rose by 9
degrees Fahrenheit, and the layer where cold water met surface
waters dropped by 300 feet. The warm water conditions persisted
for nine months, and were clearly defined from the surface to a
depth of 200 feet. The first abnormal month was September 1982.
In October through December, the temperature was consistently
9 degrees above normal. Then between January and May 1983,
the surface temperature remained high, but the temperature at

150 feet began to drop. Ocean temperatures approached normal by the following September.

Some of the damaging effects of an ENSO occur because of changes in upwellings. The process of upwelling still occurred off of Peru in the early months of 1983, but the influx of warm water managed to displace the cold upwelling waters laden with nitrate, phosphate, and silicate. In normal years the combination of nutrient-rich upwelling and sunlight in the coastal Peruvian surface waters yields an abundance of life. Microscopic algae flourish, producing incredibly high rates of productivity. This bounty is passed through the food chain, creating ideal living conditions for fish, birds, mammals, and other marine life. In fact, coastal Peruvian bird life is so abundant that the collection and processing of their fecal matter, or guano, has long been a major industry. Guano is extremely rich in nitrogen and phosphorus, and it is a valuable ingredient in fertilizers.

During the 1983 ENSO, the decline in essential nutrients in Peruvian surface waters, especially nitrate, hampered the growth of microscopic algae and led to reduced plankton growth. The effect was widespread—in equatorial ocean waters off South America, total productivity was only around one-fourth to one-fifth of normal. To tiny copepods, the "cows of the sea," and other animals that graze plankton, all phytoplankton are not created equal. Diatoms are usually more common in Peruvian waters and they have a far greater nutritional value than other kinds of plankton called dinoflagellates and coccolithophores. Unfortunately, under the warm water conditions in a severe El Niño it was the dinoflagellates and coccolithophores that fared better. The animals that ate phytoplankton were faced with smaller portions of poorer food. As populations of plankton eaters dwindled, so did the animals that ate the plankton eaters, and reverberations were felt throughout the food web.

Perhaps the most famous and dramatic ENSO-related decline in population is that of the anchovies. During an earlier ENSO, in 1972, anchovies were forced into a narrow band of cold water along the coast. Taking advantage of the dense concentrations of fish, fishing vessels caught many more anchovies than usual, nearly wiping out the population. With the decline in anchovies, sardine populations grew to replace the anchovies. However, the sardines have never been as bountiful as the anchovies, and the anchovy populations have only slowly recovered.

The anchovies were not the only casualties of the 1972 ENSO. Over half of all seabirds died in Peru, due to lack of food and nest desertion. Many other nests were destroyed by heavy rains and the flooding of sand bars. Because the birds who produce guano eat primarily anchovies, they declined as well. Death of these birds had severe effects on the South American guano industry.

Throughout the eastern Pacific, the 1982–83 ENSO wreaked havoc in coral reef ecosystems. In Costa Rica, Panama, and Colombia, the coral suffered 70 to 90 percent mortality. In the Galapagos, death rates for corals exceeded 95 percent. On the other hand, some species benefited greatly from the ENSO. The warmer waters enabled many species, such as skipjack tuna and dolphinfish, to extend their ranges into new areas. It also created population explosions for some species, such as the scallop *Argopecten purpuratus*. There were beneficial long-term effects, too. The movement of warm water down to the sea floor caused an increase in dissolved oxygen at the bottom, which created improved feeding conditions at this level. This, combined with the decreased fishing pressure, meant greater numbers of many fish species, including Pacific hake, in the long run.

Effects from the ENSO of 1982–83 did not stop at the shore. Significant changes in local weather affected areas far inland. In some places, severe drought occurred, in others, heavy rains. Panama experienced such an extended extreme drought that tropical forest trees began to wilt and even die.

Severe droughts also occurred in Indonesia, Australia, the United States, parts of Africa, and South America. In Indonesia, drought decreased the yields of crops, especially rice, and, combined with fire, damaged many forests. Three and one-half million hectares were destroyed in East Kalimantan, which contributed to the $6 billion in lost revenue from the forestry sector. This loss led to famine, disease, and hundreds of deaths. Droughts in Australia also caused both crop and livestock losses. Widespread bush fires compounded the damage. Wheat, oat, and barley harvests fell by half. Millions of sheep and cows were also lost, representing billions of dollars of economic damage.

Drought hit Brazil as well, causing declines in agricultural production. In the southern part of the country alone, the drought was responsible for $924 million in agricultural losses, 25 million tons of lost topsoil, and hundreds of thousands of homeless people. In India, drought affected over one-third of the country. In Africa, widespread drought had particularly severe effects on maize production in Zimbabwe, millet and sorghum output in Senegal, grain production in Mauritania, and corn crops in South Africa. Drought in the north central part of the United States meant losses of $3 billion for corn, $480 million for cotton, and $670 million for soybeans.

At the other extreme, the Atacama and Peruvian deserts received heavy rains. In Guayaquil, Ecuador, rainfall was almost four times normal in 1983. The increase in rainfall in Peru and Ecuador caused population explosions in all of the annual species of ground-covering plants. In 1983, this new ground cover became a food source for many grazing animals. But in other parts of Peru and Ecuador, heavy flooding caused agricultural damage. Parts of California were devastated by coastal storms and mudslides. These floods also caused $200 million in damage to the state's agriculture. Warmer ocean surface waters generated by the ENSO also caused many tropical storms. Hurricane Iwa was responsible for $234 million in damage in Hawaii. French Polynesia was blasted by six tropical storms between December 1982 and April 1983.

Air temperatures also changed during the 1982–83 ENSO event. On the bright side, the eastern United States experienced the warmest winter in 25 years. This translated to $500 million in energy savings.

The ENSO, with its associated climatic change, has been implicated in many secondary problems. These include dust storms in Australia, brush fires in the Ivory Coast, Ghana, and Australia, encephalitis outbreaks in the eastern United States, an increase in rattlesnake bites in Montana, an increase in the number of bubonic plague cases in New Mexico, and a higher incidence of shark attacks off the coast of Oregon.

Recent studies suggest that the oceanic effects of El Niños can be very long-lived. During the ten years after the 1982–83 El Niño, planetary waves moved east across the Pacific and joined the Kuroshio current near Japan, deflecting the course of the Kuroshio and increasing sea surface temperatures in the northwestern Pacific. Researchers believe that oceanic changes created by the strongest El Niño of the century may have influenced weather patterns over the North American continent in the decade following 1983.

SEA-LEVEL RISE

Studies of ENSO events show how complex and far-reaching the effects of oceanic change can be. Future warming of seawater could cause similar ecological changes and weather patterns, but a rise in sea level is perhaps the most important effect of climate change. Even a small rise could devastate many urban areas and low-lying coastal lands around the world. Sea levels change constantly throughout the world's oceans because of the tides, but there are many other reasons for sea-level change. Scientific models of sea-level rise focus on the expansion of seawater when it becomes warmer, melting of polar and alpine ice sheets, changes in the amount of fresh water stored on land, and changes in the earth's crust and movements of rock.

Recent studies have shown that sea levels have risen or fallen in specific areas. In Alaska, sea level has actually dropped four feet over the past century. When Alaskan glaciers melt, the land is relieved of its icy burden and rises. A study of microatolls in the Maldives and Cocos (Keeling) Islands in the Indian Ocean, and in the Republic of Kiribati in the Pacific, shows a slight fall in sea level over the past ten years. A study of South African sea-level measurements shows rises of nearly half an inch each decade from 1960 to 1988.

In some areas of the world, sea levels change seasonally. The Mediterranean Sea, for instance, shows somewhat regular drops and rises in sea level annually. The reason is that the sea's elevation is determined by evaporation, rainfall, and the influx of river water, as well as variable inflows of Atlantic Ocean surface water and outflow of bottom waters.

Great sea-floor earthquakes, caused by the movement of plates of the earth's crust, may have contributed significantly to sea-level rises in the past. The 1960 Chilean earthquake was accompanied by sea-floor uplift and subsidence, resulting in a reduction of ocean basin volume of more than 137 cubic miles. With less room for ocean water, sea level increased 0.07 inch overnight—about the same as the average year's global sea-level rise from other causes.

These local changes in sea level generally are of less concern than the continued global rise in sea level and its anticipated acceleration. Over the past century, global sea level has risen between one and two millimeters each year, as part of a 300-year trend. Although scientists do not agree which theory explains this rise, they generally do agree that global warming due to increasing levels of greenhouse gases in the atmosphere would accelerate the long-term trend. The Intergovernmental Panel on Climate Change, convened by the United Nations Environment Program in 1990, has predicted that future global warming will cause the average global sea level to rise 15 inches by the year 2050. This is the middle of a range of sea-level rise estimates from 9.5 to 20.5 inches.

As with global warming scenarios themselves, a good deal of contention exists about how global climatic change would affect sea level. A worst-case scenario would take place if global warming caused the Western Antarctic Ice Sheet to melt. The water from this mile-thick slab of ice the size of India could create a 10-foot rise in sea levels. Melting of Greenland ice could add from 4 to 39 inches, and melting alpine glaciers could add from 4 to 12 inches.

A change of a few inches in global sea level may seem like a trifling amount, but even the lowest predicted scenario for sea-level rise could have drastic effects on more than half of the world's population, for that is how many people live within 50 miles of an oceanic coastline. Local effects will vary depending on local or regional movements of the earth's crust, the resistance of shorelines to erosion, and ocean current patterns, but they include inundation, loss of life and property, and groundwater contamination.

The effects of sea-level rise would be particularly harmful in low-lying coastal areas. At current sea-level rise rates in Egypt, eight to ten million people could be displaced if flood waters submerge the Nile delta. With a three-foot rise, about 15 percent of the country's gross national product would be affected, with 12 to 15 percent of Egypt's arable land drowned. Nearly 80 percent of Bangladesh's land is part of the Bengal delta system, fed by the Ganges, Brahmaputra, and Meghna Rivers. This is the world's largest delta system. A three-foot sea-level rise would affect 9 percent of the country's people, destroy 11 percent of their crops, and adversely affect nearly 6 percent of the gross domestic product. Salt water could intrude up to 300 miles inland into groundwater sources, jeopardizing the survival of crops. Increased storm surges would magnify the already incredible number of lives lost during hurricanes. Inundation could cause the nation to lose 12 to 28 percent of its area, where 9 to 27 percent of the population lives.

Island nations are particularly vulnerable to sea-level rise. Maldives, a nation of 1,190 small islands in the Indian Ocean, lies just six feet above sea level. Although the land would not be flooded by the maximum rise anticipated for the year 2050, even the lowest estimated rise will jeopardize life on the islands. Among other things, these coral islands may lose their supply of fresh water. In natural reservoirs on coral islands, a pool of fresh water generally floats atop heavier salt water. Rising sea level would contaminate this pool of fresh water with salt water and could push the water out onto the land surface, where evaporation and runoff would further reduce what is already a limited water supply. By a similar means, sea-level rise may contaminate underground sources of fresh water in other low-lying coastal areas.

Rising sea levels would affect some habitats more severely than others. The most vulnerable environments are major river deltas, coastal wetlands (including mangrove forests), and coral islands. Episodic storms and floods could extend the damage farther inland. The last century's one-foot rise in sea level already has caused significant coastal erosion, with a 50–100-foot landward shift of the waterline on the East Coast of the United States. Sea-level rise increases the erosion of cliffs by the force of waves and by undercutting sediments protecting the cliffs' bases. As they erode, cliffs become vulnerable to landslides and other damage.

In estuaries, a wedge of salty water could move farther upstream into freshwater rivers, increasing salinity in the estuary and freshwater aquifers. This change could severely disrupt the spawning and growth of fish that have adapted to particular salinity levels, as well as altering the distribution of sea-grass beds, mangrove forests, and marshes, all of which would have a cascading effect on dependent fish, wildlife, and people.

A study of the geological record of the last 10,000 years showed that mangroves could keep up with a sea-level rise of three inches per century, but at rates over four inches per century, they could not adapt. Over thousands of years, coastal ecosystems could move inland in response to sea level rise, but the development of coastlines—converting forests to farms, building roads and dikes—means that there are fewer escape routes for coastal plants and animals.

STRATOSPHERIC OZONE DEPLETION

The decrease of stratospheric ozone over the South Pole is another form of global change that could directly affect marine ecosystems. Researchers have shown that there is excess ultraviolet radiation entering the earth's atmosphere through the "ozone hole" over the South Pole—which is actually not so much a hole as it is an area in which the ozone layer is abnormally thin.

The stratosphere is a layer of the earth's atmosphere located 8 to 30 miles above sea level. Within this layer is a very thin layer of ozone. The ozone layer has an average thickness of one-tenth of an inch, and ozone is only 0.0001 percent of all the gases present; however, it shields the earth from harmful ultraviolet-B radiation. Ozone absorbs ultraviolet light and retains much of it far above the earth's surface.

Ozone in the lower atmosphere is a type of air pollution produced in our cities by automobiles and other vehicles. Anyone living in a major metropolitan area has probably heard ozone levels quoted as part of air quality indices. The higher the ozone the more unhealthful the air. However, this same ground-level trash is a stratospheric treasure.

In the stratosphere, ozone is created by chemical reactions fueled by strong sunlight. Ozone is also destroyed in the stratosphere through chemical reactions with naturally occurring chemicals. Chlorine, in particular, is a major destroyer of ozone in the stratosphere.

Atmospheric concentrations of chlorine gases have been steadily on the rise, nearly doubling between 1975 and 1990. Chloro-fluorocarbons (CFCs) are the main culprits. Manufactured chemicals that can remain in the atmosphere for 40 to 150 years, CFCs have been widely used in aerosol propellants, refrigerants, cleaning solvents, and foaming agents for chemicals. They were so valued that perhaps 20 million tons of two CFC compounds have been produced worldwide. Much of this has already been released into the atmosphere and strayed up to the stratosphere. The rest will probably follow unless we are more careful about the way we retire appliances and dispose of industrial wastes. When CFCs encounter ultraviolet radiation they split apart, releasing chlorine, which reacts chemically to break down ozone.

Investigators use balloons, high-flying aircraft, and satellites to map the stratospheric ozone hole. A seasonal phenomenon, the hole is present only during the austral spring. When the ozone hole is not present, the ozone layer measures 220 Dobson units (a single Dobson unit is only 1/100 of a millimeter). In 1987, the ozone was down to 121 Dobson units. One hundred twenty-four Dobson units were measured in 1989, and 125 Dobson units in 1990. This decrease allows large amounts of harmful ultraviolet-B radiation to reach the earth's surface.

As scientists tracked the thinning of the ozone layer and increasing amounts of ultraviolet-B radiation, concern grew about increased incidence of human skin cancer, as well as harm to other animals and plants. Ultraviolet-B radiation has numerous effects on phytoplankton and other plants. For instance, there are damaging effects to growth, photosynthesis, uptake of nutrients such as nitrogen, and enzyme activity. Phytoplankton movement is impaired, and chlorophyll—a pigment necessary for photosynthesis—is bleached and destroyed by the radiation. Studies in the North Pacific have shown that excess ultraviolet-B also damages DNA in fish eggs, larvae, and animal plankton or may kill the animals outright. Because ultraviolet-B cannot penetrate far through water, surface-dwelling organisms face the greatest risk from excess UV-B.

Although much of the research into the effects of decreased ozone on the Antarctic ecosystem is in its early stages, the loss of phytoplankton due to ultraviolet radiation could be dramatic. Together with his colleagues, Ray Smith of the University of California at Santa Barbara measured the effects of ultraviolet-B radiation on productivity in the Antarctic marginal ice zone and found productivity reduced by 6 to 12 percent under the ozone hole. Using conservative figures, the research team estimated that this reduction could translate into a 2 to 4 percent loss in yearly production of phytoplankton in the marginal ice zone.

Loss of oceanic phytoplankton could have reverberations throughout the planet. These tiny algae convert approximately 104 billion tons of carbon every year, whereas all terrestrial ecosystems combined convert only 100 billion tons of carbon. Therefore reduced productivity of the phytoplankton could result in some global changes. Phytoplankton, the basis of many marine food chains, are 1,000 to 10,000 times more concentrated in subpolar regions than in either the tropics or subtropics, and therefore are particularly vulnerable to increased ultraviolet radiation.

In 1994, the production of CFCs fell as it had for the previous five years, giving hope that this global threat to the productivity of the oceans has been blunted. This decrease in their manufacture is entirely due to the rapid recognition of the danger of CFCs that was sparked by the discovery of ozone thinning during the Antarctic spring in 1985. With unprecedented speed, the countries of the world negotiated an agreement to cut CFC production in half. As more information on the gravity of the problem became available, the 87 members of the Montreal Protocol on Substances that Deplete the Ozone Layer agreed to phase out CFC production by January 1, 1996.

The Southern Ocean, located under the ozone hole, is one of the largest and most productive ecosystems in the world, contributing 10 to 20 percent of the total global oceanic production. Changes in the abundance of phytoplankton base could have serious effects on other creatures in the Antarctic community, including krill, 120 species of finfish, 80 species of seabirds, 6 species of seals, and 15 species of whales.

Protection of this rich ecosystem from increased ultraviolet radiation can only occur far away, in factories and appliance stores.

4

≈≈≈

Life in the Seas

The beauty and genius of a work of art may be
destroyed; a vanished harmony may yet again
inspire the composer; but when the last individual of a race of living beings breathes no
more, another heaven and another earth must
pass before such a one can be again.

WILLIAM BEEBE, 1906

Life in the seas seems like a strange distortion of life on land.
Oversized animals, diminutive plants, and unusual lifestyles dominate. Look closely at the seas and the life forms appear more fan-
tastic than familiar. The largest animal that has ever lived on sea
or land, the blue whale, is the definition of big. Weighing more
than 20 adult elephants, it has blood vessels so broad that a full-
grown trout could swim through them. The vessels serve a heart
the size of a small car.

At the other end of the spectrum, microscopic viruses are the
most numerous life forms in the oceans. A teaspoon of seawater
can contain millions of viruses.

The sea floor is home to organisms that seem more appropriate
for horror movies—giant single-celled organisms and herds of
overgrown meat-eating relatives of crabs. Xenophyophores are
single cells that can grow to several inches in diameter. In some
deep-sea trenches in the Pacific, scientists estimated that 30 to 50
percent of the sea floor was covered by the slimy pseudopodia
these creatures use to collect food particles. Enormous isopods, a

kind of crustacean, grow to a foot in length, and scavenge the sea floor for dead and dying animals. There are species of fish that live only in the anal cavities of sea cucumbers, fish that change sex in the course of their lives and fish that have both male and female sex organs.

Life began in the seas, and relatives of the plantlike bacteria believed to be responsible for releasing oxygen into the earth's primordial atmosphere still exist. Many other marine life forms are quite ancient. Horseshoe crabs have existed in essentially the same form for the past 135 million years, and one genus of lamp shell has survived for more than 500 million years.

A TRIP TO THE SEA STORE

Humans are relative newcomers on the ocean scene, although we have been eating products from the seas for 10,000 years and using sea life for medicinal purposes for several thousand years. The oldest written pharmacopoeia, the Chinese *Pen Tsao,* compiled in 2800 B.C., mentions many marine cures. Algae have been used to prevent scurvy, kill parasitic worms, cure goiters, dilate cervices, and supplement vitamin-deficient diets. Corals, pearls, oysters, seahorses, eels, and a variety of other fish have provided folk remedies around the world.

We still rely upon sea life to cure medical conditions and conduct medical research. Perhaps the most promising marine pharmaceuticals are Ara-A and Ara-C, both derived from chemicals in marine sponges. Ara-A is an antiviral compound and Ara-C fights leukemia. Kainic acid, used throughout the world to fight parasitic worms, is the same compound found in the red algae. Synthesized calcitonin derived from chinook salmon is used to treat postmenopausal osteoporosis, Paget's disease of bone, and hypercalcemia, a condition caused by excessive amounts of calcium in the blood. The remains of fossil fish provide some components of ichthamol, a topical antiseptic. Recent research indicates that skeletons of stony corals can be useful in human bone grafts.

Marine plants and animals have greatly contributed to medical research. Agar, the growing medium used in tissue culture, is a mixture of polysaccharides from cell walls of certain red algae. Basking sharks and other deep-sea sharks are sources of squalene, a compound similar to skin oil that helps drugs and lotions penetrate human skin. The blood from horseshoe crabs helps hospitals test for toxins in pharmaceutical products that cause septic shock, which previously accounted for half of all hospital-acquired infections and one-fifth of all hospital deaths. Studies of neurons in sea slugs and squid helped scientists learn about nervous system function. Prolific sea urchins provided material for embryological studies. Large white blood cells from smooth dogfish helped researchers discover the cause of gout.

Cosmetics and vitamins, as well as hygiene and other personal care products, commonly are based on products from the sea. We wash our hair with oils from the deep-sea orange roughy fish and drink cod liver and shark liver oils for our health. We brush our teeth with the remains of diatoms. We supplement our diets with vitamins A and D, betacarotene from algae, and calcium from ground-up oyster shells. There is even a brand of denture adhesive that is made out of kelp. Ground-up herring scales provide a luster to nail polish and lipstick.

Cruise the aisles of a grocery store and it's hard to find many products without algae and algae byproducts. Alginates help keep beer foam from collapsing when it comes in contact with lipstick. The same alginates keep pimentos firm in green olives, stabilize pulp in juice concentrates, thicken instant soups, and substitute for oil and eggs in no-fat mayonnaise. Carrageenan is used as a stabilizer in air freshener gels, anti-icers, breads, infant formula, liquid cleanser, and pumpkin pie. Betacarotene pigment provides a natural yellow-orange food coloring for cheese, butter, beverages, pastries, and popcorn. Agar is found in canned meats, jellies, and marshmallows. And in the foreign food aisle you might find dried algae.

On average, Americans eat nearly 15 pounds of seafood each year, but we are not in the major league of fish-eating. Around 100 million metric tons of food come from the sea annually, and more than half of the world's population relies on seafood for most of its animal protein. While the top ten types of seafood eaten by Americans include only a few, popular finfish, plus shrimp, clams, crabs, and scallops, people in other countries eat an amazing diversity of fish, algae, and invertebrate animals.

If this metaphorical sea store were to have a service desk, a shopper could sample from a variety of services that healthy marine ecosystems provide. Oceans are the ultimate recycler, collecting and passing along oxygen, water molecules, carbon, nitrogen, phosphorus, and a host of other elements. As much as half of all photosynthesis takes place in the sea, making marine phytoplankton more deserving of the title "lungs of the earth" than tropical forest trees are. The oceans contain 97 percent of the world's water, which can spend weeks on the surface and thousands of years in the depths. The deep oceans are also a primary storehouse for carbon.

Healthy coastal wetlands and mangrove forests also perform a number of ecosystem services, such as providing nursery areas for many animals, purifying and clarifying water, preventing erosion, and protecting against storm surges. Coral reefs also provide barriers to storm surges and build atolls.

LIFE IN THE SEAS

Although we can't easily take advantage of it, the oceans provide almost all of the living space on the planet. Around 70 percent of the earth's surface is submerged in salt water. Although it is large, this figure minimizes the sheer volume of living space the oceans afford on the planet. On land, plants and animals live in a zone that ranges from a few feet below the topsoil to scores of feet above the surface—a mere sliver compared to the volume of living space in the seas. Life in the seas ranges from the surface of the waves to depths of 36,000 feet. If we compare these two volumes, the oceans provide nearly 99 percent of the potential living space on the planet.

Life in the oceans is diverse and abundant, but very difficult to study. The difficulty in sampling the deep sea has been likened to sampling life on land by towing a butterfly net behind an airplane. Marine biologists and oceanographers are fond of saying that we know more about the surface of the moon than the ocean floor. In fact, only around one-tenth of 115 million square miles of the sea floor has been explored and charted, and biological studies have been conducted on only a tiny fraction of the portion that has been mapped. Given the technical difficulties of exploring the seas, the need for carrying our own oxygen, the pressure, inky darkness, and cold temperatures in the depths, it is not surprising that major new species and entire marine ecosystems are still being discovered.

Since so little of the deep sea has been sampled, scientists can only estimate how many species might occur there. Recent studies of the sea floor have found new species in every sample, leading some scientists to believe that diversity may be extremely high on the sea floor, perhaps approaching 10 million species. Other more conservative estimates lie closer to one-half million species.

Scientists have classified and described only a fraction of the plants and animals that inhabit the oceans today. The best estimates range between hundreds of thousands to millions of species that are yet to be discovered and described by science. While most of these may be microscopic or may dwell on the ocean floor, even the more familiar groups may yield new species.

In 1991, scientists at the Smithsonian Institution described a new species of whale from Peru. This was not a case of reclassifying a misidentified species; rather, it was a new scientific discovery. In fact, the scientists never saw the new species alive. *Mesoplodon peruvianus* was described by studying 11 specimens that washed up on Peruvian beaches or were trapped in fishermen's nets over the course of 15 years. *M. peruvianus* is a small member of the beaked whale group—with adults reaching just over 12 feet. Beaked whales are characteristically difficult to study in the wild because they live offshore, dive deep, and can stay submerged for up to an hour.

Even more remarkable than recent descriptions of new species is the fact that new phyla are being found in the oceans. In taxonomy, scientists classify plants and animals according to a hierarchical system of relatedness, in which each grouping (taxon) is broader than the one below it. From the bottom up: Similar species belong to the same genus, similar genera share a family, similar families share an order, similar orders share a class, and similar classes share a phylum. Only 33 living animal phyla have been described worldwide, and the 33rd phylum, the Loricifera, was discovered in 1983 by Danish scientist Reinhardt Kristensen.

It is not surprising that the Loricifera eluded scientists for all these years. They are microscopic and they live in between grains of sand on the sea floor, at depths of 30 to 1,500 feet below the surface of the sea. Very few details are available on the biology of Loricifera, but they appear to range quite widely through the Gulf of Mexico, the Mediterranean, and the Pacific Ocean.

BIOLOGICAL DIVERSITY

With so much left to learn about life in the seas, how can we begin to assess what might be threatened by environmental problems affecting the oceans? It is not enough to say that we can't save what we don't know, because—as with many other biological conservation issues—by the time a negative trend is observed it may be too late to halt or reverse it. So marine biologists, policy makers, and others are left with imperfect tools for measuring the impact that human actions may have on life in the seas, but they must nevertheless try to determine what should be preserved, how it will be affected by human actions, and how to balance human needs with preserving marine life.

At the molecular level—when we study DNA—all life on earth reveals a common origin. Yet it also has differences wrought by millions of years of evolution. It is this diversity that is the raw material of evolution and the keystone of life on earth. It is the many manifestations of this diversity that we seek to protect through ocean conservation.

The most familiar level of biological diversity is species diversity, or the number of species living in a particular habitat. For example, a major reason for the current emphasis on tropical forest conservation is that these forests support a tremendous number of species, making them one of the most species-diverse habitats on the planet. Using this bean-counting approach, it could be said that tropical forests have higher biological diversity than kelp forests because kelp forests harbor relatively few species.

The most species-diverse marine habitats generally occur in tropical waters, and among the tropical areas, the Indo-West Pacific—between Indonesia, Australia, and the Philippines—hosts the largest number of species. The coral reefs in this area may well be the tropical forests of the seas.

We don't know how many marine species have yet to be described, but far more species live on land than in the ocean.

Around 1.4 million species have been classified, and less than 15 percent of these can be found in the seas. The numerical dominance of land-based species is mostly due to prodigious numbers of insect species. While there are over 100,000 known species of mollusks—clams, snails, slugs, squid, octopus, and their relatives—there are around 750,000 known species of insects. The number of vascular plants on land—trees, shrubs, grasses, and their relatives—far exceeds the number of marine algae.

Nevertheless, although species diversity is often used as a symbolic value of natural ecosystems, species number is only one measure of biological diversity. Genetic diversity, ecosystem diversity, diversity of the higher-level taxa, such as orders and phyla, and diversity of the functions performed by groups of species are all meaningful ways to classify biological diversity.

The process of evolution works at the level of genetic diversity. Groups of animals with a diverse genetic makeup will be more likely to contain individuals that survive or that adapt to a changing environment. Groups with low genetic diversity will be less likely to adapt to changes in chemical composition and temperatures of seawater. With environmental changes already occurring, the conservation of genetic diversity is an important goal.

If genetic and species diversity are the fine tuning of evolution, the diversity of higher-level taxa reflects radical differences. In animals, higher-level taxonomic differences are seen in extreme changes in body plans, such as between starfish, mussels, and crabs. Marine animals are far more diverse at the higher taxonomic levels than land animals. Indeed, more than 90 percent of all classes of organisms dwell in the oceans, and nearly half of all phyla are exclusively marine. Marine biologist Sylvia Earle, a major champion of ocean conservation, compares biological diversity on land and at sea using the metaphor of a tree. She sees land animals as having many more twigs and stems, while the ocean animals have more branches and trunks.

Some scientists argue that it is more important to preserve functional diversity—the diversity of roles played by plants and animals in marine ecosystems—than species diversity. For example, in rocky intertidal areas, space is at a premium. Plants and animals that live in the rocky intertidal are constantly competing for rock space with their own and other species. In a healthy ecosystem, grazers keep algae in check, and predators keep grazer numbers from skyrocketing. In a disturbed or unhealthy intertidal area, the algae take over, leaving a much less diverse ecosystem. The focus on functional diversity recognizes the importance of diverse ecological roles.

PRODUCTIVITY

Although scientists and policy makers often evaluate natural habitats by their biological diversity, diversity is only one measure of the significance of an ecosystem. Productivity is also an important consideration. Biological productivity is the engine that drives life on land and in the sea, and it is measured by the amount of carbon dioxide taken up by growing organisms. On land, green plants convert sunlight, carbon dioxide, nutrients, and water into plant tissue and oxygen through a process known as photosynthesis. In the seas, photosynthesizing algae and plantlike bacteria are the key producers of energy from the sun. As much as half of all photosynthesis occurs in the world's oceans—between one and one-half and three times more than occurs in tropical rainforests.

Unlike the towering leafy trees, sprawling shrubs, and acres of grasses that serve as the major converters of sunlight to food on land, tiny algae are the chief photosynthesizers in the seas. Microscopic algae known as phytoplankton account for approximately 40 percent of all photosynthesis that occurs on the planet. As we indicated in an earlier chapter, plankton is the general term for small organisms—plants, animals, and algae—that are found drifting passively in the sea. The phytoplankton, around half of which are only 0.0004 inch long, live mostly in the top 300 feet of the sea, where sunlight penetrates the most readily.

As they convert light and nutrients to food, marine phytoplankton manufacture most of the organic compounds required by marine animals. Animals that eat phytoplankton reap a direct benefit from the carbohydrates, fats, and proteins converted by the tiny algae. As these animals are eaten by others, the bounty from photosynthesis fuels large and complex food webs of marine life.

Because the phytoplankton are not efficient at incorporating photosynthetic products into their tissues, some of the precious, life-supporting compounds they make are leaked directly into the surrounding water. In fact, as much as 40 percent of the organic material manufactured by phytoplankton leaks into the sea, enriching the waters for many other marine organisms. Some animals, like the reef-forming corals, actually harbor algae within their bodies in order to take advantage of the "leaky" photosynthesis. Coral bleaching occurs when the algae are expelled, causing the coral to lose their pigment and a major source of nutrition.

Productivity varies greatly in different areas of the oceans, depending upon the amount of phytoplankton, sunlight, and other nutrients. The most highly productive ecosystems are coral reefs, producing 300 to 5,000 grams of carbon per year in 11 square feet. Estuaries and kelp beds in shallow waters are also highly productive, often yielding 1,500 to 2,500 grams of carbon. In fact, the kelp forests off Washington state had the highest measured daily rate of productivity—20 grams per 11 square feet *per day*. The upper fronds of giant kelp (exposed to the most sunlight) can grow up to 2 feet per day. By contrast, shallow waters without kelp produce around 100 grams of carbon per year in 11 square feet, and the open oceans yield an average of 50 grams. On land, tropical forests are many times more productive than the open oceans, producing between 1,000 and 3,500 grams of carbon per 11 square feet per year.

Areas with high phytoplankton productivity support many kinds of animals, including fishes, marine mammals, and seabirds. In highly productive areas, masses of phytoplankton are visible to the naked eye, and large-scale patterns of phytoplankton productivity can be tracked by satellites as described in chapter 2.

In clear, shallow waters, with virtually unlimited supplies of sunlight and carbon dioxide, phytoplankton growth is restricted only by the availability of nutrients, mostly nitrogen and phosphorus. As we have seen, ideal conditions for phytoplankton growth occur in areas where upwelling currents bring nutrient-rich bottom waters toward the surface or where rivers laden with nutrients meet the sea. In many areas, seasonal changes in currents create these ideal conditions for phytoplankton, resulting in explosive growth known as blooms. A bloom in phytoplankton often feeds a bloom in the animal plankton that eat phytoplankton, and the pulse of increased abundance of food reverberates through the food web.

Although a natural abundance of nutrients is a boon for marine life, too much of a good thing can trigger a disaster. When phytoplankton receive too much nitrogen and phosphorus, and the bloom is overexuberant, plankton die before they can be consumed. The bacteria that decompose the dead plankton require oxygen, which is dissolved in the water in limited amounts. As oxygen is depleted, other animals die, compounding the problem, and soon the water is stripped of oxygen. This process is known as eutrophication.

Eutrophication is increasingly a problem in areas where poorly treated or untreated sewage flows into coastal waters, bringing prodigious amounts of nitrogen. Water runoff from agricultural areas, carrying nitrogen and phosphorus, similarly causes problems. Decomposing of the organic material generated by a single gram of nitrogen can require 15 grams of oxygen, and a single gram of phosphorus can tie up 100 grams of oxygen.

MARINE ECOSYSTEMS

Although the world's oceans are all connected, they are divided into many smaller ecosystems. Physical, chemical, and biological factors combine to make distinct marine ecosystems like coral reefs, kelp forests, hydrothermal vents, and intertidal areas. Conditions of light and temperature, bottom characteristics, currents, and chemistry vary greatly throughout the oceans, creating many distinctive living spaces.

Sunlight reaches only the uppermost part of the ocean. This area, called the photic zone, can reach to 300 feet in depth, but most of the photosynthesis occurs in the top 30 to 100 feet. With the exception of nutrition provided by chemosynthetic bacteria around hydrothermal vents, all animals below the photic zone rely upon food created in the upper, sunlit area.

Seasonal fluctuations in heat from the sun warm the surface waters but do not penetrate the deep sea. Without vertical mixing, the deepest waters are a chilly 39 degrees Fahrenheit. Because warmer water is less dense, there are generally pronounced layers of warm and cold water. Surface waters are warmer in the tropics than in temperate and polar regions. Water stores heat more effectively than air, making daily temperatures fluctuate much less in the ocean than on land. In response, marine organisms generally have a narrower range of temperature tolerance than terrestrial organisms.

Under El Niño conditions, changes in ocean currents have extensive effects on the temperature and chemical composition of ocean water. During the last severe El Niño, the marine iguanas inhabiting the Galapagos islands declined by 30 to 55 percent, most likely because of the warming of waters around the Galapagos Islands. When the El Niño caused surface waters to become warmer, the red algae disappeared and were replaced by brown algae. Although marine iguanas could eat brown algae, they could not digest them as easily as the red algae, and the lower nutritional intake caused the iguanas' decline.

Surface currents can also play a major role in shaping marine ecosystems by distributing nutrients as well as plants and animals. Indeed, there are some species whose floating larvae, (the immature form of many fish and shellfish) can hitchhike long distances on ocean currents. Sipunculan worms are bottom dwellers widely distributed through the world's oceans. Scientists believe that the tiny larvae of sipunculans are capable of floating for months, perhaps even crossing the Atlantic Ocean on the currents. Floating worms and other types of planktonic plants and animals link distinctive ecosystems found east of Florida with those in the Azores and Canary Islands and in the Caribbean.

CHEMISTRY AND GEOLOGY

Ocean chemistry is also quite variable and has a similar role to play in determining living conditions for marine organisms. Ocean salinity is generally around 35 parts per thousand, but it is considerably lower in estuaries and higher in parts of the deep sea and in some shallow seas, such as the Persian Gulf. Oxygen is more concentrated in colder seawater, although it can be enhanced near the surface by turbulence and photosynthesis. Small changes in the amount of oxygen dissolved in seawater can mean the difference between life and death for many marine organisms, as is evidenced under conditions of eutrophication. The deep sea is also the oceans' major storehouse of inorganic nutrients, such as phosphorus and nitrogen, that algae need for photosynthesis, which is why upwelling of deep water results in higher productivity in surface waters.

Bottom topography and other geological features of the oceans help shape ecosystems by influencing the flow of currents and nutrients and by providing a surface for marine life. The shallow shelves that extend from the continents are covered with silts, sands, and clays washed from the land, whereas much of the abyssal plain, the deep center of ocean basins, is covered by oozes formed from the hard-shelled remains of plankton.

BIOLOGY

Predation and competition for space are major biological factors that shape living conditions for plants and animals in the sea. For instance, interactions of grazing animals and their predators maintain a balance of life in kelp forests. Kelp are large brown algae that grow in the temperate waters along the rocky shorelines of North and South America, Europe, Asia, and Australia. Forming dense forests from the sea floor to the sea surface, kelps provide food and shelter for other types of plants and animals. Although some animals eat kelp, many use kelp for shelter or perching space. Kelp forests foster a diversity of plant and animal life: One kelp forest off Del Mar, California, hosts 38 species of fishes and 98 species of invertebrate animals, such as crabs, shrimp, snails, and worms.

Some species of animals, such as sea urchins and sea otters, play an especially influential role in kelp forests. Just as sea urchins feed on kelp, so do sea otters feed on sea urchins, among other shellfish, and keep sea urchin populations and their grazing in check. With the decimation of sea otter populations off central California by hunting in the 19th century, sea urchin populations mushroomed and some kelp forests were completely destroyed. A ban on hunting sea otters allowed a very small remnant population of sea otters to recover, and as the small population of sea otters expanded into its former range, so too did kelp beds. In Alaska, where sea otters had not been hunted so intensively, scientists found other links. Islands surrounded by kelp beds and otters also hosted harbor seals and bald eagles, whereas islands without otters and kelp beds lacked harbors seals and bald eagles also. Apparently, by keeping sea urchin populations down, sea otters maintain kelp forests that provide habitat for large numbers of fish upon which seals and bald eagles feed.

In competing for food and shelter on coral reefs, animals have developed a remarkable array of feeding and defense strategies, many of which contribute to making coral reefs as productive and resilient as they are. The sea urchin *Diadema,* for instance, plays a critical role in insuring continued growth of coral reefs by grazing on algae and other plant life, making the substrate hospitable to coral larvae. In grazing on reefs, brightly colored parrotfishes scrape up coral remains and defecate them as sand.

TIES BETWEEN ECOSYSTEMS

Even seemingly distinctive marine ecosystems are connected by currents, flows of energy and nutrients, and the movements of animals. Few groups of ecosystems are as tightly associated as mangrove forests, sea-grass beds, and coral reefs in the tropics. Taken together, these ecosystems support an incredible diversity of wildlife, fishes, and plants, and have provided food as well as clothing and building materials for coastal people for centuries. Hugging the coastline, these ecosystems are especially vulnerable.

Mangrove forests grow along many of the world's tropical coastlines. In the United States, the most extensive mangrove forests are in Florida. Mangrove trees are terrestrial plants that have invaded salt water and created one of the most productive ecosystems on earth. Growing where the water is warm, shallow, salty, and calm, mangrove trees flourish in fine-grained soils rich in nutrients. Because mangrove forests provide dense cover and ample food in a narrow area that bounds marine and terrestrial habitats, they attract a diverse community of birds and other animals. Leaf litter that accumulates on the forest floor is regularly submerged by salt water and colonized by bacteria and fungi. Broken into particles, the leaves provide a rich source of food for shrimp, crabs, and some species of fish, which in turn are fed upon by larger species of fish, birds, and dolphins.

The roots of some species of mangrove form props to the trunks of the trees and create surfaces on which algae, barnacles, and other organisms can settle. Such organisms become part of a food web that includes not only animals that remain within the forest and the waters beneath it, but fish and birds that venture into other ecosystems at different times of their lives. For instance, juvenile red drum and gray snapper take advantage of the protection and food in the prop roots of red mangroves while they grow. These fish later move into sea-grass beds or onto coral reefs as they mature.

Other species of fish, such as jacks and barracuda, can move far up tidal streams during dry periods, feeding on the rich food produced by the forest. When they return to the waters over sea-grass beds and coral reefs, they take with them the nutrients that the forests have produced. The productivity of mangrove forests can benefit adjacent ecosystems in other ways. For instance, leaf litter that is swept from mangrove forests by tides or storms introduces additional sources of nutrients to sea-grass beds and reef areas.

Taken together, through the abundance and diversity of fish and shellfish that they support, mangrove forests feed coastal people by the millions. In Fiji, as one example, about half of the fish caught in commercial and traditional fisheries use mangrove forests at one or more critical stages in their lives. Furthermore, life for people in many parts of the world is supported directly by local mangrove forests, from which they harvest oysters, clams, mussels, crabs, and crocodiles, as well as building materials and fuel.

Like mangroves, sea grasses are terrestrial plants that have adapted themselves to life in salt water. By capturing sediment and plant material, they too clear waters and build habitat for other creatures. Sea grasses in both temperate and tropical areas favor clear, protected waters.

Although some groups of animals, such as snails, fishes, wading birds, sea turtles, and manatees, may feed directly on sea grass, most animals feed upon the litter from broken leaves decomposed by bacteria and fungi. Filter-feeding animals capture the decomposed particles, while other animals such as crabs and starfish may move about the bottom feeding on the mat of leaf litter. Over

100 species of algae, as well as certain species of anemones and crabs, encrust sea-grass leaves, while fish and shellfish may deposit eggs upon the surface of the leaves. Some species of fish and shellfish feed in sea-grass beds, but use adjacent mangrove forests or coral reefs for shelter.

Often protecting sea-grass beds and mangrove forests from the brunt of tropical storms, coral reefs are known for the high diversity of species they support. Coral reefs cover about 230,000 square miles of bottom in the tropics, or about one-tenth of one percent of the earth's surface. About one-third of the reefs are found along island coasts in the so-called Asiatic Mediterranean, formed by Indonesia on the west, northern Australia on the south, the Philippines on the east, and mainland Asia on the north. About 14 percent of the world's coral reefs are in the Caribbean Sea.

The Great Barrier Reef off Australia hosts more than 300 species of coral, 1,500 species of fish, and 4,000 species of mollusks. A single reef often is made up of dozens of different species of coral that form bands of distribution reflecting physical conditions such as depth, amount of light, and currents. At the crest of a barrier reef, such as one of the thousands of reefs that make up the Great Barrier Reef, elkhorn coral may dominate, with its stout branches pointing away from the waves. Just below the crest, where the energy of waves is not so great, elkhorn coral takes on a different form, low and spreading, and other species of coral appear, such as tangled patches of staghorn coral. In these deeper waters, brain coral form masses as large as a house; other species of coral, such as delicate lettuce coral, may grow on the sheltered surfaces of these mounds. Still other kinds of coral dominate in deeper, still waters.

The great productivity of coral reefs—particularly remarkable, given how nutrient-poor tropical waters often are—depends upon the productivity of the plants that cover the reef surface or inhabit the coral polyps themselves. The dizzying array of surfaces and forms in a coral reef area offers an extraordinary range of surfaces and microhabitats for plants and animals.

Removing one element of this mosaic of ecosystems, or one element of the ecosystems in the adjacent watershed, including forests and wetlands, can severely reduce these productive associations. Degradation or loss of marine ecosystems will reduce the availability of many goods and services that directly benefit people, from storm protection to the rejuvenation that an hour of snorkeling above the colorful life of a coral reef can bring. However we may measure their value, we will surely underestimate the benefits of these and other marine ecosystems.

5

≈≈≈≈≈

Economics

Thanking the captain, I went up to the shelves.
Works of science, ethics, literature, in many
languages, were in abundance; but I did not
see a single book on economics, apparently a
subject strictly proscribed on board.

PROFESSOR PIERRE ARONNAX
in *20,000 Leagues Under the Sea*

If economics is foreign territory for most people, the economics of
marine and coastal resources is an even rarer venture. Not only is
economics popularly considered a gloomy undertaking, but the
economics of things marine is murky to boot. Conservationists
are reluctant to throw in with analysts who see the world in terms
of fungible assets, and economists are unsure of values such as
biological diversity and beauty that are poorly represented in the
marketplace. Government decision makers bridle at making a
choice between promoting economic efficiency and subsidizing
ways of life that are politically supported. Economists struggle to
gain a place at the negotiating table, except as particular interests
see that they will win or lose from a decision to conserve or
exploit.

The paucity of natural resource economists on the staffs of
ocean resource agencies reflects a general bias against the social
sciences in natural resource management. This conceit arises
partly from focusing upon the resources themselves—the mangroves, reefs, fishes—and from assuming that those who know

most about plants and animals know most about how to ensure their conservation. But the prejudice is very costly, since it inhibits understanding a critical element in the conservation equation— people. Economics cannot fully explain human behavior, but the general lack of an economic perspective is also an enormous blindspot in current conservation programs.

For nearly fifty years, economists have tried to determine the value of ocean resources and to identify the human behaviors that lead to overexploitation and depletion. The need to overcome the limitations of free markets and current accounting methods has fostered new theories and analyses that more fully represent the value of coastal and marine wildlife and habitats. Like other perspectives on marine resources, from coastal geomorphology to fish population dynamics, ocean resource economics is hampered by limited information and understanding of the major factors influencing specific situations. With all of its limitations, however, the international system of measuring economic welfare has become an important element in decision making by government and private interests.

We will be poorer in the future for having misunderstood the cost of what we have gained in the past. There will be less beauty and diversity because we have ignored how we behave with money. But economics still is considered a pariah by many conservationists, largely because prevailing accounting methods omit the value of a sunset and cannot reckon the worth of a barrel of healthy ecosystem compared with a barrel of oil. It is easy to make too much or too little of economics.

Unfortunately, our lack of a common language describing the worth of wetlands or the value of a healthy ecosystem feeds frustration with the limitations of economics in measuring the value of what we buy or sell. Until we develop that language, however, we can still apply economics in ways that promote, even secure the conservation of the oceans.

A LOOK AT SOME STATISTICS

The most commonly used general measure of economic activity is Gross National Product (GNP): the value of all currently produced goods and services sold on the market during a particular period of time. Comparing GNP in different periods provides a rough measure of trends in an economy. When adjusted for inflation, the world's economic activity grew from $15 trillion in 1978 to nearly $19 trillion in 1987. During the same period, the U.S. GNP (the largest in the world) grew at roughly the same rate, from about $4 trillion to about $5 trillion.

Measures of economic activity dependent upon ocean resources are not as straightforward. Among other difficulties, the current United Nations System of National Accounts, which countries have been using since 1968 in compiling economic information, does not include a separate account for ocean activities. Rather, marine transportation, commercial fishing, and offshore oil and gas drilling, for instance, are lumped with other business activities unrelated to the oceans. Economic information on commercial marine fishing is combined with information on agriculture, hunting, and forestry, as well as freshwater fishing. On the basis of other government records, we know that marine commercial fishing accounted for about $3.3 billion of the revenues in the $61-billion agricultural sector of the U.S. GNP in 1980.

Several years ago, James Broadus and colleagues at the Woods Hole Oceanographic Institution analyzed available information on worldwide and U.S. economic activity in the marine area from 1978 through 1987—a gargantuan undertaking. The Woods Hole group focused on expenditures associated with the four principal ocean-dependent activities: naval affairs, marine transportation, offshore oil and gas production, and commercial fishing. Taken together, the contribution of these activities to the world economy grew from $650 billion in 1978 to $733 billion in 1987, or about 13 percent—less than half the rate of growth in the world economy generally. This slower growth rate caused the marine share of the world economy to slip from 4.3 percent in 1978 to 3.9 percent in 1987.

Although world and U.S. GNP grew steadily in the 20 years covered by the study, some ocean-related activities did not. For instance, marine transport of cargo depends upon production by other industries and is very sensitive to the expansion and contraction of the larger economy. Naval expenditures, on the other hand, have grown more or less independently of the larger economy. Thus, the details of expenditures in ocean-dependent activities provide a useful perspective on our use of the oceans. (All dollar amounts are adjusted for inflation and expressed in 1978 dollars.)

Naval Expenditures: For decades, expenditures for the construction and operation of naval equipment have been nearly as great as those for all other ocean-dependent economic activities combined. Between 1978 and 1987, worldwide naval expenditures grew from $289 billion to $352 billion per year. The thawing of the Cold War in the late 1980s halted the steady growth in naval expenditures that had taken place during the defense build-up of the Reagan administration. In the early 1980s, U.S. naval expenditures had risen dramatically, from $72 billion in 1978 to a high of $114 billion in 1985, which represented a 2.5 percent share of U.S. GNP.

Ocean Freight: The seas have long been the great highways of world commerce. Each year, nearly 25,000 freighters, tankers, and bulk-carriers transport 4.5 billion tons of raw materials and finished goods, providing the vital links between sources and markets in the world economy. Ocean transport revenues grew slightly from 1978 to 1987, beginning at about $152 billion and ending at $176 billion. These figures do not include worldwide expenditures for the construction of merchant ships, which grew from $94 billion in 1978 to nearly $140 billion in 1980 before falling to just $48 billion in 1988. U.S. expenditures for ocean freight and construction of merchant ships hovered around $24 billion, or about one-half percent of U.S. GNP.

Offshore Oil and Gas Production: One-quarter to one-third of the world's reserves of oil and gas lie offshore. Most exploration and production activity has occurred in the shallower waters of the continental shelf, but drill rigs have gradually moved into the deeper waters. Offshore oil and gas revenues, which are particularly significant in the United States, Mexico, Britain, Norway, and some members of the Organization of Petroleum Exporting Countries (OPEC), have fluctuated more than revenues from the other ocean sectors as world prices for oil and gas have responded to political and market conditions.

After the 1979 price shock provoked by the second OPEC oil embargo, revenues from offshore fields due to higher prices and increased production rose to $290 billion in 1981, their highest level of the last two decades. As disagreements divided OPEC members and oil flooded the world market, oil prices fell dramatically after 1983, together with revenues, exploration, and production. By 1988, offshore oil and gas revenues were at their lowest level in more than a decade and less than half their 1981 level. Oil and gas revenues from fields off the United States have risen and fallen with the world market, beginning at about $16 billion in 1978, rising to a high of $32 billion in 1982, then falling back to a little more than $16 billion in 1987—about four-tenths of a percent of GNP.

As oil prices have fallen and environmental restrictions have increased in the United States, the interest of the offshore oil and gas industry worldwide has moved to fields off India, Malaysia, Ghana, Tunisia, the Philippines, and Thailand. Some countries, such as Thailand, have based their plans for economic development largely upon the production of offshore reserves for domestic consumption or export.

Commercial Fisheries: Although revenues from worldwide commercial landings of fish rose from $87.4 billion in 1978 to $101.9 billion in 1988, revenues from U.S. fish landings actually declined from $3.5 billion to $3.4 billion, or less than one-tenth of a percent of U.S. GNP. Most of the growth in global landings has been in species with low economic value, such as Japanese pilchards, a kind of herring used for fish meal, and Alaska pollock, used in processed seafood substitutes. The growth in landings of these lower-priced species obscures dramatic declines in those of other, more valuable species, such as Northwest salmon and Atlantic bluefin tuna in the United States.

OTHER MARINE ECONOMIC ACTIVITIES

The economic importance of ocean activities not covered by the Woods Hole analysis is even more difficult to measure. For instance, no reliable estimates exist for the revenues generated by mining hard minerals, such as gold, platinum, magnetite, or tin, from placers in river deltas, beaches, and nearshore waters. In southeast Asia, mining offshore deposits of tin ore contributed ten percent of world production in 1982. Sources of titanium are mined in offshore Australia, India, and Sri Lanka, and diamonds are mined from gravel deposits off Namibia. Offshore deposits of sand and gravel provide one-third of the construction needs of Japan and 16 percent of the United Kingdom's needs.

Seawater itself is the source of a wide variety of products. One-third of the world's supply of salt is evaporated from seawater held in ponds. About two-thirds of the magnesium used in light-weight metal alloys comes from seawater, as does most of the bromine used in pharmaceuticals, photography, and gasoline. By 1989, more than 3,500 desalination plants were processing sea-water into fresh water for domestic and industrial uses, mostly in the Middle East.

In a very few parts of the world, such as the Bay of Fundy in Canada and the mouth of the La Rance River in western France, the range between low and high tides is so great that engineers have been able to tap the energy in the ebb and flow of water to generate electrical power. Another innovative technique is off-shore thermal energy conversion, in which deep, cold water is drawn upward to mix with warm surface waters, creating vapor that drives electric turbines. For the most part, both these means of generating power will remain experimental as long as petro-leum prices are as low as they are, and their application will be limited to a few geographical areas.

Expenditures for marine recreation and tourism have increased dramatically in recent years, as personal income has grown. In the United States, estimated spending for marine boating and fishing alone rose from $5 billion in 1970 to more than $8.7 billion in 1987, outstripping the growth rate of any of the principal ocean-dependent activities discussed above.

Marine-based tourism now provides the lion's share of foreign exchange for many developing countries in the Caribbean and elsewhere. Scuba-based tourism at the Bonaire Marine Park in the Caribbean accounted for at least half of the island's economic activity in 1985. In Bonaire and elsewhere, however, a large part of the earnings from tourism do not contribute directly to the local economy, since the hotels and diving operations often are foreign owned.

In stark contrast to the growth in other areas of ocean economic activity, expenditures for scientific research and pollution control declined between 1970 and 1987 in the United States. Modest increases during the Bush administration broke a pattern of steep decreases.

SOME LIMITATIONS

One of the chief complaints about conventional accounting and GNP specifically is the way they treat natural assets. Although renewable natural assets produce goods and services that benefit us and have an economic value, conventional accounting does not place a value on the assets, nor does it recognize any economic loss if they are degraded or destroyed. Thus, conventional accounting would document the income from the building blocks mined from a coral reef, but would not document the loss of the reef itself and of the fish, storm protection, and recreation it would have provided in the future.

Likewise, conventional accounting does not depreciate the value of nonrenewable inventories, such as petroleum and other mineral deposits, as they are exploited and consumed. Rather, income from the exploitation and sale of these assets is treated as free income. In other areas, conventional accounting does recognize wear and tear on manufactured assets such as buildings and equipment by levying a depreciation charge against the income that the assets generate. For instance, old equipment eventually is replaced by new equipment and the business continues producing goods.

Furthermore, conventional accounting counts money spent by a government to clean up an oil spill in a mangrove forest as a contribution to economic welfare, yet does not deduct the loss in future income caused by the damage to the forest itself or by the reduction in the oil inventory. Rather than raising income, these and other antipollution expenditures should be deducted from the value of the final products as a cost of doing business. No accountant would record the economic activity generated by reconstructing freeways, homes, and other buildings in Los Angeles after the January 1994 earthquake without also booking the losses.

The results of this failure to recognize the value of natural assets include the loss of fisheries and wetlands, for instance, and the overstatement of income. Resource-rich Ecuador has sought to generate foreign currency by raising and exporting shrimp to the United States and other industrialized nations. In 1990, these exports generated $400 million, representing one-third of the amount of hard currency the country required to service its enormous foreign debt. The unrecorded cost of these exports is the near-permanent loss of nearly 270,000 acres of productive wetlands to shrimp ponds.

The stage seems to be set for a dramatic change in how nations calculate their economic welfare. In 1776, when the Scottish moral philosopher and economist Adam Smith published *An Inquiry into the Nature and Causes of the Wealth of Nations,* the Americas seemed to offer limitless abundance to the earth's one billion inhabitants. What was lacking was capital for the equipment and infrastructure necessary for exploiting these resources, whose price was close to zero.

Herman Daly, an economist at the University of Maryland, argues that we have moved from an age in which the lack of manufactured assets limited economic productivity to an age in which availability of natural assets has begun to limit economic productivity. For instance, landings in most fisheries are now limited not by the number of boats, but by the reproductive capacity of fish populations. Indeed, many fisheries are overcapitalized, in that they have many more vessels than necessary to harvest the sustainable yield of fish populations. As more vessels have entered fisheries, competition for the available fish has increased so much that fish populations have declined to levels well below their potential for producing more fish and income in the future.

One reason for the resistance to recognizing the increasingly important link between manufactured and natural assets arises from the prevailing theory that as resources become scarce, the market will send signals in the form of higher prices that will spur technological innovation and the substitution of other resources. In the past, when resources became scarce, new technologies were developed that allowed further exploitation. Until recently, the environmental and health costs of many new technologies went unrecognized. As an example, the wholesale logging of forests to supply fuel for homes and factories early in the Industrial Revolution caused the price of wood to rise in England to the point that technology substituting coal for wood was developed. Consumption of coal skyrocketed, fueling extraordinary economic growth, but the mining and burning of coal scarred countrysides, cost miners their health and lives, and launched us on the path to global warming.

Several years ago, economists at the World Resources Institute collaborated with the government of Costa Rica in calculating the long-term economic effects of overexploited fisheries, forests, and agricultural soils. According to the study, the loss in long-term value of these resources due to overexploitation amounted to more than $4 billion in the 1970s and 1980s. Had the value of these natural assets been treated the same way as that of capital assets, government accountants would have reduced the value of economic activity by five percent each year. To put this in perspective, a change of two percent in economic activity can make the difference between recession and economic growth.

SHIFTING COSTS

Gross National Product and other measures of economic activity and welfare are aggregates of millions of transactions at a much smaller scale. Failure to account for all costs and benefits at the national and international levels reflects the failure to do so at the level of individual activities. Local environmental damage from activities that range from dam-building to overfishing, whose costs and benefits have not been completely tallied themselves, accumulates into widespread environmental damage.

The tradition of common property ownership, in Western society especially, removes many marine ecological benefits from the marketplace and externalizes them. Benefits are considered externalized when someone gains a benefit without cost. For instance, fishermen capture the benefits from fish produced by a wetland without any investment in the wetland. Costs are externalized when they are imposed on someone who does not gain any benefit from them. Such externalization of costs and benefits severely hinders restraints on exploitation of fish populations, destruction of coastal habitats, or use of rivers and bays for the discharge of pollutants.

Sometimes, costs and benefits are externalized by the way in which boundaries between economic activities are drawn. For instance, conventional economic analysis ignores the links between watersheds and nearshore waters. Gregor Hodgson and John A. Dixon have described a telling exception in their study of the impact of proposed logging in a watershed above Bacuit Bay on the island of Palawan in the Philippines.

For many years, the waters around the island of Palawan had attracted commercial fishermen from hundreds of miles away to catch spawning yellowfin and skipjack tuna. The local fishery employed many men and operated year-round. In the 1980s, Japanese interests opened two scuba resorts that attracted a steady and well-paying clientele to the island's coral reefs, adding to its wealth. These important economic activities, however, were increasingly threatened by mining and logging, which had reduced the forested area of the island from 92 percent in 1968 to 50 percent in 1987. In 1985, logging began above Bacuit Bay, and although only 11 percent of the available forest was clear-cut, rain-driven sediment from the logged-over area poured into the bay. After a particularly heavy rainstorm, the coral reef closest to the river mouth lost nearly half its coral cover.

Field surveys of the reef and watershed revealed that continued logging would significantly damage the coral reef and other habitats of Bacuit Bay, and would thereby reduce revenue from tourism and fishing by $54 million over ten years. In that time, logging would generate only $13 million in earnings, or more than $40 million less than the cost of the damage to fisheries and reefs caused by continued logging.

Cost-benefit analyses of proposals to convert habitats to other uses, for instance, often focus only on marketable goods and services that are associated with the site in question. When the effect on offsite goods is included in these analyses, the comparative benefits of converting habitats to other uses tend to decrease markedly. As an example, a cost / benefit analysis of a proposal to convert mangrove forests to shrimp farms in Thailand found that the benefits from traditional, sustainable uses of mangrove forests were at least equal to the benefits from converting the forests to rice farms, when the value of mangrove-dependent fisheries and products from sustainable forestry alone were included. Benefits from traditional uses also compared favorably with those from shrimp farming when job creation was considered.

In the United States, Robert Costanza of the University of Maryland and his colleagues have tried to estimate the value of Louisiana coastal wetlands by including the values of goods and services that either are not traded in the market or cannot be captured by a landowner. To do so, interviewers asked individual people how much they valued various ecological goods and services provided by wetlands. Thus, Costanza's group calculated that an acre of Louisiana wetland annually provides up to $846 in commercial fishery benefits, $401 in economic benefits from trapping, $181 in recreational benefits, and $7,549 in storm protection benefits. The total calculated value—between $2,429 and $8,977—is well above the $200 to $400 that an acre of Louisiana wetland fetches on the real estate market. Although these estimates are imprecise, they show that the market is not accounting for some significant benefits from wetlands. Moreover, since Louisiana loses 60 square miles of wetlands each year, it also suffers a minimum annual loss of $93 million in economic benefits.

These estimates themselves leave out other values. For instance, as wetlands and other open coastal areas have been converted to agricultural lands, housing developments, and harbors, the residential property that is adjacent to remaining open areas generally commands a higher price than other property. By comparing housing prices and environmental quality among areas, economists can estimate the economic value of waterfront open space. Similarly, by comparing how much recreational users spend in visiting areas with different ecological features and quality, economists at the University of Maryland determined that a 20 percent improvement in the ambient water quality of the Chesapeake Bay would yield $10 million to $100 million in benefits.

The farther removed from the market such valuations are, the more vulnerable they are to being challenged. For instance, when responding to questions about their willingness to pay for the protection of an animal, individuals are often influenced by what they know about the animal and its status. Such biases undercut the authority of valuation information derived from interviews and similar techniques.

SUBSIDIES AND THE MARKETPLACE

Governments have long used economic measures to achieve narrow or broad policy goals. In the early days of the United States, when the settlement of the frontier was embraced as a national goal, the federal government provided a menu of incentives, including land grants and financial subsidies. Farmers were given wetlands on the condition that they drain them and convert them to agricultural production; as a result, millions of acres of wetland were filled. Often, subsidy programs persist long after policy goals have shifted and the subsidy has become irrelevant or counterproductive. As the limits of resources and of the capacity of natural environments to assimilate pollutants have become evident, governments have tried to withdraw from the marketplace or to introduce incentives that encourage resource conservation. But the withdrawal of subsidies is fiercely resisted by those who have benefited.

Agricultural subsidies for water, chemicals, and product prices show how damaging government intervention into apparently unrelated economic activities can be to marine and coastal resources. In the United States, the federal government enabled farmers in the arid central valley of California to grow water hungry crops such as rice, cotton, and alfalfa by setting water charges at 1/50th the cost of new water. Furthermore, these crops often received other subsidies that encouraged monocultures requiring heavy use of chemicals. If price supports and loan credits are included, rice grown in the Sacramento Valley for export to the Far East has yielded growers more than $12 for 100 pounds of a crop that actually fetches $3 on the world market and cost farmers no more than $7 to grow.

These subsidies have encouraged the impoundment and diversion of more than 60 percent of the water from the Sacramento River that would otherwise enter San Francisco Bay. In losing the water, the bay also lost a run of salmon that at the time of the Civil War supplied the first salmon cannery on the West Coast. By the 1980s, dams at Shasta, Red Bluff, and elsewhere effectively had closed off about 90 percent of the spawning habitat for chinook salmon in the Sacramento River Basin. By 1990, the winter run of chinook salmon in the Sacramento River had declined from an average of 86,500 fish in 1967–69 to only 500 fish. Pressed by conservation groups to act, the National Marine Fisheries Service listed this run of salmon as threatened under the Endangered Species Act in 1992.

The reaction of farmers in the delta and central valley of California surprised no one. Rather than acknowledge that taxpayers had supported them with the aquatic equivalent of welfare payments, some farmers characterized themselves as victims of the Endangered Species Act and resisted any change in their use of water. With passage of the Omnibus Water Bill of 1992, Congress established an elaborate process for changing price incentives from those that promote water use to those that promote conservation. Like anyone else losing a subsidy, farmers have protested higher prices and the loss of their subsidies.

By increasing the money farmers can spend to boost production and still make a profit, price supports and other subsidies encourage farmers to increase the use of chemicals, raising the risk of pollution of freshwater and nearshore waters by poisoned runoff. Subsidies also encourage practices that increase soil erosion. The offsite costs of such intensive agricultural practices are staggering. A 1991 World Resources Institute report found that eroded sediments alone caused $692 million in damage to marine recreation and $451 million in damage to U.S. commercial fishing in 1989.

Like other upstream polluters who transfer the costs of their waste to downstream users, farmers have little reason to alter their behavior as long as they do not have to bear offsite costs. Some governments are seeking to change this market failure by withdrawing subsidies, by charging true costs for providing services, and by taxing the use of chemical pollutants in agriculture so that their price better reflects not simply their cost of production, but also their cost to the environment. For instance, after eliminating an 80 percent subsidy of agricultural pesticides in 1988, the Indonesian government generated annual budgetary savings of more than $120 million and reduced use of pesticides by farmers.

Unfortunately, such wisdom is not yet typical of government policy. Thus, for example, as competition for fish escalated in the 1970s and 1980s, governments around the world launched programs to expand their fishing fleets. Deciding that fish protein could be obtained at much lower prices than other forms of animal protein, the government of the Soviet Union, for example, built hundreds of large fishing vessels that could roam the seas in search of fish and process it on board. But by 1989, operating expenses exceeded revenues by as much as $8 billion. With the fall of the Soviet Union, the subsidies that covered this deficit disappeared, and much of the fleet remained tied up at the dock. Such extravagance is not confined to centralized economies. According to the United Nations Food and Agriculture Organization, the fishing fleets of the world incur an operating deficit of $22 billion annually. A modest return on the $320 billion investment that is tied up in fishing vessels themselves would add another $32 billion to the annual deficit.

This uneconomic situation is made possible by enormous subsidies provided by governments to maintain employment or to match subsidies given to other, similar sectors of the economy such as agriculture. From 1983 to 1990, fishing subsidies in the European Economic Community rose from $80 million to $580 million per year, and 20 percent of this was devoted to the construction of new vessels.

Although some subsidies for fishing fleets in the United States have been withdrawn, others continue. For instance, the carbon tax on fuels, proposed by the Clinton administration in 1993, threatened the existing exemption from the fuel tax that commercial fishermen and farmers have enjoyed for many years. Given their estimated annual consumption of 1.3 billion gallons of fuel, the tax exemption reduces fishermen's operating costs by as much as $250 million. Like many other interests whose costs of doing business would rise with the withdrawal of such subsidies, fishermen protested, and the Clinton proposal was defeated.

Whatever broader economic or social benefits fuel subsidies may promote, they also remove an important restraint on fuel use and fishing effort. As an example, fuel use by the New Bedford,

Massachusetts, fishing fleet increased between 1970 and 1989 as the size of the fleet, the horsepower of the vessels, and the length of fishing trips grew in response to declines in fish stocks caused by overfishing. By 1988, 300 percent more fuel was being consumed to catch 30 percent less fish than in 1968.

Governments have sometimes attempted to create disincentives to environmentally damaging practices, or to charge for services provided by wetlands, for instance. However, setting tax levels that can survive political challenge by powerful interests while correctly valuing ecological services has proved to be a very difficult matter. In theory, an efficient tax would be set at the level that produces maximum benefits, spurring a polluter to cut back on emissions through reducing production or improving the production process. Of more than 50 such environmental charges by industrialized countries, most were set too low to provoke a change in behavior by polluters, according to the Worldwatch Institute. A principal obstacle to setting effective tax charges on environmentally damaging activities is the difficulty of linking a specific level of runoff pollution, for instance, to a particular polluter and to environmental or health damage. This is particularly true where the sources of pollution are diffuse, as from city streets and agricultural fields.

Whatever the obstacles, one point is clear: Continued masking of costs and benefits may be politically advantageous, but it makes little sense economically or environmentally.

RESOURCE MANAGEMENT AND THE MARKETPLACE

Collapsed fisheries, disappearing wetlands, rising pollution, and other environmental losses have inspired another kind of government intervention into the marketplace: management. Government regulation of activities that affect the direct and indirect use of marine resources has grown rapidly since the 1970s. State and federal government agencies now actively manage marine fisheries, pollutant discharges, coastal development, harbor dredging, waste disposal, and marine transport of hazardous materials, among many other human activities.

In many instances, government must intervene in the use of marine resources because, in the absence of property rights, fishermen, waste dischargers, and other resource users will inevitably though unwittingly exhaust living resources and marine environments. Government management of marine resources generally requires tremendous amounts of information that is expensive to collect and difficult to interpret. Even if funding for data collection and analysis were adequate—it never has been and never will be—government officials have little incentive to resist political pressures and to avoid measures that require change and sacrifice by a few.

Government regulation sometimes depends upon reducing the efficiency of resource users. For instance, traditional tools of fisheries management include restricting mesh sizes for nets, seasons for fishing, and discard of fish. In many instances, fisheries managers use these tools in order to reduce the ability of fishermen to catch as much fish as they could otherwise catch. However, in reducing fishing efficiency in one way, fisheries managers may inadvertently encourage fishermen to make additional investments in gear and technology in order to maintain catch levels in the face of restrictions.

Under traditional fisheries management, most fisheries have attracted so many fishermen and so much fishing effort that the profits normally flowing from productive fish populations are consumed by increased costs of harvesting. As a result, money that could be invested more productively elsewhere in the economy generates very little net benefit. By assigning transferable shares in a harvest quota, fisheries managers hope to reduce the drive to overinvest in equipment and to relieve political pressure to raise quotas so that fishermen can meet mortgage and other costs.

This new approach to fisheries management has been evolving very quickly, as it has become clear that the traditional quota system was inadequate. For example, within three years after the 1987 discovery of an unexploited population of wreckfish (a kind of bass), the number of vessels in the fishery grew from 2 to 40 and catches grew from 30,000 pounds to four million pounds. In 1990, the 40 vessels in the fishery met a two-million-pound quota in the first four months of the year, flooding the market and driving prices down, while increasing the risk of accidents on the water. Although biologists knew little about this species of fish, what they did know suggested that it was a slow-growing species that could be quickly fished out. Despite claims of economic ruination and abundant wreckfish, the government held to the two-million-pound quota and attempted to impose measures that would reduce some of the conflicts on the water. In 1991, 90 vessels entered the fishery. The intense competition to catch as large a share of the quota as possible led to the marine equivalent of the Kentucky derby. Again, fishermen caught the year's quota in four months.

After months of debate, the government established an Individual Transferable Quota (ITQ) program for the wreckfish fishery. Under this program, fishermen were allocated percentage shares of the overall quota, which were based partly on past landings. The results were dramatic. Within a year, more than half of the vessels that had participated in the open access fishery in 1991 had left, selling their shares to fishermen who remained. Instead of racing to catch as much fish as possible as early in the season as possible, fishermen began to fish when they were most likely to get the higher price that properly handled fish can fetch on the market. Arguments that the quota should be higher evaporated, conflicts between fishermen on the water ceased, and fishermen themselves began reporting violations of the rules.

These types of programs, as innovative as they may be, still require considerable governmental intervention. First, fisheries managers must collect information necessary for determining an overall quota. Furthermore, ITQ-type fisheries programs require careful monitoring of catches and landings by individual vessels. Whether fisheries managers place observers at docks or rely upon audits of landing records submitted by harvesters and processors, they must invest in effective enforcement if possession of a share of a harvest quota is to have any value on the market.

Also, allocating shares in a quota gives individual fishermen exclusive use of a public resource, for which they pay nothing to the government. The exclusiveness of this allocation only makes clearer the unusual status of fishermen and fishery resources in the industrialized world. Whether fishermen catch fish under an ITQ program or in an open access fishery, the government effectively is giving away a public resource for free. No other renewable resource is treated this way.

Like any other fishery management measure, ITQs and other types of quasi–property rights programs cannot lift the burden of setting overall quotas that promote long-term conservation. These programs can, however, eliminate the need to race for the fish and can curb the economic incentive to increase quotas.

GROWING TOWARD CONSERVATION

President Bush expressed a common view when he addressed other world leaders at the Earth Summit on June 12, 1992, and said: "Twenty years ago, some spoke of the limits to growth. Today we realize that growth is the engine of change and the friend of the environment." Indeed, middle- and upper-income countries have been able to increase their expenditures for abatement of the pollution caused by their economic growth. In the United States, the share of GNP devoted to pollution control more than doubled between 1972 and 1990. These expenditures brought some significant improvements in environmental quality, including the near elimination of lead from automobile exhausts and a dramatic reduction in the discharge of raw sewage.

Elsewhere in the world, a rapidly growing human population seeking the pattern of consumption enjoyed and advertised by the industrialized countries is drawing upon a natural inheritance that developed countries like the United States have already exploited in their own development. Without great assistance and a reduction in consumption by the industrialized countries, developing countries will have to perform technological miracles to avoid catastrophic ecological destruction in building a future for their peoples. According to the World Bank, manufacturing output in the developing countries will have to increase sixfold to meet the basic needs of 3.7 billion more people in the year 2030. If increased pollution from this additional economic activity is to be avoided, manufacturing and power generation processes will have to reduce the emission of air and water pollutants by 90 percent. This leaves aside the greater pressures to exploit renewable and nonrenewable resources to meet today's needs for food, shelter, and energy.

Promoters of continued economic growth as the key to a more habitable world in the future rely heavily on promoting free trade, as well. According to the theory, developing countries will benefit from the sale of their goods in developed countries and from the purchase of the best that the developed countries have to offer. The wealth generated by trade will enable developing countries to invest in measures to protect their environmental quality from the damage that is so often a by-product of economic growth.

Critics point to several sizable obstacles to achieving this goal, which assumes that developing countries can best develop as the developed countries have. For instance, trade barriers in industrialized countries and large foreign debt have inhibited the growth of processing industries, as for seafood and other marine products, in many developing countries. In order to earn hard currency, these countries have exploited natural assets such as forests, mineral deposits, and fisheries and exported the products at the low prices that unprocessed goods fetch. Unlike the United States, which had the benefit of enormous natural resources at home and abroad, and until recently little or no foreign debt, many developing countries, particularly in Latin America, have already tapped heavily into their natural resources and face a future of servicing enormous debts. Without economic assistance, these countries will be unable to husband their natural assets while generating the kind of economic development that will benefit their citizens.

Furthermore, investors can move large amounts of money much more quickly and freely than in the past. Since the international community has imposed few restrictions, investment money will flow wherever the advantage is greatest, and will not discriminate between a business that achieves lower costs through efficiency and a business that seeks an advantage through lowering wage, health, safety, and environmental standards.

A country that internalizes the environmental and social costs of economic growth will be at a competitive disadvantage to a country that does not, since its prices will likely be higher. In order to eliminate this disadvantage, free trade proponents must make the unlikely assumption that all trading partners will incorporate the environmental and social costs of their economic activities. The only alternative is to modify free trade rules to insure that these costs are addressed, whether through countervailing duties or other mechanisms. But the international community has refused to incorporate environmental concerns in the trade rules that were first formulated long before the environmental implications of international trade were apparent.

INCENTIVES FOR CONSERVATION

Incentives matter, whether they are economic, political, social, or psychological. Unrestricted access to fisheries creates an incentive for a fisherman to keep fishing, lest another fisherman catch more fish. Reducing the financial risk of building on storm-beaten barrier islands and providing roads, bridges, sewer hookups, and power all create a powerful incentive for converting dunes, forests, and wetlands to condominiums and shopping malls and for rebuilding after destructive storms. The fierce opposition to the Clinton administration's proposals to raise grazing fees or to charge royalties for minerals from federal lands gives one measure of how seriously people take incentives. Yet, the use of incentives to promote conservation has received little study and still less support from people concerned about conservation.

As the following chapters will demonstrate, incentives have played a critical role in the decline of coastal areas, water quality, and fisheries. Reforming the current pattern of incentives must be part of efforts to restore where we can and to conserve what we still have. As Paul Hawken notes in *The Ecology of Commerce:*

> Just as every act in an industrial society leads to environmental degradation, regardless of intention, we must design a system where the opposite is true, where doing good is like falling off a log, where the natural, everyday acts of work and life accumulate into a better world as a matter of course, not a matter of conscious altruism.

6

Coasts

Little drops of water
Little grains of sand,
Make the mighty ocean
And the pleasant land.

JULIA A. FLETCHER CARNEY,
Little Things

Years before Saddam Hussein released a massive oil spill into the
Persian Gulf, hundreds of square miles of salt marsh, sea-grass
beds, and mud flats along the Saudi peninsula had been buried
beneath garbage and dredge spoil. Once the gulf's most productive habitats for fishes, shrimp, dugongs, and sea turtles, these
waters were victims not of armed aggression but of careless economic growth. Where shorebirds once fed, petrochemical, fertilizer, steel, and plastic manufacturing plants now joined houses,
streets, and parking lots. The Persian Gulf may recover from Saddam Hussein's oil spill, but the Saudi smothering of the seabed
with industrial and residential development is probably irreversible.

The civilizing of the Saudi coastline in the past 20 years follows
a worldwide pattern that dates back hundreds of years. Offering
rich fisheries and forests, scenic beaches and seascapes, ready
transportation to ports around the world, and a handy repository
for waste, coastal lands and waters have attracted more people
and business activity than any other areas of the world.

Since the 1960s, governments have intervened more and more

deeply into private uses of coastal lands and waters, if only to reduce conflicts at the shoreline between fishermen and condo-minium developers, between beach-goers and beach owners, or between any of the many interests vying to enjoy the benefits that coasts offer. In the United States alone, hundreds of millions of dollars have been spent to study and mediate conflicts at the shoreline, where public interest and private property interests clash ever more intensely, as coastal areas become more crowded and the costs of ignoring the vulnerability of coastal construction rise into the billions of dollars.

For decades, government commissions and hearings have pointed to the need for expanding the view of the coastal zone to include entire watersheds and adjacent coastal waters. The initia-tive in the Chesapeake Bay region that we discussed in chapter 1 is just one of several dozen recent attempts to manage human activities that damage coastal lands and waters, wherever those activities may be taking place. But these initiatives are crippled by resistance within government, industry, and citizens' groups to broadening perspectives and acknowledging the geographical, ecological, social, economic, and political links among water-sheds, coastlines, and coastal waters.

As developing countries around the world seek to better the lot of their citizens, watersheds and coastal waters are being threat-ened by many of the same types of activity, patterns of economic development, and fragmented government programs that already have cost developed countries, including the United States, much of their coastal inheritance. At stake are some of the earth's richest and most diverse marine ecosystems, which have supported coastal residents for centuries.

The Land's Link with the Sea

Everyone lives within a watershed—the land area that drains rain-water and snowmelt into the tributaries of a river system. Whether moving across the surface in creeks and rivers or beneath the ground in aquifers, water transports enormous amounts of mineral elements, soil, and debris. Eventually, much of this mate-rial reaches coastal waters. In the right amounts and at the right time, a river's load of chemicals can feed a profusion of plant life in coastal waters that will in turn feed an abundance of animal life, from bait fish to blue whales. When drought reduces the flow of water and with it the flow of nutrients, the survival rates of young fish and shellfish decline dramatically, with effects on fish abundance that may reverberate through an ecosystem for many years. On the other hand, the discharge of excessive amounts of nutrients, or too great a volume of sediments, can also be a disruptive change.

It would be easy to underestimate the capability of water to transport materials over great distances. The Ganges and Brahmaputra Rivers of the Indian subcontinent annually discharge two billion tons of sediment into the coastal waters of Bangladesh. In recent years, the sediments accumulating in the Padna-Meghna estuary have built 1,500 square miles of islands—an area nearly one and a half times the size of Rhode Island. Very little of this soil is drawn from lands within Bangladesh. Rather, beginning in the Himalaya Mountains, hundreds of miles from the coastal plains of Bangladesh, water collects sediments from deforested hillsides and farmlands in the half million square miles of the rivers' drainage area that is outside Bangladesh. Indian scientists estimate that as people have occupied broader and broader areas in these river basins, the amount of sediment carried by rivers into the Bay of Bengal has increased 100-fold in the last century.

Additional evidence for linking watersheds with coastal waters comes from the downstream effects of changes in the mosaic of ecosystems within watersheds. Elimination of wetlands in upland areas of a watershed may dramatically increase the volume of water entering coastal waters. One study found that watersheds without wetlands discharge water at five times the rate of watersheds with 40 percent wetland cover. Clearing land in northern China for farming has increased the amount of sediment carried to the sea by the Yellow River ten times over. Around the world, where extensive logging and road cutting have removed vegetative cover from the land, increased sediments have buried coral reefs and sea-grass beds offshore.

Finally, economic linkages argue for a broader definition of the coastal zone that includes entire watersheds. Just as clearing mangrove forests for shrimp ponds reduces the yield of offshore fisheries, so can pollutants and floods released by upstream activities, such as agriculture, manufacturing, forestry, and urbanization, jeopardize the success of aquaculture operations, fisheries, and coastal tourism.

From this broader perspective, the transformation of coastal habitats becomes a more complex drama. The stage for this drama is no longer a narrow strip of land where human stubbornness and ingenuity resolutely battle against irresistible forces of wind and wave. Rather, the stage includes many more landscapes and natural forces, and the drama involves many more actors and many more agendas.

FORESTS

In an uncut forest, the leaves, branches, and roots of trees and bushes as well as leaf litter all act like a great sponge, absorbing as much as 90 percent of rainwater and snowmelt. Water is then slowly released into the air as vapor or gradually enters rivers from creeks and streams or from pools of groundwater. As a result, the flow of water in rivers of forested watersheds is relatively steady, although it may fluctuate between dry and wet seasons.

Clear-cutting forests for wood products, for farming, or for suburbs removes one of the most effective regulators of water flow in a river basin. Without leaves and branches to break their fall, raindrops loosen soil and run across the soil surface rather than soaking into the ground. Especially where compacted surfaces such as logging or construction roads crisscross hillsides, running water picks up momentum and carries soil and debris into streams and rivers. Much of the soil and debris eventually reaches coastal waters.

In the study of the Philippine island of Palawan described in chapter 5, the amount of sediment discharged by a river in a logged watershed was 100 times greater than the amount discharged by a river in an unlogged watershed. The rush of water discharged during a rainstorm formed a distinct layer over the salt water and carried the sediment farther offshore, where it smothered coral reefs and sea-grass beds.

In all, the marine resources of 36 tropical countries, from Belize to Tanzania, are potentially at risk from sedimentation due to logging alone. In the last several decades, the reduction of inland forest cover from 80 percent to 20 percent in the Philippines has contributed to the widespread destruction of coral reefs and reef fisheries through siltation, causing the loss of important sources of food and jobs for tens of thousands of fishermen and their families.

In temperate areas, common logging practices have contributed to the decline of anadromous fishes (those that migrate up rivers from the sea to spawn) by silting up pools and gravel areas critical to successful spawning. A recent congressionally mandated report concluded that existing forest management practices in the Pacific Northwest of the United States are likely to cause the extinction of still more fish populations.

The pattern of deforestation and careless logging practices is so persistent partly because those responsible do not pay the full cost of the trees or of offsite damage. As elsewhere around the world, the fees paid by timber companies to the U.S. government for logging public lands are below the market value of the trees themselves. Indeed, these fees do not even cover the costs incurred by the federal government in building the roads used in removing cut timber. Although different logging practices might reduce some onsite and offsite problems, including siltation of stream and coastal habitats, these and other benefits would likely be more effectively gained from insuring that the price for felling trees included the full range of costs.

WETLANDS

Since the time of European settlement, nearly 60 percent of the original 350,000 square miles of wetlands in the lower 48 states have been drained and filled. More than 85 percent of these wetlands were filled to create new agricultural lands with such government encouragement as the Swamp Land Act of 1849, which deeded wetlands to private individuals on the condition that the wetlands be drained. From the obliterated swamps of the Limberlost in the Midwest to thousands of acres of smothered salt marshes in Puget Sound, we soon drained much of what was wet and wild before we knew what it was.

Between 1950 and 1980, farming that often produced surplus

crops continued to account for most of the annual wetland losses of 700 square miles in the lower 48 states. Since then, agriculture's share of wetland loss has fallen somewhat, most dramatically since passage of the Food Security Act of 1985, which removed some subsidies to farmers who drained wetlands or farmed highly erodible lands.

Until recently, the drainage of freshwater wetlands and other agricultural practices generated little concern for the conservation of coastal resources. Like logging in distant watersheds, the destruction of upland wetlands and soil erosion caused by conventional tillage practices exert an indirect, though very important, influence upon the health of the coasts. This influence becomes plain when rivers, swollen with rainwater that wetlands once stored and brown with sediment from eroding agricultural fields and other disturbed lands, disgorge a plume of sediment into bays, estuaries, and more distant coastal waters. Fish may flee the cloud of soil and debris, but sea-grass beds, reefs, and oyster beds must await clear water, if it ever comes, or face destruction.

This scenario may seem extravagant, but even a partial accounting for coastal resource damage from conventional agricultural practices is sobering. According to the U.S. Department of Agriculture, soil erosion from agriculture causes more than one billion dollars in damage to marine recreation and commercial fishing alone each year. Where many rivers drain into densely populated coastal areas, as along the coast of New England, the damage is particularly high.

Since most prime agricultural lands already have been brought into production or converted into suburbs and cities, subsistence and commercial farmers have been turning to marginal lands besides wetlands, including steep hillsides and forests. As an example, just above Elkhorn Slough near Monterey Bay, California, immigrant farmers now cultivate strawberries on steep hillsides that were blanketed with oak trees less than a decade ago. Even moderate rain sends torrents of topsoil down the service roads alongside the rows of strawberry plants and into the slough, often carrying fumigants, pesticides, and fertilizers. Annual damage from erosion and sedimentation runs into the millions of dollars.

Like their counterparts elsewhere around the world, these marginal farmers do not own the land they work. Nor do they or the landowners bear the cost of water pollution. From the rice fields of central California to the coconut plantations of Thailand, government policies and subsidies have discouraged farmers from looking beyond short-term gain to the benefits of conserving their soils. These government policies often reflect a desire, particularly among less developed countries, to generate hard currency through international trade. Such worthy national goals generally do not recognize the lost value of coastal recources caused by decreased fisheries landings and destruction of amenities, such as coral reefs and clean beaches, sought by tourists.

URBANIZATION

Since World War II, the growth and spread of cities has accompanied population growth and increasing affluence in many countries. Worldwide, urban populations have been growing twice as fast as rural populations since at least 1963. Cities replace a porous, yielding, breathing mosaic of plants and soil with hard, impervious surfaces that rush water toward rivers and bays. The asphalt and concrete of city streets and buildings also collect the wide range of pollutants that urban life generates and raise stream temperatures above the tolerance of native plants and animals. As a result, urbanized streams generally are warmer and pollutant levels can be one to two orders of magnitude higher than in forested watersheds. With these changes, the diversity and abundance of organisms in urban streams, including anadromous species such as shad, herring, striped bass, trout, and salmon, have plummeted.

Besides crowded cities, population growth and movement have led to vast, sprawling suburban settlements, from the outlying tenements of Calcutta and Rio de Janeiro to the exclusive subdivisions and shopping malls of the United States. Governments in many industrialized countries have encouraged suburban sprawl by subsidizing the needed services, such as roads, sewer, water, and power. Although suburbs often do not disturb watersheds and streams as acutely as densely populated cities do, they may through their sheer extent affect far larger areas.

Like logging and agriculture, the expansion of cities and suburbs around the world continues to transform watersheds and affect the flow and chemistry of waters entering coastal areas. Government policies generally fail to recognize this link, relying on the common assumption that rivers and oceans are unaffected by inland changes.

DAMMING THE COAST

Until recently, river water flowing to the sea has been viewed as wasted unless it has first irrigated fields, cooled powerplants, quenched the thirst of city-dwellers, or carried away the human and industrial refuse of our towns and cities. As the number of people has grown in river basins around the world, the demands upon the surface and underground waters that eventually feed coastal waters have grown as well. For instance, the world's annual withdrawal of fresh water for irrigation alone more than doubled between 1950 and 1985, to the equivalent of five years' flow of the Mississippi River.

Dams are built principally for domestic and industrial water supply, energy production, irrigation, and flood control. In 1992, nearly 45,000 dams more than 50 feet high impounded the world's rivers. In the last 40 years alone, more than 15,000 large dams have been built. Large dams now control about 15 percent of the global runoff of rainwater and snowmelt and intercept up to 90 percent of the sediments that would otherwise enter coastal bays and estuaries.

In focusing their attention upon the agricultural and industrial benefits of dams and diversions, governments and investment banks generally have not considered the environmental costs, including damage caused by reduced amounts of sediments, nutrients, and fresh water entering coastal waters. These environmental and economic impacts often have been catastrophic and irreversible.

The southern seas of the former Soviet Union are typical casualties of water projects aimed at growing monsoon crops such as cotton and rice on arid lands. Dams and diversions of water from the Volga, Dniester, Dnieper, and Don Rivers have reduced the annual flow of fresh water into the Caspian, Azov, and Black Seas by roughly 50 percent. As a result, salinity has quadrupled in some adjacent estuaries. Furthermore, as much as 90 percent of the sediments that once carried nutrients into the waters of these seas now are captured behind dams. In changing river flows and the chemistry of adjacent estuaries, in blocking migration routes, and in damaging spawning grounds, these dams have nearly eliminated formerly valuable commercial fisheries in all major rivers and estuaries of the area. Michael Rozengurt, formerly of the Federal Oceanographic Institute in Moscow, has estimated that fishery losses alone in the Black and Azov Seas amount to at least $800 million and perhaps to as much as $1.5 billion annually.

Governments have also diverted rivers in order to protect towns and cities in floodplains and low-lying coastal areas. For more than 40 years, the U.S. Army Corps of Engineers has constructed and maintained levees and other flood-control structures along much of the Mississippi River in order to protect cities along the river, particularly New Orleans, which sits below sea level on a former marsh near the river's delta. Much of the sediment that would otherwise spread out and replenish the millions of acres of wetlands at the river's mouth is now diverted outside the delta or is carried onto the continental shelf by the flow of the straitjacketed river. Furthermore, the loss of fresh water flowing over the delta has exposed brackish water and freshwater marshes to the devastating intrusion of salt water.

The diversion of sediment and fresh water has aggravated wetland losses caused by channels cut for construction and maintenance of oil and gas fields, so that wetlands are no longer formed at the same rate as they are lost. Between 1971 and 1989, the annual loss of coastal wetlands in Louisiana nearly quadrupled, from 16 to 60 square miles. The Organization for Economic Cooperation and Development estimates that $3 billion worth of land in the delta has already been lost.

Elsewhere, water projects have so reduced the flow of sediment into coastal waters that the erosion of beaches and barrier islands has accelerated. Annually, the High Aswan Dam on the Nile River captures as much as 110 million cubic yards of silt, accelerating erosion along the 120-mile-long perimeter of the delta. Although some areas actually gained land, overall erosion along the delta

(RIGHT) Oyster fisherman and tongs, Chesapeake Bay: Landings of Chesapeake Bay oysters are now just one percent of what they were at the turn of the century. (Skip Brown)

(BELOW) Baltimore Harbor: International trade has fueled the growth of coastal cities around the world. (Martin Rogers/ Woodfin Camp)

(ABOVE LEFT) A CTD sampler and a rosette of sampling bottles allow oceanographers to measure water temperature and salinity at different depths.

(BELOW LEFT) Before research submersibles, such as the *Johnson Sea Link,* scientists could study ocean life in the depths only with nets and other samplers. *(Harbor Branch Oceanographic Institution)*

(ABOVE RIGHT) Beachcombers collected these shoes that were spilled from a freighter and carried across the North Pacific by currents. *(Diane L. Nordeck/ Smithsonian Institution)*

(BELOW RIGHT) Storm surf pounding a breakwater in Santa Barbara, California. *El Niños,* periodic phenomenona affecting the Pacific Ocean, alter weather, currents, and wildlife over much of the Earth. *(Chuck Place)*

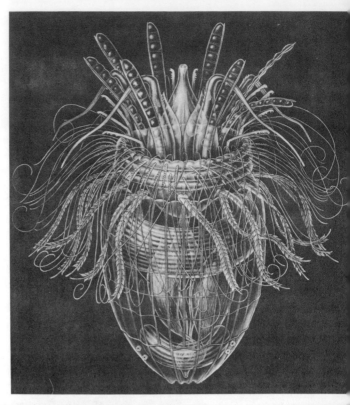

(ABOVE LEFT) Artist's depiction of a microscopic loriciferan. Discovered in 1989 living between sand grains, *Loricifera* were so different in design that scientists created a separate phylum for these animals. *(National Museum of Natural History)*

(BELOW LEFT) Like coral reefs in tropical waters, temperate water kelp forests provide shelter and food for myriad species of marine life, such as these blue rockfish. *(Norbert Wu)*

(ABOVE RIGHT) The oil tanker *Crown* navigates a harbor area. In 1992, more than four million barrels of oil were imported into the United States by sea from the Organization of Petroleum Exporting Countries. *(Luc Cuyvers)*

(BELOW RIGHT) Recreational fishermen squeeze together at Rollover Pass, Texas to take advantage of a fall run of fish. Affluence and inexpensive equipment have led to explosive growth in saltwater sport fishing. *(Robert Parvin)*

(ABOVE LEFT) Cleared mangrove forest on San Marco Island, Florida. Environmental protection laws have only slowed the destruction of coastal wetlands in the United States. *(Bianca Lavies/National Geographic)*

(BELOW LEFT) Bonneville Dam on the Columbia River. Built to provide cheap power and water, Bonneville and 55 other dams on the Columbia also depleted rich salmon fisheries and coastal communities that depended upon them. *(Chuck Place)*

(ABOVE RIGHT) Sandy Hook, New Jersey, 1991. Raw or partially treated sewage and urban runoff still close thousands of acres of shellfish beds to harvesting in the United States. *(Bruce Wodder/The Image Bank)*

(BELOW RIGHT) Like rivers, winds transport pollutants from land to coastal waters and the open ocean, hundreds of miles from their sources. *(U.S. Fish & Wildlife Service)*

(ABOVE LEFT) Once a cheap
source of protein, Atlantic
cod now fetches the price
of beefsteak in supermar-
kets, when it can be found
at all. *(Mark Lovewell)*

(BELOW LEFT) Stilt fishing
near Galle, Sri Lanka,
1983. Most of the world's
fishermen still rely on little
more than their ingenuity
and tradition. *(Heather
Angel)*

(ABOVE RIGHT) Memorial
Day at Virginia Beach, Virginia, 1984. By 2020,
three-quarters of the
world's population will live
within an hour's drive of
the seashore. *(Karen Kas-
mauski/Woodfin Camp)*

(BELOW RIGHT) Barrier
island development crowds
New Jersey's Island Beach
State Park. Government
subsidies for insurance and
infrastructure has encouraged development in these
and other vulnerable
coastal areas. *(Robert
Perron)*

(ABOVE) Monitoring water and sediments in coastal areas is the unglamorous basis for identifying environmental problems. *(Puget Sound Water Quality Authority)*

(BELOW) Storm-drain signs remind Baltimore residents that careless disposal of waste into storm drains can harm the Chesapeake Bay. *(David W. Harp)*

increased 800 percent just between 1978 and 1984. At the Rosetta Promontory, erosion now averages about 100 linear yards per year.

Although the pace of building large dams and water diversions has slowed, increasing numbers of people and economic growth will lead to increased freshwater withdrawals by existing and future water projects. The cost of reversing past and future damage to coasts caused by water withdrawals will only increase as well.

AT THE SHORELINE

Until the 19th century, beaches and coastal wetlands in the United States and Europe generally were left to those few men and women who made their living from the sea. By the end of the 19th century, however, attitudes had changed enough that President Theodore Roosevelt could claim, "A man would not be a good American citizen if he did not know of Atlantic City." From the French Riviera to Waikiki Beach, tourist resorts, second homes, and eventually entire communities have been transforming coastlines.

Now, two-thirds of the world's population lives within 50 miles of a coast, a band that accounts for about 8 percent of the land area of the earth. In the United States, people have been migrating to the coasts since World War II, especially. Already, more than half of the nation's population lives in coastal counties, which make up just 11 percent of the land area of the lower 48 states, and the density of people in coastal counties is several times that of other parts of the country. By the year 2025, three out of every four Americans will live within a hour's drive of the shoreline.

This concentration of people along the coasts means that a tremendous amount of economic and social activity takes place in a small geographical area. In the United States, at least one-third of all economic activity and a slightly larger part of total employment were generated in coastal counties in 1985. By far the largest part of this activity was generated without reliance on coastal resources. Only one percent depended directly upon coastal resources, such as sites for ports or fishing. The remainder was economic activity associated with having so many people in one place. This imbalance makes fisheries, wetlands, and other wild areas vulnerable to being sacrificed for uses that are more attractive economically, such as residential or industrial development.

Each year for the last 20 years, housing the growing number of coastal dwellers accounted for 700,000 housing units or nearly one-half of all new housing units nationwide. Providing jobs, goods, and services entailed construction of about 325,000 new office and industrial buildings during the same period. To handle the 46 percent of the nation's retail sales that took place in coastal areas, 300,000 retail stores were built near the coasts.

But coastal areas have never been all business. In 1990, more than 5,000 coastal marinas and 600,000 moorings serviced a fleet of nine million recreational boats. In 1982, coastal counties spent $4.5 billion in supporting outdoor recreational opportunities. Four of every five new hotels in the United States were built in coastal counties in the last two decades, as were almost half of all theaters, athletic and social clubs, and other recreational facilities. Each year, millions of Americans travel from far and wide to experience the special rejuvenation that only the coast can provide.

After World War II, the population surge of the "Baby Boom" as well as rising affluence increased the demand for housing and for vacation homes and resorts. Some of this demand was met by building along the very fringe of America's coast. Between 1950 and 1970, urban development caused 90 percent of all coastal wetland losses in the United States. Indeed, as progress has conquered ever more wet, teeming places along the coast, people have vied to get their very own plot of dark and mucky space, or have escaped to resorts offering them a taste of the solitude, quiet, and wilderness that once made wetlands seem less than worthless.

With their near elimination in some coastal areas, wetlands have gained in real estate value, leading some investors and developers to argue, topsy-turvy-like, that these remnant wetlands are too valuable to preserve. In California, for instance, where coastal wetlands have been reduced from about 100,000 acres in 1900 to less than 14,000 acres now, the demand to convert remaining fragments of wetlands into residential and commercial developments is especially intense. As an example, four years after the California Coastal Commission banned residential and commercial development in a 66-acre strip of wetland in southern California, two groups of investors purchased the land for $465,000 per acre. Although they were aware of the ban on development, the investors claimed that the ban will deny them the ability to sell lots for homes—yet to be built—at twice the price they paid.

BATTLING THE SEAS

The shoreline is an unstable place in many areas. In the United States, each of the 400 sandy barrier islands that line more than 2,600 miles of coastline from Maine to Texas are cases in point. Sometimes slowly, sometimes rapidly, a sandy barrier island conserves itself by migrating up a gentle coastal plain, as winds, waves, and storms move sand from the ocean side to the landward side of the island. As the ocean beach erodes, shallow waters and wetlands on the back side of the island fill in, and the island seems to roll over on itself.

However slow the process may seem in human terms, it is inexorable. On the broad continental shelf of the Gulf of Mexico, for instance, some coastal barriers have retreated as much as 80 miles. As Edisto Island off South Carolina retreated before rising seas, the 19th century town of Eddingsville Beach became an underwater ghost town.

As seemingly relentless has been the steady march of property owners toward barrier islands. Before World War II, less than ten percent of these islands and spits had been settled, but postwar affluence and government subsidies for roads, bridges, water, sewage treatment, insurance, and other services provoked an explosion in development. By 1982, 42 percent of these islands had seen some construction, and more than 5,000 acres of barrier island forest, scrub, wetland, and dunes were falling to development each year. Only a bitterly fought withdrawal of federal subsidies from undeveloped areas slowed the urbanization. For decades, people who settled on barrier islands have tried to protect their homes and businesses against rising seas, erosion, and storms. In doing so, they have often aggravated the very problems they have sought to solve.

Although fierce storms account for the most dramatic changes in the coastline, long-term erosion has regularly whittled away beaches and buildings, even when they have been armored with tons of sand or rock or concrete seawalls, generally at taxpayer expense. In the United States, the National Academy of Sciences concluded in 1990 that coastal erosion would claim about 750 beachfront buildings in the next 10 years and another 5,000 in the next 60 years in North Carolina alone. The problem extends beyond North Carolina: About 80 percent of the nation's sandy beaches are eroding. In many areas, erosion rates have been aggravated by upstream impoundment of sediment behind dams or by coastal impoundment by jetties and rocky groins. Jetties and other measures to maintain inlets between barrier islands are thought to cause 80 to 85 percent of the erosion along the Atlantic coast of Florida.

Hurricanes, nor'easters, and other types of storms are only more dramatic in overwhelming efforts to protect private property that hugs the coastline. Hurricane Hugo, one of the worst natural disasters of the century in the United States, was born as a cluster of thunderstorms above warm ocean waters off the coast of western Africa in September 1989. On September 22, Hurricane Hugo came ashore near Charleston, South Carolina. The air pressure in the storm's 50-mile-wide eye was so low that ocean waters were lifted 20 feet, creating enormous storm tides that flooded whatever they did not wash away. By the time it left the South Carolina shoreline and continued its destructive path through West Virginia and western New York, Hurricane Hugo had become the costliest hurricane in history, causing more than $7 billion in damage in South Carolina alone. By June 1990, the federal government had paid out nearly $320 million in claims by more than 15,000 holders of federal flood insurance policies.

The enormous damage was due partly to the violence of the storm, but also to the swarm of resorts and second homes that had been erected on the barrier islands of South Carolina during the lull in hurricane activity of the previous 35 years. The value of insured property in South Carolina coastal counties alone had increased 83 percent between 1980 and 1988, as people forgot the state's last major hurricane in 1954, which had caused $1.4 billion in damage. Nationwide, insurance liability for such storm damage is the second largest source of liability in the federal budget, after Social Security.

Like many other states, South Carolina has come to depend upon tourists visiting barrier islands as a source of income. In 1986, tourists in South Carolina spent 58 percent of their $3.9 billion in expenditures in coastal counties. The rush to house and entertain tourists fueled much of the construction on the coast. In 1988, the U.S. Army Corps of Engineers estimated that hotels and resorts facing the Atlantic along one 37-mile stretch of barrier island were worth $1.2 billion.

By the spring of 1990, many of the houses destroyed by Hurricane Hugo were being rebuilt in the same or more hazardous areas with the permission, and often the financial assistance, of state and federal governments. Unlike other types of insurance, federal flood insurance premiums do not increase in response to repeat claims. Rather, premiums for insurance to rebuild, even in very hazardous areas, have remained well below their market price.

DIRECT LOSSES IN THE NEARSHORE

Although landside activities greatly affect nearshore habitats such as coral reefs and sea-grass beds, these areas have also been the victims of direct assaults such as dredging, mining, boat traffic, and groundings. The degradation and loss of these less visible pieces in the coastal mosaic have already contributed to losses in fisheries and in attractions such as clear water, upon which coastal tourism depends.

Sea-grass beds are a once-common link that provide food and shelter for fish and shellfish inhabiting coral reefs, mangrove forests, or salt marshes at other times. In the tropics, for instance, shrimp and spiny lobster spawned offshore take up residence in sea-grass beds early in life before moving to other habitats as adults. Other species exploit the abundant prey of sea-grass beds. As these predators move to adjacent habitats, they take with them the nutrients generated in sea-grass beds.

Sea-grass beds have often found themselves in the path of progress. Just between 1959 and 1979, Galveston Bay lost nearly all of its sea-grass beds, which once contributed to valuable shrimp and finfish fisheries in the bay and offshore. With the loss of sea-grass beds, fisheries and water clarity often decline. In the 1930s, the collapse of the bay scallop fishery and the catastrophic decline of migratory brant in the Chesapeake Bay coincided with the disappearance of eelgrass. The decline in eelgrass beds was provoked partly by pollution from landside activities.

In the Chesapeake, as elsewhere, dredging for navigation and other purposes has directly destroyed sea-grass beds. As navigation channels in ports and marinas fill with sediment, dredging resumes, its environmental costs multiplied by the disposal of dredge spoil. The amount of sediment dredged from harbors and navigation channels in the United States alone is staggering. In 1986, Congress authorized deepening six large harbors and 32 smaller harbors, which together would require the disposal of millions of tons of dredge spoil.

A no less serious assault on sea-grass beds in the United States arises from the widespread availability of motorized pleasure boats and a growing coastal population that can afford them. Besides the losses caused by creation of private marinas and docks to service pleasure boats, sea-grass beds in heavily populated areas such as the Florida Keys are lacerated by propellers and strangled by sediment kicked up by boat wakes. These cumulative losses may now be matching losses from dredging.

Other nearshore habitats, such as coral reefs, have also suffered direct damage in the United States and elsewhere. According to the United Nations Environment Programme, coral reefs off nearly 70 countries are being sacrificed to navigation channels, airport runways, tourist resorts, and industrial parks. In many areas of the world, coral reefs are still mined for building blocks or as a source of lime for cement. About 40 percent of the lime used by the cement industry in Sri Lanka, for instance, is mined from coral reefs and coral sand—more than 16,000 tons annually.

Entire sections of reef have also been removed for navigation of vessels large and small. Such projects often have unintended effects. As an example, several years ago, a section of fringing reef off the north coast of the Dominican Republic was blasted to provide vacationing windsurfers with easier access to windier offshore waters. In removing this natural breakwater, the resort also lost its beach as tides and waves gained access to once-still waters and carried away the sands that had slowly accumulated on shore.

Finally, coral reefs are becoming victims of their own appeal near many resort areas, where divers and snorkelers descend onto the reefs and slowly, unwittingly kill colonies of coral with the uncalculated touch of their thousands of hands and fins.

DEVELOPMENT IN DEVELOPING COUNTRIES

Like other developed countries, the United States has exploited its rich coastal resources in its economic development, often at the cost of long-term sustainability. Until seeming abundance gave way to scarcity and loss, coastal resources provided a cheap source for fueling economic growth.

As less developed countries now seek to meet the needs of their growing populations and to prevail in international trade, they too are turning to the rich and complex mix of coastal resources. Individual resources, such as mangrove forests, coral reefs, and fisheries, have been mined with little or no thought to the impact upon other resources or other parts of the economy and society. In this, these developing countries are suffering from the same fragmented view of the coast that has already cost the United States some of its richest natural heritage. However, the damage is occurring much more rapidly than it did in the United States, partly because of the much larger size of the world economy now and of the density of human settlement along the coasts.

Though the pattern is playing out in dozens of countries, none exemplify the risks and difficult choices better than Indonesia. At 200 million people, Indonesia was the world's fourth most populous country in 1994. It is a land of coastal superlatives. Besides being the world's largest archipelago, Indonesia lies in an area of such exceptional coastal biological diversity and abundance that it is sometimes called the Fertile Triangle. Scientists have identified more than 2,200 species of fishes, 3,200 species of mollusks, and 488 species of corals alone in this area. Fish and shellfish from waters surrounding Indonesia's 13,700 islands provide 60 percent of the country's protein supply. Much of this marine productivity depends upon Indonesia's extensive mangrove forests, the largest in the world. A rough calculation suggests that in 1987, economic activity in coastal and marine areas of the country accounted for 22 percent of Indonesia's Gross Domestic Product—more than half of that share from extraction and refining of oil and gas.

Increasing population and economic activity in coastal areas, which is growing at twice the rate of other economic activity in Indonesia, already have taken their toll on some of Indonesia's richest natural inheritance. Between 1974 and 1985, the total area of mangrove forest converted to fish and shrimp ponds, called *tambak* in Indonesia, increased by 30 percent, and by 1987 *tambak* covered 925 square miles along the coasts of Java, Sulawesi, Kalimantan, and northern Sumatra. The Indonesian government intends to continue expanding aquaculture at a rate of more than 11 percent per year, partly by converting some of the remaining 2,300 square miles of suitable mangrove forest into *tambak*.

Besides damaging mangrove forests indirectly by altering the flow of fresh water and sediment into estuaries, upland activities also are leading to direct destruction of mangrove forests. On Java, for instance, the annual conversion of 380 square miles of upland arable land to towns and industrial parks is increasing pressure to convert mangrove forests and other coastal areas to agricultural uses, although poor soils and drainage prevent predictable yields.

One type of exploitation offers particularly graphic evidence of short-sighted, single-use exploitation of Indonesia's rich mangrove habitats. Since 1975, more than 770 square miles of mangrove forest have been felled to produce wood chips, principally for export to Japan, where they are used in the production of paper pulp and rayon. In all, human settlement, shrimp pond and port construction, forestry and agriculture, as well as diversion of fresh water in uplands, have reduced Indonesia's mangrove forests by more than 50 percent.

Converting mangrove forests to wood chips for export to Japan or to shrimp ponds for shrimp exports to the United States and western Europe has come at the cost of losing valuable ecological goods and services. First, destruction of mangrove forests removes critical habitat for an extraordinary diversity of plants and animals. Conversion of mangrove forests to wood chips or shrimp ponds also causes losses in offshore fisheries. Although an acre of *tambak* produces an average of 250 pounds of shrimp for export, the loss of the acre of mangrove forest results in an annual loss of roughly 425 pounds of fish and shrimp. Only the high value of shrimp on the world market makes economic sense out of this loss. However, the world market does not account for the loss of other important functions of mangrove forests, such as storm protection, erosion control, waste-water cleanup, and wildlife habitat, as well as the generation of renewable products including construction materials, fodder for cattle, and medicines.

Indonesia's reliance on offshore oil and gas production and refining for much of its foreign exchange has already caused obliteration of thousands of acres of mangroves and sea-grass beds in the construction of ports and refining facilities. Besides directly destroying mangroves, sea grasses, and coral reefs, construction of navigational channels for ports and refineries also has disrupted the flow of fresh and salt waters in nearshore waters, leading to changes in animal and plant species and loss of productive habitats.

Meanwhile, Indonesia's beaches and coral reefs are being whittled away by a variety of generally small-scale economic activities. As in many other tropical countries, Indonesian coral reefs are mined for production of lime and cement, sometimes with dramatic results. Mining has reduced the size of two coral islands, Ubi Besar and Nirwana, by half.

Destructive fishing practices, such as dynamiting, have destroyed sections of reef elsewhere in Indonesian waters, as has mining of corals for the international curio trade. Sandy beaches have also been mined for building materials, again with dramatic consequences. Between 1972 and 1975, erosion of the beach at Cilincing on Java, for instance, accelerated from 80 feet per year to about 285 feet per year, as local builders removed 200 to 300 truckloads of sand each day.

Indonesia's coastal and marine resources may still be abundant and in no immediate danger of catastrophic loss. Nonetheless, if coastal development in the United States and other developed countries offers any guide, this happy situation will not last. As elsewhere, the very richness of the coastal zone is likely to continue attracting Indonesia's growing population and incompatible economic development. By the year 2000, Indonesia's coastal population is expected to double, greatly increasing the demand for space, food, shelter, and economic well-being.

Furthermore, the government of Indonesia is looking to the coast for siting expanded industrial activity, including the production of shrimp, petrochemicals, pulp and paper, palm oil, steel, and fertilizers. If the government succeeds in its plans, the coast of Indonesia will also be supporting many more international tourists, who already provide the fifth greatest source of foreign exchange. Constructing the roads, airports, hotels, and other facilities necessary for hosting tourists already has led to some destruction of the very coastal amenities that attract tourists.

Like most other governments around the world, the government of Indonesia has not developed a coordinated approach for the use of its coastal resources. Rather, individual agencies promote uses of coastal resources with little regard for the effect of these uses on other uses. In some cases, as in the conversion of mangrove forests to shrimp ponds or to wood chips, one use completely excludes another, renewable use. Often, this narrow approach does not reflect a decision to promote single rather than multiple use of coastal resources, so much as an ignorance of the multiple goods and services that a coastal area may offer.

Until decision makers confront the trade-offs involved in using coastal resources in one way to the exclusion of others, coastal forests, beaches, reefs, and fisheries will continue to be exploited unsustainably in Indonesia, the Philippines, Ecuador, and dozens of other countries, as they already have been in the United States and other industrialized countries.

COASTAL RESTORATION

No other society has equaled the coastal engineering works of the Dutch. In the 17th century, Dutch settlers first began claiming large stretches of land from the North Sea by ringing a body of water with a dike and using the power of windmills to drain the water into surrounding canals. In 1852, steam-powered engines drained the 45,000-acre Lake Haarlem. Just 60 years ago, Dutch engineers enclosed the Zuider Zee with a massive dam, turning it into a freshwater lake and providing protection from the North Sea for the drainage of still more farmland. Where shallow waters once incubated fish and shellfish for the North Sea, villages and farmlands now stretch to the horizon.

The most massive of coastal works was yet to come. In February 1953, an intense North Sea storm pushed a 15-foot wall of water over dikes built to protect settlements in southwest Netherlands, killing more than 1,800 people and sweeping away farms and cattle. After years of study, the Dutch government decided to build an enormous barrier to future storm surges. Unlike earlier dikes, however, this barrier would consist of 62 movable steel gates as tall as a 13-story building, which could be lowered to block storm tides. At other times, fresh water from the Maas and Rhine rivers feeding four of Holland's great estuaries could continue to mix with the tides of the North Sea. On October 4, 1986, Queen Beatrix dedicated the $2.4 billion Delta Works, the most ambitious coastal engineering project ever undertaken.

For the last decade, the Dutch have debated the wisdom of spending more than $400 million annually to pump water from reclaimed lands and $3.5 billion in farming subsidies for the crops that are grown on them. Besides its cost, pumping has also caused reclaimed lands to sink as they dry out and compress. Given that the sea level is expected to rise a foot or more in the next century, the subsidence of these lands is a trend that the Dutch wish to reverse. Proud of their image as leaders in wildlife conservation, Dutch citizens' groups and government wildlife agencies also have pressed to reverse the loss of lakes, marshes, and shallow estuarine waters that devastated populations of birds and other wildlife, such storks and river otters.

In 1990, the Dutch government and private conservation groups adopted an ambitious plan to return 600,000 acres of farmland to forests, marshes, and lakes. It is a plan that makes ecological and economic sense.

7

Pollution

And all the water that was in the Nile turned
to blood. And the fish in the Nile died, and the
Nile became foul.

Exodus 7:20–21

In December 1982, in the cold, cavernous Old Post Office building in Washington, D.C., a bearded poster-maker named Friedens-
reich Hundertwasser ruffled a crowd of marine lobbyists and
policymakers with the exhortation: "Treasure your shit!"

Some of those attending the fundraising reception thought his
remarks were crude. Most of the crowd was confused, but continued ingesting fresh scallop and shrimp appetizers. Certainly,
none of the festive consumers thought that Mr. Hundertwasser's
plea had anything to do with them or the oceans.

Few if any of Mr. Hundertwasser's targets later read a World
Bank report that urged the same principle in these antiseptic
terms: "Human excreta should be regarded as natural resources
to be conserved and reused rather than discarded." Peter
Edwards, the author of the World Bank report, could make such
a provocative statement, knowing that daily, for decades, even
centuries, people in villages and cities from Munich to Taiwan
have not discharged their sewage into rivers and coastal waters,
but husbanded it in ponds to feed plants and fish for later
human consumption.

Cultural prejudices often overcome common sense in defining
and dealing with pollution of ocean waters. As a consequence of

our prejudices about human waste, for instance, cities and towns have fertilized coastal waters in many parts of the world with billions of gallons of nutrient-rich waste water that foster algal blooms and deplete coastal waters of their oxygen.

In producing consumer goods and food, industry and agriculture have relied increasingly on synthetic chemicals whose unintended impacts are seldom tested before they are released into the environment, either as waste from the production process or as waste from consumer use. The social catharsis that seems to mark each major oil spill continues to divert attention from much greater sources of oil pollution—everyday automobile use, paving of watersheds, and routine tanker operations. Indeed, degradation of coastal waters, especially, has less to do with the exotic or infrequent than with the insults of everyday living.

As human population and consumption grow, we become more deeply committed to an enormous environmental experiment. In some areas it already has strangled productive coastal waters with nutrients and sediments, and in other areas it has nearly eliminated native species of plants and animals through the intentional and unintentional introduction of exotic species. In meeting the needs of increasing numbers of coastal dwellers, industry and agriculture have been moving larger and larger amounts of nutrients and metals from inland areas to the coasts, where they eventually enter rivers and coastal waters. The same process has fed the introduction of chemicals entirely new to coastal environments and their inhabitants, including people, whose health they compromise to a degree that we are only now coming to grasp.

The types and amounts of pollution have increased far more quickly than scientific, much less popular and political, understanding. Rather than reducing the risk of damage by reducing our production of pollution, we have relied on technology to segregate and treat wastes. As technological limitations become clear, we seek ever more expensive and futile methods of attempting the impossible: to make our wastes disappear.

Ocean and coastal waters and wildlife are resilient. But in many areas, the limits have been reached. Treating or sequestering wastes once they are produced is cheap and convenient only for a short time. Progress in reducing marine pollution most likely will come only from reducing the production of waste and learning to manage waste as a resource.

SOME BASICS

There is no such thing as destruction of matter or energy—only changes in its form. Sewage treatment plants, for instance, don't destroy the waste discharged by households and businesses into sewers and gutters. Among other things, modern sewage treatment produces sludge, which itself must be managed. As an example, incineration transforms some of the sludge into gas, some into particulates that may be carried miles through the atmosphere, and some into a potentially toxic residue. Incineration itself produces additional wastes from the combustion of fuel, which themselves must be managed.

Manufacturing and other uses of materials and energy are inevitably inefficient. Whether producing automobiles from steel, leather, and plastic, or energy from coal, oil, or food, transforming materials and energy into goods and services also produces residuals, such as steel cuttings, waste heat, and human excreta.

Releasing residuals into the environment has been the rule partly because recovery and use of residuals, such as wood chips for lumber or sewage for fertilizer, has appeared to be more expensive than use of other material, such as timber and chemical fertilizers. This is partly because the discharger of wastes has not borne any cost in using the environment for disposal. Rather, society at large and people living downstream have absorbed the cost of degraded environmental quality in altered ecosystems, reduced fisheries, or unswimmable waters.

Discharge of a waste does not necessarily pollute. Up to a point, discharges may actually increase the productivity of marine areas, as sometimes occurs around sewage outfalls. Even without such beneficial effects, water can so dilute and assimilate waste materials that they cause no harm. But determining the capacity of a body of water to render wastes harmless is very difficult in practice, partly because we can neither agree upon nor detect acceptable levels of pollution damage. In many instances, however, the growth in population and in consumption has led to volumes and types of wastes that have clearly overwhelmed the ability of estuarine and coastal waters to dilute and process. Assimilative capacity in most coastal waters is an idle concern.

Whether plants, animals, or humans are at risk from pollution in a particular area depends upon a number of factors. What wastes reach the area at what times of year? Does the waste degrade or persist? Does it accumulate in animal tissue or does it dissolve in water? Does it become more or less harmful with exposure to sunlight, acidic water, heat? Do organisms such as fish or bacteria make it more or less harmful as they digest it? Does the waste affect some species of plants and animals but not others? Is the waste toxic at any level or is there a threshold level above which the waste causes harm? What are the principal sources of the waste? Is it usually transported in the air, surface waters, or groundwater? Does it accumulate in coastal sediments or in wetlands plants?

Movement and Fate of Wastes

Until recently, pollution control efforts emphasized point sources, principally large industrial facilities, municipal sewage treatment plants, and operations for dumping of material dredged from harbors and shipping lanes. In the industrialized countries, pollution from many of these sources has been greatly reduced, although the cost of further reductions has slowed additional progress in treating waste once it is produced, whether in the home or at a factory.

In recent decades, the attention of scientists and government officials, at least, has turned to runoff, which has millions of sources that cannot be so easily identified as discharge pipes from a factory. Runoff from urban and agricultural areas, mines, and clear-cut forests, for instance, is a major contributor of sediments and organic wastes, as well as phosphorus and some metals, such as lead and chromium, and pathogenic bacteria from animal wastes. Wastes that are discharged from automobile exhausts, home fireplaces, and the smokestacks of industrial and utility plants often are transported hundreds of miles before they fall on water or land. Rain and snow later sweep these deposits from streets and parking lots into storm drains and, eventually, into streams, rivers, and the sea.

Whether discharged from automobile tailpipes, sewage outfalls, or agricultural sprayers, wastes often are moved great distances by winds, water, and animals. DDT has been found in the fat of Antarctic penguins, and heavy metals released by factories on the North American continent have been found on the surface of the North Atlantic Ocean hundreds of miles from land. Even so, many wastes from human activities settle into coastal waters and sediments, especially in estuaries where water circulation is restricted. From the Gulf of Thailand to the Gulf of Mexico, hot-spots of pollution cluster in waters near major urban and industrial areas.

The ultimate fate of a waste also depends upon a number of physical factors, some of which can be greatly influenced by human activities. Stripping a landscape of its vegetation, for instance, greatly increases the amount and velocity of runoff from land and, with that, the likelihood that a waste will be swept into coastal waters. Pesticides that might remain on land and degrade during the dry season may be washed into creeks and coastal waters when applied during the rainy season. In reducing the flow of rainwaters and snowmelt, dams and irrigation diversions can radically change the chemical environment of estuarine organisms by allowing the incursion of salt water, by intercepting the supply of nutrients from land, and by reducing the seaward flow of pollutants.

In its 1990 review of the marine environment, a United Nations group of experts found widespread evidence of wastes carried by prevailing winds and deposited on coastal and ocean waters. For eons, winds have lifted dust from deserts, volcanoes, and forest fires and deposited it over land and sea alike. What is new is the potpourri of industrial chemicals, remains from fossil fuels, and other wastes that are discharged into the atmosphere and carried by high-altitude winds over thousands of miles. According to the UN group, 98 percent of the lead dissolved in the oceans and most of the cadmium, copper, iron, and zinc, not to mention nearly all PCB and DDT waste in the open oceans, falls from the sky. Although more nitrogen enters coastal waters from rivers, most of the nitrogen entering open ocean waters appears to come from the atmosphere.

Although calculations are imprecise, there are clear trends in the distribution of atmospheric wastes on the ocean surface. For instance, the amounts of metals such as lead and cadmium that annually fall on the North Sea, Baltic Sea, and western Mediterranean are as much as ten times higher than the amount falling on the open North Atlantic, and ten to 100 times higher than the amount falling on the open North Pacific. The influence of human activity clearly emerges from the significantly lower amounts of organic compounds such as PCBs and DDT that enter southern hemisphere seas compared with those in the northern hemisphere, where these compounds have had a longer history of use.

Even though chemical wastes may be moved about by water and wind, they also tend to accumulate in certain areas and in the body tissues of animals. Trace metals and many organic chemicals that bind to sediments tend to settle in water bodies such as estuaries, where weak circulation and layering of fresh and salt waters encourages particles to stick together and sink more quickly. Currents, winds, and the topography of an area also can combine to capture pollutants. The counterclockwise currents of the Persian Gulf carried much of the oil released during the Gulf War south until it reached the Abu Ali peninsula, which confined the slick against the Saudi coast.

TYPES OF POLLUTANTS

Each of the principal types of marine waste—metals, synthetic chemicals, oil, marine debris, exotic species, nutrients, and sewage—behaves in a different way and presents different threats to ocean resources. Even within types, there are differences. For instance, most metals remain in their mineral form and do not accumulate to toxic levels in animals. Slightly toxic mercury, on the other hand, may be transformed into highly toxic methylated mercury by bacteria in coastal waters and sediments. When accumulated in the tissue of predator species such as sharks and swordfish, methylated mercury poses a health risk that mercury itself does not.

Leaving nutrients and sewage for separate consideration, let us look more closely at each of the other principal types of marine pollution.

Metals: Life in the oceans evolved depending upon natural supplies of metals like cadmium and mercury as trace elements for physiological functioning. Mining as well as metal processing and use have significantly increased the amounts of metals entering marine waters. Whether these increased amounts of metals, particularly arsenic, cadmium, lead, and mercury, will affect animals and plants depends upon several factors. First, metals must be in a form that can be taken up by organisms. When in the form of particles, metals tend to cling to sediments and settle on the sea bottom. Metals bound in bottom sediments may be released by storms and dissolve. Once dissolved, metals may bind with other molecules, becoming more or less available or toxic to animals.

Once ingested from the water by filter feeders or from prey by predators, metals may pass through the gut of an animal or accumulate in tissues or organs. Cadmium and mercury tend to accumulate in animals, while arsenic and lead do not. If predators at higher levels of a food chain consume animals that have accumulated metals in their tissues and organs, the predators themselves may store and accumulate the metals stored by their prey. Repeated consumption of contaminated prey gradually increases the concentration of metals in the predator's tissues. Through such biomagnification, top-level predators such as swordfish, sharks, and some marine mammals may accumulate metals at levels potentially affecting their health and that of human consumers.

Synthetic Chemicals: Every year, about 1,000 new chemicals join the ranks of 65,000 chemicals already available to industry and agriculture. About 10,000 of these chemicals are regularly used in some agricultural or industrial process. Little is known about what happens to such chemicals when they enter water. Some persist and accumulate in the tissues and organs of aquatic animals, others may be metabolized or excreted. Some are toxic enough to cause massive fish kills, others have chronic effects that are difficult to identify. Very few have received any study at all.

The success of the Green Revolution in boosting agricultural production around the world has depended largely upon the application of chemical fertilizers and a new, evolving line of pesticides. The first generation of these new chemicals, called chlorinated hydrocarbons, included DDT, chlordane, dieldrin, mirex, and endosulfan, all of which have either been banned or greatly restricted in the United States, although they still are widely used abroad. As effective as these new insecticides were in eliminating pest species, they also had very significant disadvantages, which were acknowledged only after damage had been done to habitats and wildlife. Since the banning of DDT in the United States in 1972, the early wonder chemicals have been replaced by new products that appear to be less damaging.

Whether any industrial or agricultural chemical is likely to damage marine life depends partly upon certain characteristics of the chemical, principally its toxicity and whether it accumulates in animals in concentrations that increase at higher levels of the food chain. For instance, although so-called organophosphates, such as malathion, degrade relatively quickly, they are very toxic to fish and other vertebrates. Because of their chemical complexity, the early chlorinated pesticides resist bacterial degradation and persist in the environment, sometimes for years. In waters off southern California, bottom-feeding fish were still accumulating high levels of DDT 20 years after dumping was halted.

Most recent agricultural chemicals remain in soil for less than half a year. Those that dissolve in water, such as atrazine, may be diluted by rainfall or snowmelt and washed into surface waters or groundwater. Chemicals that are less soluble in water, such as endosulfan, often bind to soil particles and plant debris. If they are not ingested by filter-feeding or scavenging animals, they accumulate in soils or in estuaries and other protected coastal waters. Agricultural and industrial chemicals that dissolve in fatty tissues can accumulate in the muscles and digestive organs of animals. As animals higher in the food chain consume prey with high levels of fat-soluble chemicals in their bodies, they themselves may accumulate and increase the concentrations of the chemicals to levels well beyond what is found in surrounding waters.

The revolution in agricultural chemicals after World War II was accompanied by a similar revolution in industrial chemicals. None of the new chemicals received careful environmental evaluation before commercial use. Like agricultural chemicals, industrial chemicals differ in their persistence in the environment, in their tendency to accumulate in animal tissue, and in their effects on the health of aquatic life. As an example, because of their chemical stability the polychlorinated biphenyls (PCBs) attracted widespread use until 1970, frequently as insulation in electrical power transformers. This same chemical stability, together with their solubility in fat, meant that PCBs, like other chlorinated hydrocarbons, have accumulated in the environment and in animals. Since PCBs are toxic, they now represent a clear health hazard to humans.

Oil: Although estimates vary, tankers and freighters are the source for 42 percent of the estimated 25 million barrels of oil entering the oceans every year—about 100 times the entire spill from the *Exxon Valdez* in 1989. Two-thirds of the oil from marine transportation comes from routine operation of vessels, including the discharge of oil in ballast water, of oil washed from tanks for storing oil, and of the sludge from fuel oil used to power these vessels. On average, spills from tanker accidents release nearly 3 million barrels of oil into the oceans each year.

Discharges of oil from sources on land account for about 32 percent of the oil entering the oceans annually. Of this, 5.1 million barrels, or more than half the total, comes from municipal sewage treatment plants, and about one-quarter comes from refineries and other industrial activities. Offshore production of oil and gas releases an estimated 360,000 barrels of oil in routine and accidental discharges each year. Winds carrying wastes released into the atmosphere in the refining and combustion of oil deposit another 2.2 million barrels of oil onto the oceans. Finally, another 1.8 million barrels of oil flow from natural seeps in the ocean floor.

The environmental effect of oil depends greatly upon its chemical composition and other factors such as wind, currents, and temperature. Types of oil that enter the seas vary from very heavy crude oil to light refined oil products. Crude oils themselves differ greatly in how they behave when spilled. For instance, high winds broke up the 29 million gallons of Norwegian light crude spilled by the *Braer* off Scotland in January 1992, whereas winds could not break up the heavier Alaska crude spilled by the *Exxon Valdez* in March 1989. Unlike other crudes, the Norwegian light crude resisted forming tar balls and mats.

Refined oil products such as kerosene and fuel oil generally evaporate quickly after being spilled. Very soon after the Greek tanker *World Prodigy* ran aground off Rhode Island in June 1989, all but one percent of the 7,200 barrels of Number 2 fuel oil that spilled from its tanks had evaporated and formed a layer of smog over the southern end of Narragansett Bay. When it is not broken up by winds and currents, oil remains as a slick on the surface of the water, coating plants and animals that come into contact with it. Oil slicks also prevent gas exchange between the air and water and reduce light penetration to plants. When oil comes ashore, it can smother plants and animals.

Once oil is spilled, it undergoes various chemical changes, whose rate is greatly influenced by environmental factors such as temperature and wind. Many of the toxic elements in crude oil, such as benzene and toluene, can kill marine animals, particularly eggs and larvae, almost instantly. Because these lightweight toxic elements evaporate very quickly, particularly in warmer climates, animals such as marine mammals can inhale them, severely damaging their lungs. In colder climates, the process of degradation slows greatly and marine animals are exposed to harm for longer periods. As time passes, oil that remains on the water's surface weathers and forms tar balls or foamy mats. About one percent of the crude oil and most of the routine discharges from vessels forms tar balls that can harm animals by entrapment or ingestion.

Legal, routine discharges from vessels are a cocktail of oily wastes. Ships often fill cargo tanks with water to serve as ballast during a voyage. Unless treated before discharge, this ballast water will be contaminated with the remnants of the previous cargo. Vessels also discharge the waste that collects in their bilges and the sludge that fuel filters separate from the oil burned in their diesel engines. These fuel oils have become increasingly contaminated with carbon residues generated in the refining process and with contaminants such as heavy metals and solvents remaining in the waste oils from automobiles and other sources that are used to produce fuel oils. Each seagoing ship entering a port carries about seven barrels of waste oil, if it has not discharged it at sea.

Marine Debris: For centuries, sailors and city-dwellers alike have discarded garbage in the sea. While much of this debris may have been unsightly, most of it decomposed with time and exposure to the elements. The advent of plastics and other synthetic materials, valued for their toughness, lightness, and low cost, changed this. Now, large numbers of plastic cups, bottles, ropes, nets, fishing lines, packing bands, bags, and balloons are discarded into rivers, coastal waters, and the open ocean each year. Like other synthetic products, plastic debris may persist for hundreds of years.

Most debris enters the ocean near coastal cities, where vessel traffic, sewage discharges, and land runoff are concentrated. While much of this debris sinks or collects along drift lines in the ocean where currents collide, much of it washes ashore on beaches. In an International Coastal Cleanup in 1992, sponsored by the Center for Marine Conservation, more than 160,000 volunteers in 33 nations and territories collected more than five million pieces of debris.

Concern about plastic debris in particular increased in the 1980s, when government scientists suggested that entanglement in fish netting was responsible for the deaths of as many as 30,000 northern fur seals each year. Additional investigations found that some species of sea turtles mistake plastic bags especially for food, and sometimes die when ingested bags block their digestive tracks. Similarly, many species of seabirds were found to mistake plastic resin pellets for fish eggs, although it is unclear whether ingestion of the pellets has affected health.

Exotic Species: Together with an increase in marine shipping has come an increase in the introduction of exotic species into coastal areas around the world. In taking on ballast water in harbors for trim, stability, and maneuverability, ships inadvertently take on planktonic plants and animals that often survive even the longest passages across the oceans. Once at their destination, ships discharge their ballast water and their planktonic stow-aways. Although most of the stowaways do not survive in the new environment, some do. In some instances, an exotic species will flourish because of the absence of natural controls such as patho-gens, parasites, and predators. Exotic species may also move about attached to hull surfaces or may enter new waters through navigation canals.

The accidental introduction of exotic species has greatly altered the community makeup of bays around the world. The small South Slough estuary in Coos Bay, Oregon, now hosts 32 exotic marine organisms. In 1986, after floods greatly reduced popula-tions of native clams and mussels in San Francisco Bay, Asian clams invaded and within two years reached a density of 12,000 clams per square yard in some areas.

SEWAGE

In June 1832, cholera bacteria, which had begun their journey west from Indonesia in 1817, arrived in the port of New York City—no doubt as unknown and unwanted companions of a pas-senger or crewman on an ocean-going vessel. In the next four months, the lethal dehydration caused by cholera took the lives of more than 4,000 New Yorkers. The cholera pandemic already had killed millions of people in western Europe and Russia after its arrival at the port of Astrakhan on the Caspian Sea in 1823. For the next century, Asiatic cholera revisited cities around the world, killing hundreds of thousands more.

Of all types of marine pollution, contamination by sewage is most closely associated with people wherever they live and what-ever standard of living they enjoy. On the face of it, sewage should be easy to handle in comparison with modern industrial chemi-cals. Yet, after billions of dollars of research and sewage treatment plant construction in the industrialized countries, sewage remains a substantial threat to coastal waters, in particular. Believing per-haps that the approach to sewage in the industrialized countries is progressive, many developing countries now are investing in sophisticated sewage treatment works. With sewage as with other types of pollution, our habit of seeking a solution in treatment of waste has been a futile one, guided principally by convenience and short-term cost.

The rapid growth of cities in the industrializing world of the 19th century provided ideal conditions for the spread of cholera bacteria, which relies on humans as hosts and on water as an intermediary. As cities became more crowded, pit latrines and collection of nightsoil gave way to more convenient flush toilets and indoor plumbing, whose outflow pipes emptied into common canals carrying fecal matter contaminated with the cholera bacteria and other pathogens into cesspools and rivers.

Then, 19th-century urban engineers began diverting raw sewage collected by pipes from individual houses into surface waters, confident in water's capacity to dilute. But the growing volume of waste generated by growing numbers of people eventually overwhelmed the ability of rivers, lakes, and bays to dilute and decompose all the waste.

As the population of London grew from 750,000 inhabitants to more than two million in the century between 1750 and 1850, the River Thames became so foul that the British government took to hanging sheets soaked in disinfectant in the Houses of Parliament to smother the stench. In 1856, Parliament reacted by establishing the modern world's first sewage district, with the mission of preventing sewage from flowing into the Thames River within the metropolitan district of London. By 1865, the Metropolitan Board of Works had achieved this goal by collecting the sewage that otherwise drained into canals throughout the city, and by discharging it outside city limits during ebb tide—into the Thames estuary. The theory that outgoing tides would whisk sewage away proved as misguided in London as it would later prove in New York, Boston, Bangkok, Calcutta, and elsewhere.

The year 1889 marked a fundamental change in the approach to handling human waste, for in that year, the Metropolitan Board of Works commissioned its first sewage treatment plant, which aimed at improving the quality of the water discharged into the River Thames. But early improvements in the quality of discharges were overwhelmed once again by the increased volume of sewage generated by a population that had grown to more than eight million people before World War II. By 1945, the River Thames was fishless—without the runs of shad, smelt, sea trout, and salmon that had supported commercial fisheries just a century before.

Together with a ban on phosphate detergents, improvements in the methods of treating raw sewage did restore the quality of water in the Thames River. Now more than 80 species of fish inhabit the Thames. Even so, some of the five million tons of sewage sludge that is dumped at the mouth of the estuary each year moves back up the river, depositing bacteria, chromium, copper, lead, mercury, and other pollutants on the riverbed. Furthermore, the significant reductions in phosphorus discharges have not been matched by similar reductions in nitrogen—the nutrient that most influences the growth of marine algae.

SOURCE REDUCTION

From the earliest days of modern sewage collection, water has been used as a convenient and plentiful vehicle for carrying all manner of wastes from households and businesses to sewers and eventually to treatment plants and rivers or coastal waters. Thus, raw sewage is a varying mixture of human wastes, bath water, kitchen cuttings, toilet paper, household and industrial chemicals, and other refuse.

But sewage is mostly water, lots of water: Before the introduction of low-volume toilets in 1982 in the United States, for instance, a single flush used five to eight gallons of water to dilute and transport a cup or less of waste via sewers to sewage treatment plants. The principal business of a sewage treatment plant then is to separate water from the wastes it has transported. Some of the solids can be separated from the water by screens or settling. Other solids dissolve with liquid wastes and make even partly treated sewage a potion with many origins and attributes that change as society and industry change. Sewage treatment technology has generally lagged behind these changes.

While bans on phosphate-based detergents significantly reduced the amount of phosphorus discharged with treated sewage in many areas, similar reductions in nitrogen discharges have not been achieved. Nitrogen levels in effluent can be reduced up to 90 percent by mimicking the decomposing processes of swamps, where aerobic and anaerobic bacteria break down ammonia, nitrite, and nitrate into gaseous nitrogen. But many older sewage treatment plants cannot spare or afford the space necessary for holding sewage for longer periods.

Water conservation might overcome this obstacle, since it is the volume of water entering sewer lines that determines the capacity requirements of a treatment plant. However, applying this principle is socially and politically difficult. In New York City, where per capita water use increased from 100 gallons per day in 1900 to 207 gallons per day in 1985, resistance is building toward recent efforts by the city government to meter water use and charge for the actual amount used rather than a flat fee for each household.

Two other design flaws undermine the effectiveness of conventional sewage treatment systems in reducing the discharge of pollutants into coastal waters. First, the Congressional Office of Technology Assessment has calculated that 160,000 industrial facilities discharge more than a trillion gallons of waste water containing hazardous wastes into municipal sewers each year. Besides hampering bacterial degradation of wastes in sewage treatment plants, metals and chemicals released into sewer systems contaminate not only discharges from sewage treatment plants but also much of the 325 million tons of sludge produced by sewage treatment plants in the United States each year. As a result, sludge that might otherwise be applied on agricultural fields must be restricted to areas that pose no health risk, such as highway median strips. This problem looms ever larger as the volume of sludge needing disposal increases with population and conversion of sewage treatment plants to higher levels of treatment.

The only practical way of preventing the contamination of sewage treatment works and sludge by trace metals and organic chemicals is to keep them out of sewers in the first place. Since 1978, the Clean Water Act has required that businesses remove hazardous chemicals from their sewage before discharging it into municipal sewers. But the requirement went unenforced until 1990, when the Environmental Protection Agency required the city of New York to reduce discharges of mercury and copper from its 14 sewage treatment plants.

A second flaw is commonest in older cities that constructed their sewers to handle both domestic sewage and storm-water runoff. Even a relatively small rainstorm can swell the volume of sewage entering a sewage treatment plant well beyond its capacity. The Field's Point treatment plant on Narragansett Bay in Rhode Island, which was designed to handle about 77 million gallons of waste water per day, may receive more than 200 million gallons per day with just one inch of rain. The excess waste water, which carries not only household wastes but also wastes from city streets, bypasses the sewage treatment plant and flows untreated into Narragansett Bay. Annually, about 2.5 billion gallons of raw sewage flow into the bay and its tributaries in this way, closing about one-quarter of the bay to shellfishing.

More than 1,100 cities in the United States rely on such combined sewer overflows, or CSOs, as backup systems to move waste from 43 million people. Of the 15,000 to 20,000 outfall points from CSOs, thousands are in coastal areas. Discharges from CSOs regularly close beaches to swimming and shellfish areas to harvesting. In 1989 and 1990, CSOs were implicated in 2,400 beach closures and the closure of nearly 600,000 acres of shellfish harvesting areas in ten states. According to a report by the State University of New York, CSO discharges cost the states of New York and New Jersey $3 billion to $7 billion in lost jobs, lost fishing days, and forfeited economic opportunities in the last decade.

Even during dry weather, increased volumes of domestic sewage alone can trigger discharges of raw waste water from CSOs or reduce the level of treatment of waste water leaving a sewage treatment plant. For instance, the volume of sewage entering six of 14 sewage treatment plants serving New York City regularly exceeds their capacity. The volume of waste water entering these treatment plants has increased with increases in the number of people served and with an eight percent increase in the amount of water used by people during the 1980s.

Finally, aging sewage works and pipes are breaking down more frequently as cities fall behind in maintenance and repair. In 1993, a ruptured sewage pipe spewed millions of gallons of raw sewage into waters near San Diego, California, closing beaches for miles. This incident and others have given more and more people reason not to indulge in one of southern California's great attractions— going to the beach.

NUTRIENTS

From Long Island Sound to Calcutta, growth in sewage discharges, increased use of fertilizers, and acid rain have dramatically increased the amount of nutrients, principally nitrogen and phosphorus, entering coastal waters. For instance, the amounts of nitrogen and of phosphorus entering the North Sea have increased by factors of four and eight respectively in the last two decades. Broad areas of this sea are now affected by eutrophication, a condition in which elevated levels of nutrients provoke blooms of algae that may damage plant and animal communities and pose human health threats.

Among other consequences, eutrophication may change the ecological balance of an area. For instance, as nitrogen levels increased in waters off the west coast of Sweden in the mid-1970s, several species of annual red algae gradually established themselves and inhibited the normal growth of large perennial brown algae. Weakened, the brown algae were consumed by large numbers of mussels that moved into the area. Starfish then entered and completely eliminated mussels and brown algae, leaving a much degraded ecosystem based on annual red algae.

Increased levels of sewage discharges probably have contributed to more frequent and widespread blooms of toxic algae that can kill marine life and threaten human life. Toxic algal blooms are not a uniquely modern phenomenon. But in 1946 a massive bloom along 150 miles of the Gulf coast of Florida killed 500 million fish and drove tourists from hotels with its nauseating spray. Thereafter, investigations of the causes of such "red tides" accelerated and continue today as blooms affect more coastal waters. Around the world, reports of algal blooms that have damaged commercial fisheries and tourism are on the rise.

Toxic algal blooms generally are composed of one or another species of dinoflagellates. These algae secrete substances that may be toxic to some organisms that consume them and not to others. Shellfish, for instance, can consume toxic species of dinoflagellate and store the toxins in their organs without any effect. However, humans who consume the shellfish may suffer a mild to severe toxic reaction. As an example, mussels and scallops can store saxitoxin, one of the most deadly of all biotoxins, with no effect on their own health. However, the same poison, consumed by humans or other animals, causes paralytic shellfish poisoning, which can lead to respiratory paralysis and death within 24 hours. Other biotoxins, such as domoic acid, ciguatera, and brevetoxin, may not be fatal. However, their effects can range from mild discomfort to permanent brain damage.

Concern about toxic algal blooms has been growing with their increased frequency and with the appearance of species of toxic dinoflagellates previously unknown in certain waters. In the mid-1980s, for instance, a previously unreported species of algae bloomed in Long Island Sound, wiping out eelgrass beds and a scallop fishery. In 1978 to 1982 alone, dinoflagellates that produce paralytic shellfish poisoning spread into eight new areas in Japan.

So, just what might be causing the spread of toxic algal blooms? There are several theories, none of them comforting. All of them more or less assume that the foreign species of algae are finding conditions in their new homes very much to their liking, largely because of an overabundance of nutrients.

Ocean currents may well be responsible for the spread of various species of dinoflagellates. The organisms can also be transported in the ballast water of freighters and discharged into the waters of distant ports. Alternatively, the spread of toxic algal blooms may reflect, not the introduction of exotic species, but simply the blooming of resident species that were previously unnoticed. The same hardiness that enables dinoflagellates to survive transport in ballast water or ocean currents also allows them to survive for long periods of dormancy in sediments. Given the right conditions, these species may break out of their dormancy and affect the healthfulness of fish and shellfish.

Quite by accident, Edward J. Noga of North Carolina State University found that at least one species of dinoflagellate behaves like a deadly hit-and-run driver. When fish were placed in laboratory tanks with the cysts of this dinoflagellate, the cysts broke open, releasing a powerful toxin. The fish turned sluggish and spasmodic, and died soon afterwards. The dinoflagellates then fed on the flesh of the dead fish, and upon exhausting their food supply, fell to the bottom, where they formed cysts again or took on the form of amoebas. Scientists now believe that this species of dinoflagellate may be responsible for dozens of fish kills along the Atlantic coast over many years. In May 1991 alone, Pamlico Sound in North Carolina suffered nine major fish kills, one of them killing more than one billion fish.

Algal growth fostered by excessive nutrients from human activities or natural events such as seasonal upwelling of bottom waters can also combine with stagnation of waters to create areas bereft of oxygen and unsuitable for all but the most opportunistic plants and animals. Under normal conditions, consumers of algae, from oysters to menhaden, maintain a rough balance with the growth of algae. When excess nutrients provoke an algal bloom, however, the consumers are overwhelmed and much of the algae sinks to the ocean floor, where bacteria decompose the algae, consuming oxygen in the water and sometimes producing toxic hydrogen sulfide.

In Long Island Sound, where calm summer weather encourages layering of water by temperature and salinity, and rainfall washes high levels of nutrients from heavily populated watersheds, low oxygen levels can cover as much as 40 percent of the sound's bottom, with devastating impacts on marine life. Late in the summer of 1989, oxygen levels were so reduced in an area of more than 500 square miles that 90 percent of the bottom-dwelling finfish and shellfish had either left the area or been smothered, so that the area was effectively closed to fishing.

DEMONSTRATING DAMAGE

As a practical matter, addressing pollution of the air, water, or land involves a complex and often frustrating interplay between science and public attitudes. In most cases, science can only assign probabilities of damage and levels of risk to the discharge of a waste. More often than not, public perception of risk differs greatly from that of the scientific community. This is partly because scientists often do not communicate research results in a way that most people can understand. Not understanding that science progresses by disproving theories it had previously accepted, the public becomes impatient with the seeming contradictions. Political and industrial leaders bring their own set of assumptions and desires to the process.

This interplay of interests, information, and assumptions has produced very different results in different circumstances. In 1932, the Chisso Corporation began producing acetaldehyde, used principally for silvering mirrors, at its chemical manufacturing plant on the southeastern coast of the island of Kyushu in Japan. As in the past, Chisso discharged the effluents from its operations into the poorly flushed but rich waters of Minamata Bay, where fishermen had harvested fish and shellfish for centuries. Within a generation, however, the bay's fisheries had been destroyed, more than 100 people had been killed and hundreds more crippled by mercury poisoning, and Minamata had become synonymous with environmental disasters.

Signs that something was seriously amiss in Minamata Bay began accumulating as early as 1947, when a rash of birth defects was reported in the town, and shellfish and seaweeds began declining after a series of fish and shellfish kills. Within five years, birds began dropping out of the sky. Cats and dogs staggered about the streets, before collapsing dead or throwing themselves into the bay. In 1956, six people suffering from slurred speech and delirium checked themselves into a local hospital, provoking the admission of another 30 cases, many of whom had been suffering silently for many years in fear of being ostracized and of bringing shame upon their families.

In 1957, a simple if gruesome experiment established the link between the waters of the bay and "Minamata disease." Investigators found that cats who ate fish transplanted from a nearby bay into Minamata Bay developed the characteristic symptoms of the lethal disease. Nonetheless, the government refused to place restrictions on the consumption of fish from the bay or to investigate the effluents from the Chisso plant. Furthermore, residents were reluctant to challenge so important an employer.

Chisso mounted its own research program, which emphasized the uncertainties regarding any linkage between their effluents and the disease, and suggested other causes, including ammonia compounds released by decaying fish—themselves victims of the mercury poisoning. But in 1958, when Minamata disease struck in a nearby river to which the chemical plant's effluents had been diverted, even the Chisso Corporation finally admitted that its effluents were responsible for the disease.

In 1959, before methylated mercury was identified as the chemical cause for Minimata disease, the Chisso Corporation began treating its effluents, but ineffectively, and residents continued eating shellfish from the bay. Indeed, the discharge of effluents contaminated with mercury did not end until 1968, after residents of the town of Niigata on the island of Honshu successfully sued to stop mercury contamination from another chemical plant.

Eventually, more than 100 residents of Minamata died from mercury poisoning, and more than 700 suffered permanent neurological damage. As recently as 1991, Minamata residents were deeply divided between those who wish to forget the past and those who seek additional compensation in the face of government opposition.

Although mercury has accumulated in estuaries and bays elsewhere in the world, there has yet to be another mercury poisoning on the scale of Minamata. This is partly because monitoring techniques can now detect mercury and other heavy metals in effluent well before they become a health threat on the scale of Minamata, where fishermen, fish consumers, birds, cats, and dogs all served as unwitting and ignored monitors.

TRACING LINKS

In the industrialized countries, where many of the grossest forms of pollution have been curbed, evidence for remaining types of damage from pollution is seldom so clear as in the Minamata mercury disaster. The growing ability to detect contaminants in water or tissue at levels of a few parts per million or less is outstripping our ability to detect biological damage that those levels and greater might be causing. Only recently have scientists achieved some success in linking pollution with sublethal effects, such as damaged reproductive capability, immune deficiency, genetic damage, or growth inhibition. The comfortable assumption that the end of fish kills is the end of concern for contaminants is slowly dissolving.

Less than a decade ago, Usha Varanasi and her team at the National Marine Fisheries Service's research center in Seattle began systematically tracing the link between specific toxic chemicals and specific physiological effects on marine life. Varanasi first examined groundfish from several bays in Puget Sound, whose sediments were known to be heavily contaminated with the typical urban stew of industrial chemicals, including polycyclic aromatic hydrocarbons (PAHs), and chlorinated compounds such as DDT and PCBs, as well as trace metals and sewage wastes.

It seemed reasonable to expect that groundfish, which spend a lot of time in contact with sediments and consume prey that feed on the sediments, would accumulate pollutants from their prey. As suspected, investigators found that as the level of aromatic hydrocarbons in sediments increased, so did the number of fish that suffered from liver tumors. Groundfish from uncontaminated areas that were exposed experimentally to sediments from contaminated areas developed many of the same tumors.

But until the mechanism by which the contaminants provoked the tumors was discovered, the correlation between the pollutants and the tumors was circumstantial. Rather than finding high levels of PAHs in the tumored livers, the investigators found mere traces. They did find high levels of PAHs in their bile, the liquid secreted by the liver. Apparently, the fish metabolize the hydrocarbons rather than accumulate them in their tissue.

Later investigation revealed that some of the metabolized hydrocarbons bind themselves to the genetic material in the livers of the fish, damaging them in a way characteristic of cancer. Further investigation found that contaminated sediments also correlated with reduced reproductive success of groundfish. English sole from contaminated areas showed impaired development of ovaries and were less than half as successful in spawning as fish from uncontaminated areas. Fish from the contaminated sites also had lower levels of female sex hormones in their blood. Statistical tests showed that the level of PAHs in the bile of groundfish correlated with both these conditions. Furthermore, fish from uncontaminated sites developed these conditions when exposed to sediments from contaminated areas.

Over several years, investigators found other correlations. For instance, female sole in contaminated areas had only a 40 to 50 percent chance of reaching sexual maturity and most of those that did mature did not spawn. Also, an unusually high percentage of the larvae from these spawners showed abnormalities. Larvae of sole from uncontaminated waters did not exhibit similar defects.

This groundbreaking research cannot determine whether crippling the reproductive ability of so a large percentage of the female sole population greatly reduces the size of sole populations in these contaminated areas. Although the assumption is a fair one, the dynamics of fish populations are not so straightforward: Fish populations rise and fall in response to a great variety of factors, from fishing to climate, any one of which may overwhelm pollution as a factor. Determining whether contaminants are, in fact, jeopardizing the capability of the English sole stocks to maintain their numbers awaits a separate, detailed assessment.

More recently, evidence has been accumulating that some kinds of synthetic chemicals disrupt hormonal functions in wildlife and people in sublethal ways that are difficult to detect. As an example, scientists have found that young salmon in the Great Lakes, which have been contaminated with PCBs, DDT, and other synthetic chemicals, have enlarged thyroid glands and produce eggs with poor survival rates, among other effects. Birds that feed on Great Lakes fish produce offspring that die early at unusually high rates.

Together with her colleagues, Dr. Theo Colborn of the W. Alton Jones Foundation and the World Wildlife Fund has also reported on alarming effects in children of women who regularly ate Great Lakes fish for years before and during pregnancy. These children exhibited a variety of symptoms including lower birth weight, behavioral problems at birth, and impaired memory. Children of women with the highest PCB concentrations in their breast milk refused to cooperate during testing and became intractable.

None of the protocols that industry and government use in testing the toxicity of new chemicals seeks to detect such effects. Rather, chemicals that pass government-approved tests are assumed to pose no threat to wildlife or people.

Once again, our lack of caution and curiosity about our own inventiveness has created problems that we have scarcely begun to perceive, much less solve.

THE FUTURE

What had been a disease that could strike anyone has become a disease of the poor. On January 23, 1991, cholera bacteria arrived at the Peruvian port of Chimbote, perhaps in the ballast water of an Asian ship. The bacteria took up residence in fish and shellfish later eaten raw in *ceviche*, a marinated fish salad. Using humans as hosts and canals polluted with sewage as highways, the bacteria spread through the slums of Chimbote, Lima, and other Peruvian cities. By the end of 1992, the bacteria had infected more than 750,000 people and killed 6,400 people from Mexico to Argentina.

Peru and most other South American countries share an impossible task with much of the world: protecting their citizens by investing scarce funding in the treatment of growing amounts of sewage. The Pan American Health Organization has estimated that the Peruvian government would have to increase expenditures for sewage and water treatment to ten times their current levels over the next ten years to protect the country's 22 million inhabitants from cholera and other waterborne pathogens.

In 1980, more than 600 million people lived in large coastal cities such as Lima, and with few exceptions, sewage from these settlements was discharged raw into coastal waters. In the Caribbean region, less than 10 percent of the sewage discharged into coastal waters has been treated. Only 30 percent of the sewage discharged into the Mediterranean is treated, compared with next to nothing in southeast Asia, the South Pacific, and west and central Africa. By the year 2000, waste from another 380 million people is expected to flow, treated or untreated, into coastal waters.

Investment in sewage treatment might well prevent economic losses that are becoming substantial in many areas. For instance, the presence of pathogens introduced by sewage cause millions of dollars in fishery losses in Thailand each year. Coastal tourism in Thailand is also suffering losses due to contamination of beaches and swimming waters by sewage, much of it produced by once-booming tourist resorts. In the Caribbean, fish kills have nearly eliminated fish from the Bay of Cartagena in Colombia and the Bay of Havana in Cuba.

In trying to reverse the flood of sewage that increasingly under-mines the future health and prosperity of coastal residents, many governments can leap over conventional sewage treatment toward husbanding the resources sewage has collected instead of dumping it, treated or not, out of sight and out of mind.

Perhaps it was to be expected that the town of Arcata on the coast of northern California, known for its leanings toward alter-native thinking, would adopt an alternative approach to handling its sewage. In the 1980s, the town of 15,000 residents trans-formed a former garbage dump into a series of ponds into which the town's partially-treated sewage flows. After several days, dur-ing which the solids in the sewage settle out, the waste water is released into adjacent marshes, where plants and bacteria con-sume the wastes, cleansing the water further. The nearshore waters support thriving oyster bars, and the former garbage dump now is a wildlife hotspot, visited by picnickers and birdwatchers.

But the Arcata example is not as novel as it sounds. Although cities and towns around the United States are only now adopting techniques for handling sewage that rely more on the biological potential of sewage than upon the ability of engineering to treat and sequester it, cities and towns around the world have been doing so for centuries. In his World Bank study, for instance, Peter Edwards reviewed uses of sewage to support aquaculture in Ban-gladesh, China, Germany, Hungary, India, Indonesia, Israel, Malaysia, Taiwan, Thailand, and Vietnam. The city of Calcutta, India, operates the world's largest single waste-fed aquaculture operation. There, sewage fed into two lakes covering 6,200 acres provides nutrients for the growth of algae that feed the 8,000 tons of fish annually delivered to the local market.

Since 1972, the federal government alone has invested $57 bil-lion in sewage treatment, most of it for the construction of indus-trialized sewage treatment plants. As federal funds decline and sewage treatment plants wear out, cities and towns are casting about for less expensive alternatives. The town of Picayune, Loui-siana, recently decided not to spend $11 million to repair its sew-age treatment plant, but opted to construct a $350,000 system of ponds and green plants to treat sewage from its 12,500 residents. Although these approaches may be beyond the reach of some large cities along the coast, where land is at a premium and past investment in traditional treatment facilities amounts to billions of dollars, they provide an alternative to degrading coastal waters as coastal sprawl spills sewage into previously protected areas.

Failing to use a waste as simple as sewage will bode ill for using the myriad other wastes we seem determined to produce.

8

Fisheries

The rapid view of the [cod] fishery enables us
to discern under what policy it has flourished
or declined in the hands of other nations, and
to mark the fact, that it is too poor a business
to be left to itself, even with the nation the
most advantageously situated.

THOMAS JEFFERSON,
Message to the First Congress,
February 2, 1791

In preparation for negotiating a new treaty to conserve the Antarctic marine ecosystem in 1978, the U.S. State Department convened a meeting of scientists and managers from federal agencies. Early in the five days of meetings, the administrator of the National Oceanic and Atmospheric Administration, Bob Schoning, suggested that the new treaty should rely on the traditional standard of fisheries management called maximum sustainable yield or MSY. Expressed either as numbers or as weight of fish, MSY is an estimate of the largest amount of fish that can be harvested annually from a species or population of fish.

All of the heads in the State Department meeting room nodded in agreement with Dr. Schoning's suggestion—except one. The executive director of the Marine Mammal Commission, John R. Twiss, Jr., objected, arguing that using MSY in the Antarctic would be absurd. Among other things, the U.S. government's objective of managing the Antarctic ecosystem as a whole would fail if it did not take into account the impacts of harvesting krill on populations of great whales recovering from commercial hunting. Nations such as the Soviet Union, Japan, and Poland, whose enormous fleets of fishing vessels were seeking new sources of fish, were making plans to exploit untapped populations of Antarctic krill—a shrimplike creature about three inches long that can form enormous swarms stretching for miles. Twiss was concerned that harvesting so important a food source would jeopardize the recovery of great whale populations in Antarctic waters, now that they were no longer pursued with harpoons.

Twiss pressed for the approach to management of wildlife populations—set forth in the Marine Mammal Protection Act—that recognized the interdependence of species and populations, one that included a safety factor in management decisions to allow for our lack of understanding of ecosystems and for the imperfections of human institutions. Eventually the position presented by the Marine Mammal Commission had become the position of the U.S. delegation.

Conditions among the member nations of the Antarctic Treaty were ripe for accepting the new approach to conservation of the marine living resources in the Southern Ocean. Besides the near exhaustion of great whale populations by commercial whaling fleets in previous decades, members of the Antarctic Treaty had witnessed the depletion of populations of Southern Ocean finfish by Soviet trawlers in the late 1960s. Only grudgingly accepted by those members of the treaty who were looking forward to new sources of fish in the Southern Ocean, the new approach found its way into the treaty. The agreement required not only that fisheries avoid reducing a species below a level at which it no longer plays its role in the ecosystem, but also that decisions take account of species that are dependent on the fish or shellfish that is being harvested. The treaty also called for avoiding changes in the Antarctic ecosystem that cannot be reversed in two or three decades.

Although this shift in paradigm has yet to penetrate most management of marine and coastal resources, it does reflect broader shifts in perspectives. In the 1960s and early 1970s, when fisheries scientists predicted ocean catches of fish four times higher than today's predictions, many commission reports and conference proceedings identified the greatest obstacles to more fish for more people as excessively conservative management and outdated technology.

But the collapse of great whale populations and other formerly thriving fisheries undermined the confidence of scientists and managers that the seas were virtually inexhaustible and mechanistic. Instead of viewing marine ecosystems as smoothly functioning, efficient, self-contained, and sensible systems that tended toward stability and predictable production, scientists began to see ecosystems as dominated by uncertainty and influenced by external factors, from global climate patterns to fishing, that interact in complex ways and produce inconsistent outcomes.

However reasonable this approach may be, it does require a shift in priorities and short-term costs to insure long-term benefits. The payoff from rebuilding fisheries by erring on the side of conservation could be considerable. The National Marine Fisheries Service has estimated that the long-term yield of U.S. fisheries could be more than 25 percent greater than it now is.

The Race for the Fish

Of the 17 major fisheries that the United Nations Food and Agriculture Organization tracks, four are depleted and nine are declining. In the United States, 67 of 156 fish stocks are overexploited, according to the National Marine Fisheries Service. Among these are bluefin tuna, swordfish, summer flounder, Nassau grouper, oysters, hard-shell and soft-shell clams, and bay scallops in the Atlantic, red drum, red snapper, brown and white shrimp in the Gulf of Mexico, all five species of Pacific salmon, and North Pacific albacore tuna.

Among the most common reasons for overexploitation is the unrestrained access to fishery resources enjoyed by fishermen in many parts of the world. Because anyone has access to marine fish, a fisherman cannot claim to own a fish until he has caught it. As a result, a fisherman has no assurance that he—and not another fisherman—will reap the benefit of leaving fish in the water for a later day, when it may have reproduced or grown to be of higher economic value. Instead of investing in the long-term renewability of a fish population by leaving young fish in the water, a fisherman in an open access fishery is compelled to catch the fish and hold it, at least until he catches larger fish with which to fill the boat's hold. The only investment that seems to make sense is equipment and fuel that increase a fisherman's chance of catching a fish before a competitor does.

On the face of it, the decisions to invest in a bigger boat or in more sophisticated technology seem to make sense. When fishermen begin exploiting a new resource, catches are high and are gotten at low cost and effort. As word of great profits spreads, more fishermen enter the fishery. Although total landings may remain high, the increasing number of fishermen reduces most fishermen's share in the fishery. Through investment in larger, faster vessels and more sophisticated gear, fishermen try to maintain or increase their share in the catch even as they increase their costs and reduce their profits. As more vessels enter the fishery and competition for the fish provokes competition in technology and vessel size, the abundance of fish declines.

In a perverse response that reflects how poorly the marketplace signals the vulnerability of renewable resources harvested on a first-come basis, higher prices reward fishermen for investing in the means to catch more and more of less and less fish. Eventually, entry of new vessels into a fishery slows and the fleet reaches an unprofitable equilibrium with the fish stocks, resulting in two to three times as many boats as are necessary to catch the available fish sustainably.

As stocks decline together with fishermen's revenues, political pressure builds to raise quotas and relax conservation measures. The uncertainty that arises from imperfect information about the complex interactions among various species, environmental factors, the behavior of fishermen, and economic decisions provokes doubts among political decision makers, who must address strongly held views of fishermen arguing that scientists have been wrong in the past. Protesting that they are conservationists who would never do harm to the resource and themselves, fishermen often dismiss arguments for increasing economic efficiency and long-term economic health and insist that their very way of life is at stake.

These potent political arguments generally prevail, particularly since so little is generally done beforehand to create alternatives and opportunities for fishermen who must make the transition from a chosen way of making a living. Focused on a resource and economic crisis, decision makers address the lack of certainty by erring on the side of continued exploitation.

And ingenuity always seems to find a way to find more, if different, fish. Now, new, more powerful tools are coming into the hands of fishermen in industrialized countries. Tuna and billfish fishermen can now take much of the guesswork out of finding their prey by consulting temperature maps, based on satellite sensing and sent to them by facsimile machine. Airborne laser scanners that can detect schools of fish beneath the surface have been used for several years by Russian fishermen and are being introduced to U.S. fisheries. Whatever may be said for the increased efficiency these technologies give a fisherman, they also remove another level of protection from vulnerable fish populations.

THE NATION'S FIRST INDUSTRY

Although no one openly suggests that fishermen should catch as much as they can as soon as they can and the future be damned, that is what happens much of the time. Fish populations that have not been overfished are uncommon. Although the path leading to overfishing, economic loss, social hardship, and ecological havoc has been trod many times before, fishermen, government administrators, legislators, and anyone in the public who is paying attention to fisheries seems to enter on the path as if they were bushwhacking into new territory.

Any one of dozens of fisheries could offer a case study of the pattern. But few offer as rich a history of the interplay among human aspirations, technology, and changing tastes as the New England groundfish fisheries.

The waters off New England are the western branch of a broad arch of very productive waters extending from Cape Cod to the British Isles. Along this archway of shoals broken by canyons, cold Arctic waters butt up against the warm Gulf Stream, creating an oceanic boundary and collecting nutrients that build stores of food for creatures great and small. Within these waters, enormous schools of herring, cod, haddock, flounder, mackerel, halibut, and others have swarmed to the amazement of fishermen since the 16th century.

The fish that defined the New England groundfish fishery for its first 300 years was the Atlantic cod, which can weigh as much as 200 pounds but averages between 6 and 12 pounds. Caught at first with single-hooked lines by fishermen in narrow, 15-foot dories close to shore, beginning in 1624 Atlantic cod was salted for an international trade that united England, her molasses-rich Caribbean colonies, and the industrializing American colonies.

The governments of the colonies recognized the importance of this trade. In 1639, the General Court of Massachusetts rewarded cod fishermen with an exemption from military duty and from taxes on their gear and vessels, while prohibiting the use of cod or striped bass for fertilizer. The industry flourished and generated much of the wealth that sustained the early colonies, drew the suspicion of England, and fueled the Revolution.

The Revolutionary War devastated many New England fishing communities, but the opening of the fishery on Georges Bank, just 100 miles from Cape Cod, led to renewed growth of the New England fishing industry after the war. By the time of the Civil War, however, those fishermen restricted to nearshore waters began complaining that the nearshore cod populations were being depleted by offshore fishermen. In 1871, Congress responded by creating the United States Fish Commission located at Woods Hole, Massachusetts.

Then began a series of innovations and introductions of fishing gear that changed forever the balance between people and the abundance of groundfish in the Northwest Atlantic. In the late 1870s, more and more hooks were added to longer and longer lines—as many as 500 hooks on a line miles long—to form line trawls. The new gear spread through the fleet, and landings increased from 46,000 tons in 1879 to more than 146,000 tons in 1880. Meanwhile, Spencer Baird, the first commissioner of the United States Fish Commission, was busy trying to introduce gill nets from Norway. This gear, more efficient than either handlines or line trawls, didn't catch on, however, until gill-netters arrived from Michigan in 1908.

Shortly, fishermen learned to use otter trawls, which are sock-shaped nets of various dimensions long used in European waters with devastating results. Indeed, in 1367, the British parliament had debated a measure to restrict the use of trawls, and in the course of the controversy, created the first royal commission to investigate the state of fisheries affairs in England. But the trawls of 20th century America were even larger and more effective at catching anything that swam in their path, since they were steadily dragged along the ocean bottom with the same power that made much of the Industrial Revolution possible—the steam engine.

With steam power, fishermen at last freed themselves of the vagaries of windpower that the finest sailing ships could not overcome. Fishermen exercised their new freedom to catch groundfish almost at will. Landings of cod, which had fallen from the highs experienced soon after the introduction of line trawls just 30 years before, nearly doubled. With the extension of railroad lines to such ports as Montauk on Long Island and Gloucester, Massachusetts, the market for fresh cod expanded and sent fishermen as far away as the waters off Greenland to meet the demand.

In other industries, increased efficiency might have led to reduced numbers of operators. But in the New England groundfish fishery, as in most other fisheries, increased efficiency meant increased profits, which attracted even more fishermen. Without quotas, the combination of more fishermen and more efficient fishing gear soon overwhelmed the capacity of fish populations to produce more fish.

World Wars I and II gave New England and other Atlantic fish stocks the only respite they would enjoy this century. Soon after the armistice ended World War I in 1918, fishing resumed. In the mid-1920s, diesel and gasoline engines made it possible for more fishermen to drag otter trawls. At the same time, U.S. Bureau of Fisheries' Harden F. Taylor, together with Clarence Birdseye of frozen-vegetable fame, succeeded in developing a process that enabled fish processors to quick-freeze fillets of cod that could be shipped to homes throughout the northeast, from Bangor, Maine, to New York City. Frozen-food trucks, frozen-food lockers in grocery stores, and convenient packaging all expanded the market for Atlantic cod and other groundfish even farther.

By the 1930s, Atlantic cod had become scarce enough that the haddock, which had been considered the fare of the poor, became respectable fare at middle-class dinner tables when Boston fish distributors first began filleting, rather than salting or drying it. In less than a decade, landings of haddock in New England more than tripled, amounting to more than 146,000 tons in 1929.

About the same time, two other previously scorned groundfish were introduced to the American dinner table: the yellowtail flounder and redfish. Like many other fishes of the sea, the yellowtail flounder owes its popularity to the decline of a cousin, in this case the winter flounder. To meet the demand for flounder fillets after the decline of winter flounder, processors encouraged the landing of the yellowtail flounder, which they had once considered too thin to fillet. Landings tripled from about 11,000 tons in 1938 to nearly 35,000 tons in 1942.

An unappealing look had protected the rosy, slow-growing redfish from overfishing. Because its spines discouraged fish processors, redfish was mostly discarded by fishermen who inadvertently caught these and other species of marine life in their trawls. But the fate of redfish changed dramatically when a way was found to fillet and sell it as ocean perch, thus trading on the popularity of its similar-tasting relative, the freshwater perch. A mild-flavored white fish, freshwater perch had become a market favorite after sea lamprey, entering the Great Lakes through navigation canals built in the 19th century, decimated the Great Lakes populations of lake trout.

By 1950, ocean perch dominated the groundfish fishery at 102,000 tons. As fishermen found an unfished population, they did what most fishing fleets have done: They caught the largest, most productive fish, fished until the returns for their effort were fewer and smaller, and then moved on. The redfish fishery collapsed. Unlike other species of groundfish, which mature relatively quickly, redfish are slow to mature, making their recovery much less likely.

Technological innovation continued. Military research and development during World War II contributed new materials and technologies to the rapidly industrializing fisheries of the North Atlantic, including more powerful engines and lighter hulls. Synthetic materials enabled netmakers to produce much larger, lighter, more durable nets than ever before. Electronics engineers created technology that enabled fishermen to locate their position with a precision never before possible and to communicate with each other. But even these developments—so dramatic at the time—did not give warning of the developments to come.

FACTORY FISHING

Early in the 1950s, European shipyards began building fishing vessels reminiscent of the whaling vessels that had worked in Antarctic waters for decades. These new vessels were not outfitted with harpoons, but with enormous trawls that could be pulled up a stern ramp just as great whales had been. Besides larger nets made possible by synthetic materials, the keys to the success of these vessels were quick-freezing equipment and automated filleting machines. As long as a football field, these early factory trawlers could catch as much as 500 tons at a time and process half that amount in one day. With comfortable crew quarters and other amenities, factory trawlers could fish distant waters for weeks before returning home with high-quality frozen fish fillets.

Word about the success of the first factory trawlers spread rapidly, except in the United States. By 1974, the Soviet Union had built the largest distant-water fleet in the world, with 710 factory trawlers and hundreds of supply and service vessels. The Soviet Union was not alone in sending these extraordinarily effective fish eaters to the productive waters of Georges Bank and elsewhere in the Northwest Atlantic. In 1974, more than a thousand factory trawlers from 14 countries caught more than 2,200,000 tons of groundfish off New England—10 times the catch of U.S. fishermen.

The profitability of factory trawlers depends upon finding large concentrations of a single species of similar size for ease of processing. At first, factory trawlers focused their efforts on Atlantic cod. Soviet trawlers were well known for collaborating in finding and fishing large concentrations of cod. As William Warner describes it in *Distant Water,* Soviet trawlers swept through great schools of cod in a pulse of exploitation. Spanish pair trawlers, with half-mile-broad trawls stretched between them, caught cod for their salt holds and discarded ton after ton of fish that were too small or the wrong species. Most of this bycatch was dead or dying. In the late 1950s, West Germans perfected mid-water trawls that were able to overtake huge schools of herring and mackerel, landing in one haul twice as much fish as traditional trawlers would land in a week.

This onslaught provoked protest from American and Canadian

fishermen. In 1972, the International Commission for the Northwest Atlantic Fisheries (ICNAF) recommended quotas and closed areas to fishing. These measures may have been responsible for a brief recovery between 1974 and 1977, when groundfish stocks increased 86 percent on Georges Bank, the most productive of New England's fishing grounds.

As the United Nations Conference on the Law of the Sea struggled with developing an international framework for protecting marine fisheries on the high seas and in coastal waters, Congress was pressed on two sides to take action: by New England fishermen, who wanted to end foreign access to U.S. waters, and by West Coast tuna fishermen, who wanted to maintain open access to waters in the eastern tropical Pacific. After several years of hearings and debate, Congress passed the Fishery Conservation and Management Act of 1976, now known as the Magnuson Act in honor of Washington Senator Warren Magnuson, who played an important role in its passage.

With the passage of the Magnuson Act, the United States led a growing number of countries that asserted jurisdiction over living marine resources within 200 miles of its shores, an area that has become the Exclusive Economic Zone or EEZ. The act also thrust the federal government actively into the management of fisheries in the EEZ but outside of state waters, where the states retained primary jurisdiction. Finally, the Magnuson Act established eight regional fishery management councils, which have come to be dominated by fishing interests. These councils were given the responsibility of initiating and preparing fishery management plans for fisheries in their regions.

The New England Fishery Management Council wasted little time in preparing a fishery management plan for groundfish, which limited fishermen to fixed quotas for cod, haddock, and yellowtail flounder and soon excluded foreign trawlers from U.S. waters. But the plan encountered difficulties from the start. When the fishery closed on August 12, 1977, fishermen protested. There were plenty of fish to catch, they said.

There certainly were lots of fish, but they were mostly juveniles born in 1975, the largest year class of groundfish in a decade. Leaving these fish in the water would have been a good investment that fishermen could have profited from many times over in the future. But fishermen pressed to take advantage of the profit immediately before them, and the council relented, juggling quotas and seasons so that fishermen could continue to fish these young fish down. By 1982, the council had eliminated quotas on groundfish altogether, substituting gear restrictions that have seldom worked anywhere in the world. The Secretary of Commerce, who must approve fishery management plans developed by the councils, concurred.

The race to cash in on the riches apparently deeded to American fishermen by the Magnuson Act accelerated. Bankers walked docks in New England talking to fishermen and consulted scientists about the potential riches of Georges Bank. In the feverish growth of the fleet, old boats were replaced by bigger, faster boats, and some fishermen built small fleets of trawlers. The New England fleet grew from 825 trawlers in 1977 to 1,662 in 1990. The increased number of vessels together with new electronics and other technological innovations more than doubled the amount of fishing effort directed at New England groundfish.

Whatever recovery in groundfish stocks the management program of ICNAF may have caused were erased by these efforts to "Americanize" the fishery. Between 1977 and 1987, the population size of the principal species of groundfish declined 65 percent. But the race continued and distrust of warnings by scientists deepened. In 1990, New England fishermen took advantage of the large number of fish born in 1987 and landed more Atlantic cod and yellowtail flounder than they had since 1984. The once-scorned haddock is now on the brink of commercial extinction (landings were just 2,600 tons in 1992), and ocean perch landings in 1992 were just 933 tons, less than one percent of their level just 40 years ago.

A lawsuit by the Boston-based Conservation Law Foundation in 1991 broke the pattern of endless discussion about the collapse of New England's principal fishery. A settlement between the foundation and the Department of Commerce, which provoked threats of intervention by the New England congressional delegations, required the New England Management Council to prepare a plan to end overfishing and to rebuild groundfish populations. After months of stormy public meetings, the council proposed reducing the amount of fishing for New England groundfish by 50 percent over five years. While conservationists gave the plan grudging approval as a first step, many industry leaders predicted the plan would destroy family fishing businesses and cause thousands to lose jobs in the already stressed New England economy.

How could it be otherwise in a fleet that had grown as if there were no tomorrow?

THE COSTS OF EFFICIENCY

Foreign and American overfishing of New England groundfish exacted a tremendous economic, ecological, and social tax on present and future generations of Americans. As the Massachusetts Groundfish Task Force showed in 1990, revenues from trawlers are at their lowest point since the Magnuson Act was passed. The task force calculated that "Americanized" overfishing of groundfish has reduced annual landings by more than 66,000 tons and gross revenues by $350 million, while causing the loss of 14,000 jobs.

The costs of overexploitation are felt in other ways. Consumers who have been sold on eating fish by industry promotional campaigns now pay more for less fresh fish. Cod and haddock, which once cost no more than chicken, now cost as much as the finer cuts of beef. Once-proud fishing communities have been severely weakened, as families who have fished New England waters for generations have had to seek jobs elsewhere. And in a pattern that has been repeated time and again around the coasts, economic weakness has moved fishing fleets to the margins in many towns as condominiums and resort hotels convert working docks into picturesque playgrounds.

The heavy fishing for groundfish radically changed the mix of species in New England waters as well, with profound consequences for the future. In reducing the relative abundance of groundfish from 55 percent in 1963 to 11 percent in 1986, the groundfish fleet created an ecological vacuum, which has been filled by skates and by spiny dogfish, a kind of shark. The abundance of these species, which accounted for only 24 percent of the catch in a trawl 30 years ago, accounted for 74 percent of the catch in 1986. The growing dominance of skates and dogfish, which prey upon young cod, haddock, and flounder, may hinder the recovery of these stocks.

Michael Sissenwine of the National Marine Fisheries Service has raised the notion of diverting fishing from groundfish to skates and dogfish, in order to reduce their abundance and recreate the niche that groundfish once filled. This proposal to undertake what is called adaptive management sparks heated discussion, partly because it carries some ecological risk and partly because Americans still feel squeamish about serving such things as skates and dogfish to their dinner guests. Difficulty in processing these fishes has prevented American fishermen from supplying the lucrative European trade, including fish and chips shops in England, where dogfish is known as rock salmon.

Even where strong measures have restored fish populations, as in the Pacific halibut fishery, we have had a knack for making the worst of a good situation. Under one of a few fishery management programs that have taken the necessary steps to restore a depleted fishery, Pacific halibut rebounded from a low of 24,000 tons to more than 38,000 tons in 1954 and has remained relatively abundant in the North Pacific ever since. But the commission that imposed quotas on the amount of fish that could be caught did not restrict the entry of more fishermen into the fishery.

Predictably, the recovery of the halibut population attracted thousands more fishermen to vie for the fortune that could be made in seasons that last as little as eight hours. So intense has the race for the fish become that the successful fisherman often leaves unbutchered halibut on his boat's deck, losing its taste and its value. Once at the dock, the quality of the fish declines even more, as processors, overwhelmed with the flood of halibut from other fishermen, must process and freeze fish that would fetch a higher price and give more enjoyment to the consumer if only the fishery weren't run like a destruction derby that cost eight fishermen their lives in 1993.

In 1993, after nearly a decade of deliberations, the North Pacific Fishery Management Council adopted an ITQ scheme, like the one described in chapter 5, for ending the economic and biological waste of derby fishing for halibut. Based on past performance, owners of the thousands of vessels in the fishery will be given a percentage share of each year's quota. If this new scheme follows the pattern in other fisheries where individuals have been allocated transferable quota shares, as in the Canadian halibut fishery, fishermen will enjoy the choice to fish when they wish or to sell their shares and get out of the fishery altogether. Fishermen who stay will likely receive a higher price for their fish, since the quality will not have been destroyed by poor handling, and consumers will be able to buy a long-forgotten seafood: fresh halibut.

COSTS OF OVERFISHING

In seeking out the larger, older, and more valuable individuals in a fish population, fishermen engage, willy-nilly, in a breeding experiment that produces fish populations that mature younger and smaller. For instance, the average size of several species of reef fishes off the southeastern United States has shrunk over the last 20 years of increased fishing. Red snapper, which weighed 19 pounds on average in the 1960s, now weigh five pounds. Similarly, the average weight of snowy grouper has fallen from 18 to four pounds. Since younger, smaller fish generally produce fewer eggs than older, larger fish, depleted snapper and grouper populations are in even greater trouble than their absolute numbers might suggest.

Catching and discarding fish can have as telling an effect as catching and keeping them. In the 1960s, fishermen supplying pet food manufacturers in the Gulf of Mexico captured groundfish of several ages and sizes. This diversity disappeared with the doubling of shrimp fishing effort in the Gulf of Mexico that followed upon the closing of Mexican waters to U.S. shrimp fishermen in the 1970s. Thousands of shrimp fishermen sweeping the Gulf of Mexico regularly caught and discarded millions upon millions of groundfish—on average, 10 pounds of fish for every pound of shrimp caught and retained. By the 1980s, shrimp trawls had so completely scoured the Gulf of Mexico for so long that croaker and other groundfish rarely survived more than a year or two. Besides contributing to the demise of the groundfish fishery, bycatch and discard of croaker and other groundfish may well have changed the ecosystem of the Gulf of Mexico into one based on detritus and dominated by shrimps, crabs, and sharks.

As human population continues to grow, we cannot afford to discard so much protein. In the United States alone, per capita consumption of food fish has increased from 12.9 pounds in 1976, when Congress passed the Magnuson Act, to 14.8 pounds in 1992. Other countries rely much more heavily upon fish for animal protein; on average, each of the 5.3 billion people on earth consumed nearly 30 pounds of fish annually in 1990, up from an average of 27 pounds consumed by 4.1 billion humans in 1976.

After peaking at nearly 86 million tons in 1989, the worldwide catch from the oceans fell to 82.5 million tons in 1992—a small fraction of potential harvests predicted just 20 years before. Wild sources to meet greater demand are few and expensive. Southern Ocean krill, schooling oceanic species, and deepwater fishes such as lanternfishes are relatively abundant, but expensive to catch and process. The deficit in fish protein could be partly met by salvaging the millions of tons of fish that are now incidentally captured and discarded because they are the wrong species or size, but taking advantage of this protein source will require changes in fishing practices and advances in processing technology.

Despite the decline in many fisheries around the world, large and small fishing boats continued to be constructed and outfitted with more sophisticated ways of chasing down and catching fish. Worldwide, the number of boats and vessels increased at twice the rate that catches did in the 1980s. Besides depleting fish populations, this growth in fishing power so raised the costs of fishing that the world's fishing fleets have been losing tens of billions of dollars a year. The fleets have remained afloat largely by the grace of government subsidies. Between 1983 and 1990, the member countries of the European Community increased subsidies to their fleets from $80 million to $580 million, and 20 percent of that money was dedicated to building new boats or making old boats more efficient.

Some countries, including members of the European Community, are pulling vessels off the water, recognizing the economic lunacy of continuing to scour the oceans for fish with such intensity. But if the vessels are not turned into scrap or sunk as artificial reefs, they will likely find a way to continue fishing. For instance, hundreds of foreign fishing vessels have been registering in countries, mainly in Central America and the Caribbean, that ask few questions and are not signatories to key fishing treaties. International law does not prevent these vessels from fishing in areas that are off-limits to vessels registered in countries that are bound by relevant treaties.

Coastal countries are striking back. On April 2, 1994, Canadian fisheries enforcement agents seized the *Kristina Logos,* a large trawler crewed by Portuguese but registered in Panama. With a wink at international law, Canada seized the vessel because it had been catching cod and flounder just outside Canada's 200-mile zone, despite a ban by the Northwest Atlantic Fisheries Organization. Diplomatic protests against Canada's bold action were tempered, perhaps because two years before, the Canadian government had imposed a moratorium in its own waters, keeping as many as 24,000 fishermen in port drawing a government check.

DAMMED RIVERS, DAMNED FISH

The 1992 Pacific salmon season was a short one. Indeed, some people believe that Pacific salmon runs from central California to the Canadian border need a complete rest. Trollers and gill-netters in the small towns along the coast were selling their boats to anyone who would buy them, and looking for some justice in a debacle they had only a small hand in making. An El Niño, some believed, had suppressed the usual upwelling of cold, nutrient-rich water and had blocked the return of even the small number of young salmon that had escaped their drought-stricken natal rivers a few years earlier. Everyone knew, however, that the demise of the Pacific salmon fishery had begun many years before with the exploitation of the region's timber and water resources—and of the salmon themselves.

Like other anadromous fish, adults of the five species of Pacific salmon—chinook, coho, sockeye, chum, and pink—ascend rivers and enter small streams, where females lay several thousand eggs in gravel areas. After the male fertilizes the eggs, both adults die. Successful hatching of the eggs and survival of the fry require clean, well-oxygenated water at cool temperatures. Depending upon the species, the young salmon, called smolts, remain in the stream for one or more years and gradually descend toward the ocean. Recent research suggests that the survival of the salmon smolts depends greatly upon abundant food in nearshore waters. In most years, coastal upwelling provides the nutrients necessary for producing the plants and animals that the salmon smolts need. When upwelling does not occur, as during El Niño episodes, prey is sparse and the survival rates of salmon smolts decline.

Over millions of years, Pacific salmon have adopted as spawning grounds gravel beds in hundreds of streams and creeks, sometimes hundreds of miles from the Pacific Ocean. Through a mechanism that still escapes explanation, most salmon that hatch in a particular stream and survive at sea return years later as adults to that stream. Over the generations, salmon from individual runs have developed genetic traits more or less unlike those of salmon of the same species but from different runs. But in the millennia of experimentation and adaptation, neither Atlantic nor Pacific salmon acquired the ability to leap dams, to survive hydroelectric turbines, to avoid being pumped into cotton fields, or to reproduce in streams choked with organic waste from clear-cuts or wood-pulp mills.

In the last half of the 19th century, the Pacific salmon fishery was the nation's largest, supporting more fishermen, canneries, and vessels than any other. But the explosive economic development of the region carried the seeds of decline in this fishery. In 1852, a pioneer named Sherwood was among the first to extirpate a run of sockeye salmon when he built a little dam on a creek flowing into Mason Lake near the Hood Canal in Washington state. Hydraulic mining reduced chinook salmon runs on the Feather, Yuba, and American Rivers from 12 million fish in 1882 to two million in 1891, and eliminated them by the end of the century.

Earlier losses of Atlantic and Pacific salmon were little noted in the economic and social desperation of the 1930s, as the U.S. government invested the considerable water resources of the Columbia River basin in agriculture and power generation. The Columbia River basin, which covers about 260,000 square miles and includes thousands of miles of streams, now hosts 59 dams that have turned the mighty Columbia into a series of gigantic lakes. Federally subsidized water diversions irrigate nearly 13,500 square miles of agricultural fields that produce $8–12 billion worth of crops.

Nearly $2 billion has been invested in fish ladders and other mechanisms for mitigating the effect of Columbia River dams on salmon migration. Although these measures produced enough fish for a much reduced fishery, they could not address the continuing loss of diversity in salmon stocks. Petitioned by Shoshone-Bannock Tribe, the National Marine Fisheries Service determined in 1991 that the Snake River sockeye salmon was an endangered species. Within the year, two more runs of chinook salmon were added to the list of threatened and endangered species, and petitions to list still others were under review.

The dirty little secret of the Columbia River was in the open, and government institutions responsible for economic development and for natural resource management scrambled to find a way around the extinction of still more runs of valuable Pacific salmon. The Northwest Power Planning Council, a consortium of generators and users of the electrical power, spoke of committing one billion dollars to a last-ditch effort on behalf of the Columbia River's salmon runs. Scientists gathered to discuss a plan of action.

But the focus of discussion and commitment has been on survival of the runs. The age of abundant salmon has passed in the Pacific Northwest, as it had decades before in New England.

AQUACULTURE AND THE ENVIRONMENT

As the limits of ocean fisheries have become plainer, aquaculture has grown in popularity as a means of maintaining supplies of fish and shellfish. Worldwide, more than 181 freshwater and saltwater fishes and shellfishes are cultured now. By 1990, farms and ranches produced more than 18 million tons of fish, shellfish, and plants, almost half of it marine species. In 1982, pond-raised shrimp accounted for only five percent of the world's production of shrimp; by 1989, it accounted for nearly one-quarter, and more than 80 percent of it was raised in Asia. Aquaculture of Atlantic salmon, principally in the Scandinavian countries, rose from 55,000 tons in 1984 to nearly 300,000 tons in 1989.

In developing countries particularly, growth in aquaculture has been aimed at producing shrimp and other more expensive species for foreign markets. The markets are large and have grown with increasing affluence in some industrialized countries. For instance, Japan's consumption of shrimp increased 50 percent between 1980 and 1988, and 90 percent of the supply was imported. In the United States, imports accounted for the entire 66 percent increase in shrimp consumption from 1981 to 1990. Shrimp exports to the United States, Japan, and Europe brought Ecuador $400 million in foreign exchange in 1990, and were exceeded only by petroleum as a source of hard currency. Other developing countries, particularly China, Thailand, Indonesia, India, and Taiwan, have invested heavily in shrimp aquaculture.

The dramatic expansion of aquaculture has come at considerable environmental cost and faces daunting limitations in the future. For instance, between 1976 and 1990, Ecuadorean shrimp farmers cleared more than 420 square miles of mangrove forests to build shrimp ponds. In doing so, the farmers reduced a complex, productive ecosystem to a monoculture, and at the same time eliminated sources of food and building materials for thousands of coastal people, who were plunged into a cash economy based on supplying the farmers with the small shrimp they needed for their farms.

Aquaculture can have other environmental effects. In intensive farming of shrimp or salmon, farmers apply food pellets, generally manufactured from such oily fishes as menhaden and herring. Inevitably, much of the food is not eaten, but falls to the bottom. Studies of salmon farms in Scotland suggest that only one-quarter of the nutrients from pellets are eaten by the penned salmon, while the other three-quarters settles to the bottom. Unless strong currents carry this uneaten food away, it decomposes with fecal matter and other organic material, robbing bottom waters of oxygen and releasing toxic hydrogen sulfide.

Producing feed for aquaculture is a big industry, converting one kind of fish into a more marketable kind of fish. Feed for aquaculture operations is the fastest growing sector of the global feed market, which includes the sizable poultry market, and rose from about 1.9 million tons in 1980 to more than 3.9 million tons in 1988. Since it takes about five pounds of fish to produce one pound of fish meal, the amount of fish cooked, dried, and ground up to be fed to shrimp and salmon is considerable. The International Fish Meal Manufacturers Association in London estimates that fish meal production will decline by about five percent by the end of the century because catches are declining.

Farmers who seek to reduce their costs by crowding large numbers of animals into ponds or pens also must mix a variety of additives into their feed, including vitamins, trace elements, amino acids, medications, and even appetite stimulants. Sometimes, even sophisticated feed cannot prevent diseases that can spread quickly through crowded monocultures. Each year, Norway loses about 20 percent of its salmon production to disease. Farmers have fought viral diseases with applications of antibiotics, some of which have been banned for use in the culture of other animals. In Norway, use of antibiotics by salmon farmers rose from 19 tons in 1985 to 530 tons in 1987—more than the combined use of antibiotics in human and veterinary medicine in Norway. As on land, marine viruses develop strains resistant to antibiotics, posing a threat to cultured and wild populations.

Aquaculture can also jeopardize the diversity of wild stocks of fish. Already, the genetic heritage of salmon reared in Norwegian pens has been reduced, from salmon strains coming from 40 different rivers to only one or two strains. In some Norwegian rivers, salmon that have escaped from pens outnumber wild salmon, and Canadian researchers suggest that such escapees can eliminate the genetic distinction among native runs of salmon within four generations. In 1989, more than one million salmon escaped from farms in Norway and bred with wild fish, possibly transmitting the changed spawning and feeding behavior that has been observed in pen-reared salmon.

Unintentional introduction of exotic species also has often accompanied intentional introduction for aquaculture or stocking in the wild. Leading all other candidates in this category is the Japanese oyster, which has been introduced on the West Coast of the United States and in Atlantic waters to meet the great demand for oyster meat. The problems that have arisen are not so much with the oysters themselves, but with what has accompanied them, including diseases and organisms such as the oyster drill, against which native species cannot defend themselves. Unintentionally introduced with Japanese oysters into European waters in 1966, the fast-growing brown seaweed *Sargassum muticum* has spread from France as far as the Skagerrak coast of Norway. Wherever it has floated ashore, this seaweed has established extensive colonies in far deeper waters and has grown far larger than in Japan. Scientists are concerned that this large, canopy-forming seaweed will disrupt, then dominate some hard-bottom communities of the North Atlantic and Mediterranean. For now, they can only observe this unintended but massive experiment.

Like many other modern manufacturing activities, aquaculture would benefit from a cradle-to-grave analysis of materials and energy used and produced, beginning with sources of food and ending with products and waste. As we discussed in chapter 7, aquaculture could play an important role in processing the growing amounts of sewage that will otherwise be discharged by the growing number of coastal communities around the world. Yet, the fragmented way in which we view coastal resources and pollution has prevented meaningful consideration of this holistic approach to producing food and handling wastes.

FISHING IN OTHER CULTURES

Fishermen of the industrialized countries represent less than ten percent of the world's fishermen. Most fishermen fish from small boats with simple gear close to shore, using far less energy than their counterparts in the industrialized world, and they land nearly half of the world's catch of fish for human consumption. In southeast Asia, small-scale fishermen provide three-quarters of the animal protein.

Unlike the tuna purse seiners of the eastern tropical Pacific or the trawlers off Alaska or New England, small-scale fishermen must rely upon personal and community knowledge rather than advanced technology to locate their prey. Because they are not mobile, they are out of luck if they fish out their prey. By contrast, a factory trawler on the Grand Banks can move to the Bering Sea in search of groundfish.

In many traditional societies, regulations and laws as we know them are absent. In their place there often operates a pattern of active and passive restraints that are a part of, not apart from, the everyday life and history of the community. These restraints, which are passed from generation to generation, have evolved over time, no doubt in response to hard lessons. The rules that control fishing in these traditional societies are not published in books, but are part of the social fabric that sustains a community confronted with scarce resources.

Rather than an expression of individualism, fishing may be a communal activity. In Polynesia, the fisherman who catches more than the community needs, or who does not share a particularly valuable catch such as a tuna or a turtle, comes under great scorn and may be ostracized. In the James Bay region of Canada, Cree Indians are well enough equipped to catch as much fish as they would like. Rather than overharvesting, however, Cree fishermen catch only what the community needs, and leave some areas as refuges for fish.

Other measures in traditional societies reduce the demand for rarer finfish and shellfish or vulnerable nearshore resources. On the island nation of Kiribati in the South Pacific, giant clams benefit from prohibitions on their consumption that are explained as a way to avoid balding. Pregnant women are told to avoid flounder, which may give a baby a malformed face. As odd as these measures may seem, they effectively enabled sustained harvesting of nearshore fish and shellfish in many parts of the globe for thousands of years. By relying on a far greater variety of seafoods than we in the United States can even imagine, these traditional communities reduced their reliance upon any one species.

From the Indians of the Pacific Northwest to the island peoples of the South Pacific, communities often have held tenure over animals, plants, and habitats as part of their ancestral inheritance. This inheritance often included lagoons and marine waters in a seamless unity with community lands. Within its boundaries, a community controlled access by kin and outsiders. For some communities, rocks, channels, or reefs were manifestations of ancestral beings, whose presence was taken so seriously that the death of village men responsible for their protection might be explained by violation of these areas by foreign fishermen.

Exporting technology and approaches to fisheries that had

demonstrably failed in their own waters, foreign aid agencies of the industrialized countries have introduced cash economies and industrial fishing practices, such as large-scale trawling and gill nets, into many of these societies with little regard for social and cultural disruption. As fishermen begin to fish for cash rather than for meeting the subsistence needs of their community, the community's interest in restricting catches to sustainable levels often is overcome by the desire for more cash, and fishing itself becomes individualistic. With few exceptions, aid agencies have not accompanied funds for expanding the capabilities of fishing fleets with funds for putting management programs in place.

In northern Java, fishermen used to capture scallops by using small encircling nets deployed from sail-powered canoes. Seven years after the introduction of motorized vessels that could pull dredges, the scallop fishery collapsed and has never recovered. On Tokelau in the South Pacific, abundance of giant clams declined after the introduction of freezers on the island by a foreign aid agency.

Small-scale fishermen may also be victimized by the efficiency of larger, industrialized fishing fleets operating off their shores. In the 1980s, large shrimp trawlers began working closer and closer to shore in Indonesia. Like shrimp trawlers in many other parts of the world, these trawlers captured and discarded many tons of young finfish, upon which the small-scale coastal fishermen relied. Bitterness over the waste and loss of their livelihood prompted the coastal fishermen to confront the trawlers in several violent incidents. The government of Indonesia reacted by banning trawling from the western two-thirds of the country. Other countries have reacted by placing artificial reefs in nearshore waters as barricades to the operation of these trawlers. Elsewhere, fleets of large foreign trawlers still ravage nearshore fisheries within sight of small-scale fishermen.

As coastal populations grow along with demand for fresh fish and for foreign exchange, the nearshore fisheries that had supported small-scale fishermen for centuries are collapsing in many countries. These are losses not only of natural resources, but of a tremendous investment of human ingenuity in learning to live with the sea.

Vanishing Fish, Vanishing Cultures

In the United States and many other countries, fishermen's working lives are dominated by uncertainty: Not only does their catch fluctuate from tow to tow and year to year, but the rise and fall of the prices they receive for their catch are beyond their control. Their way of making a living is a gamble that may cost them not just their vessels, but their lives. Indeed, there is no occupation so hazardous as that of a commercial fisherman, with a death rate seven times the national average.

Although risk-taking makes for heroes in some societies, fishermen are more often viewed as a breed apart, reckless and unpredictable. Spending long hours, even days and weeks at sea, fishermen cannot participate in family and community life as others can. Their long absences make them strangers to their communities and place tremendous strains on their families. As much as they long for home when they are at sea, they find landside society strange, even hostile to their view of the world. Increasingly affluent neighbors scorn their dirty, smelly business and sometimes accuse them of plundering the seas. Fishermen respond by insisting they have to be conservationists in order to continue to make a living—a claim weakened by the race for the fish.

Quite often, fishermen struggle unsuccessfully with the business end of their lives. As a result, wives often manage the affairs not just of the family, but of the business, and build whatever ties they can with the community. Even so, fishermen have lost their fortunes for centuries to people whose business is not fishing so much as it is capital.

At one time, for instance, the fishermen of Marblehead, Massachusetts, thrived on the wealth created from fishing and farming in different seasons. But merchants from Boston and Salem gradually gained control of fishermen's boats and homes by selling supplies at high prices and offering easy credit. By the 18th century, most of the fishermen of Marblehead were landless peons.

Whether a fisherman is operating a 100-foot shrimp trawler off Brownsville, Texas, or a sail-powered canoe in the South Pacific, fishing is more than a way to make a living. It is a way of life that deserves more respect and careful study than it has received. As important as our understanding of fish population and behavior is, effective conservation measures depend upon an understanding of the values and desires of fishermen. But government fisheries agencies have only tentatively engaged the social sciences in developing an understanding of this side of the conservation equation. For the most part, managing fishermen has been left to a political process that often is satisfied with meeting the short-term needs of angry constituents and deferring difficult decisions to some future day.

In developed countries, understanding the motivations and desires of a widening range of interests is growing in importance. For instance, marine recreational fishing, which claims more than 17 million participants, has become a powerful force in fisheries in the United States. From California to New York and Florida, recreational fishermen have sought game status for striped bass, red snapper, and other prized species. In other fisheries, bitter battles between commercial and recreational fishermen for shares in the catch have increased overall quotas, as government agencies have attempted to meet the demands of both interests.

While our numbers were few, fish populations were large and coastal environments intact and healthy, fishing for a living enjoyed all the freedom that abundance can provide. But the coasts are much more crowded now, and the natural systems that once produced abundance have been weakened through years of human use.

These losses have narrowed our freedom to pursue the romantic tradition of fishing as if there were no tomorrow and no limits. It is time to put aside the conceit of the Dutch lawyer Hugo Grotius, who wrote in 1609: "Everyone admits that if a great many persons hunt on the land or fish in a river, the forest is easily exhausted of wild animals and the river of fish, but such a contingency is impossible in the case of the sea."

9

~~~~~~~~

Population

Nos numerus sumus et fruges consumere nati.
We are just statistics, born to consume the
fruits of the Earth.

HORACE (65–8 B.C.)

In 1998, the earth will be asked to serve six billion consumers. For the first 99.9 percent of human history, the earth had to share its wealth with ten million people at most. But advances in health and agriculture in the 18th century largely eliminated the checks on population growth that had kept people and the environment in a rough balance. Since then, people have grown in number by more than five billion and have become a major force in transforming the environment, not just locally but globally as well, on land, in the air, and in the oceans.

Growing population accounts for only a part of people's transforming influence. Depending upon their level of wealth and available technology, people and countries consume more or less resources, creating more or less waste, and doing more or less damage to the environment. With the Industrial Revolution in the 18th century, economic activity in a handful of countries began consuming resources and generating wastes at phenomenal rates, even as new industrial technology made it possible to generate unprecedented wealth and welfare.

Discussing population growth and economic development has provoked strong debate for as long. On one side are those who believe that the rate of growth in human numbers inevitably will exceed the rate of growth in resources. On the other side are those who believe that human progress and ingenuity will overcome apparent limitations in resources, including those for the disposal of waste. The means for reducing the rate of population growth also inspire debate between those who insist that economic development alone reduces birth rates and those who do not. In the United States, proposals to manage growth provoke bitter controversy, partly because they touch upon how people use their land or where they work and how they get there.

Until recently, the role of population and consumption in the loss and degradation of coastal and marine resources received scant attention. This is partly because these losses seldom have been caused by the kind of catastrophic events such as oil spills that rise above the din of news reports about wars, urban violence, and political scandal. Rather, coastal wetlands, productive fisheries, and the health of ocean waters have suffered from millions of seemingly minor, often indirect insults, from dredging wetlands acre by acre to dumping used motor oil quart by quart. Ignorance about these subtler, smaller injuries is pervasive.

As important as it is to analyze the dynamics of population growth and consumption, identifying steps to reduce environmental losses requires a very different approach. At its core, this task must seek to understand the aspirations and motivations of people in the United States and abroad, whose values and circumstances often are very different from our own. We cannot afford to confuse the mathematical calculations of population dynamics and consumption patterns with the people who animate those dynamics and patterns.

POPULATION, CONSUMPTION, AND POLLUTION

Before 500 marine conservationists in a darkened lecture hall at the Smithsonian's Museum of Natural History, Jonathan Cole of the Institute of Ecosystem Studies in New York displayed a graph of points gently sloping upward from left to right. The points represented population and river pollution. Cole and his colleagues had combed dozens of reports to estimate the number of people living in watersheds surrounding 42 of the world's major rivers. They had also compiled records on the levels of nitrate that these rivers pour into coastal waters. As the sloping line of points indicated, more populated watersheds release greater amounts of nitrates to coastal waters than less populated watersheds. Human sewage or air pollution from burning fossil fuels alone could account for all of the nitrates, which can feed damaging algal blooms.

The study also found that as the number of people living in the watersheds of the Rhine River in Germany and the Mississippi River in the United States increased, so too did the amount of nitrate disgorged into coastal waters. Cole estimated that the anticipated doubling of the human population in the next 40 years would lead to a 55 percent increase in the amount of human-generated nitrates entering the oceans from rivers.

Regional and global impacts from population growth and consumption have a local side as well. In the last half century, the number of family and vacation homes has increased tenfold in the watershed surrounding Waquoit Bay on the southern shore of Cape Cod. Together with the homes came septic tanks, which cleanse sewage of bacteria but not nitrogen. Carried by groundwater, the nitrogen has been entering the bay as nitrate for decades.

Research conducted by scientists at the Waquoit Bay National Estuarine Research Reserve has drawn links between the increase in septic tanks, as well as recreational boats with or without functioning latrines, and a catastrophic decline in water quality. Since 1950, eelgrass beds in the nitrogen-enriched waters of the bay have declined by 80 percent, while mats of algae now cover large parts of the bay bottom. In these areas, the number of fish species has fallen by more than half. In 1987, 1988, and 1990, thousands of dead fish and shellfish lined the bay shoreline as the result of fish kills caused by algal blooms. Since 1950, the number of shell fishermen making a living from the bay has fallen from 80 to one. And the losses have not ended: Another 30 years will pass before the last of the nitrate that already has infiltrated groundwater from septic tanks reaches Waquoit Bay.

Growing population and consumption mean not only increased pollution, but also greater demands upon renewable resources, from coastal forests to fisheries. In trying to meet the needs of growing populations, the governments of many developing countries have sought to take advantage of markets in developed countries by encouraging the conversion of mangrove forests into everything from charcoal and paper pulp to shrimp ponds. The world's industrialized and traditional fishing fleets have already reached if not exceeded the level of catch that most fisheries can sustain. In many developing countries, where fish offer the principal source of animal protein, collapsed fisheries raise the risk of malnutrition among growing coastal populations.

Population growth and levels of consumption play different roles in the contribution of different countries to the decline of marine resources. Recently, attention has turned from the explosive growth in the number of people in many developing countries to the disproportionate consumption of natural resources that continues to fuel economic growth in the developed countries. Although past population growth and patterns of consumption and of economic development already have set us on a course that will cause yet more degradation and loss of marine fisheries, wetlands, and waters, the degree of damage and the potential at least for slowing current trends still is very much a matter for everyone's attention.

POPULATION TRENDS AND DISTRIBUTION

For most of history, disease and food shortages held death rates high even as the human desire to bear many children sustained high birth rates. The world's population did not reach 100 million until 500 B.C., and took another 700 years to double. But with the beginning of the Industrial Revolution in the late 18th century, the balance between nature and human culture shifted dramatically. Improvements in food supply, increased use of vaccination, and declines in diseases such as smallpox greatly reduced death rates in Europe especially, while high birth rates continued.

In 1825, the human population reached one billion for the first time. By 1925, the human population had doubled again, to two billion, adding as many people in 100 years as had been added in the previous 500,000 years. This record was surpassed in 1975, when human numbers doubled yet again to four billion, adding more people in 50 years than had been added in all of human history.

Although the rate of population growth is likely to slow in coming years, the world's population will continue to grow in absolute numbers. Just how many more people there will be will depend in gross terms on birth rates and death rates and the coming-to-age of the extraordinarily large number of children born in the last several decades. Based on reasonable assumptions about these rates, the Population Reference Bureau in Washington, D.C., estimates that world population will reach 7 billion by 2010 and nearly 8.4 billion in 2025, twice the number of people alive 50 years before.

Population growth rates will vary greatly from country to country. Population growth rates in developing countries are six times those in developed countries. Populations are declining in several eastern European countries, including Russia and the Ukraine. In contrast, the populations of other countries are growing at very rapid rates. Many countries in western Asia, including Iraq, Syria, Oman, Jordan, and Kuwait, are growing at annual rates two to three times greater than the world average of 1.6 percent. Some island countries in Oceania and the Indian Ocean, which are particularly vulnerable to population growth, will double their population in less than 25 years.

If the human population were evenly distributed over the earth's land surface, about 109 people would inhabit every square mile. As it is, population density of individual countries in 1993 ranged from two people per square mile in the western Sahara to more than 15,000 in Singapore. On average, 327 people inhabited each square mile of China, the world's most populous country at 1.2 billion people. Population density in the United States, the world's third most populous country at 258 million people in 1993, was just 73 people per square mile.

Ignoring political boundaries reveals other patterns of distribution. Most of the world's large cities, with their concentrated populations, are in coastal areas. By 1998, 18 of the 25 largest cities in the world will be coastal. In the United States, seven of the largest ten cities are in coastal counties, including New York City. The Big Apple may stagger many people with its crowds and highrises, but its population density is only about 11,400 people per square mile. Consider Lagos, Nigeria, where 143,000 people squeeze into a square mile.

Population density in coastal cities reflects broader features of population distribution and trends. Depending upon who is counting and what boundaries are drawn, one-half to three-quarters of the world's population lives near the coasts. Like the world at large, more than one-half of the U.S. population lives in coastal areas, covering just 11 percent of the country's land area outside of Alaska. In 1988, coastal population density stood about five times above the national average.

The continued migration of people to the coasts is as troubling. The Population Reference Bureau has reported, for instance, that the population of U.S. coastal counties increased by 43 percent in the last thirty years alone—a rate greater than that for the country generally. The population of Dade County, Florida, where the city of Miami is located, grew from 5,000 people in 1900 to almost two million by 1990 as northern retirees and immigrants from the Caribbean and Central America streamed into this fragile coastal area.

As inland agricultural soils are destroyed by drought, salinization from irrigation water, and excessive tillage, millions flee to coastal areas of many countries hoping to eke out a living from the sea. Expecting to find a better standard of living in coastal cities, nearly 100 million Chinese are believed to have moved from interior areas of the country to the coast. The population of Shanghai alone increased 13 percent between 1982 and 1990, and two-thirds of that growth was due to migration from the countryside.

In moving to the coasts, people bring not only their need for jobs and housing, but also their wastes. Generally, by importing food from areas far from the coast, cities also import large amounts of nutrients into coastal areas. Eventually, these nutrients enter streams and coastal waters as human sewage or food wastes. In most areas of the world, cities cannot keep up with the flood of sewage, and coastal waters are showing it.

CONSUMPTION: THE GREAT EQUALIZER

With some cause, people in developing countries become impatient with lectures on population growth. For many of them, any

discussion of unsustainable population growth must be accompanied by a discussion of disproportionate consumption in developed countries. In their lifetimes, Americans will have 30 times
greater impact on the earth's environment than will their counterparts in India. On average, Americans and other members of the
developed world consume 1000 calories more food each day than
their counterparts in the developing world. Americans also consume 15 times as much paper and 10 times as much steel as the
4.3 billion people who know little of the consumer goods we take
for granted.

Although developed countries account for only 20 percent of
the world's population, they consume 70 percent of the world's
energy. In 1992, the average American consumed enough energy
to drive an automobile twice around the equator—nearly five
times as much energy as is used yearly by the average individual
in other parts of the world. In 1987, sources in the United States
released four times as much greenhouse gas into the atmosphere
as India did, although the population of the United States is just
one-quarter the size of India's population. The list goes on and on.

Besides ethical issues of equitable use of natural resources, from
clean air to oil, the disparity in consumption patterns raises issues
about the future well-being of the billions of people to come and
about how many billions more people the earth will be serving in
the next century. Many people believe that economic growth fuels
a demographic transition from high population growth rates to
low population growth rates. In the first stage, counterbalancing
death rates and birth rates hold a country's population stable. In
the second stage, economic growth allows improvements in social
welfare that reduce death rates. A country then experiences rapid
population growth. In the third stage, birth rates begin to decline
until they match death rates and a country's population stabilizes.

The prevailing model of economic development, upon which
the future stabilization of population in some developing countries may be staked, requires technological advances and fossil
fuels in staggering amounts. In the 19th century, much of the
extraordinary growth in the economies of such countries as
England depended upon coal, especially after European forests
were exhausted in feeding the fires that powered the Industrial

Revolution. Other industrializing countries followed England's path. From 18 million tons in 1800, worldwide coal use increased to 700 million tons in 1900.

Now, in hot pursuit of the economic growth that its growing population demands, China is following the same course that proved so successful for its capitalist rivals. Burning damaging high-sulfur coal with abandon, China has maintained an economic growth rate four to five times higher than the industrial democracies. Still, per capita income in China is just one-sixth that in Mexico, and less than two percent of the per capita income of U.S. residents.

If China were to achieve what has never been achieved in the past—maintaining its current level of economic growth, while stopping population growth completely—it could reach Mexico's per capita income in two decades. To do so, China would consume one billion tons more coal in the year 2010 than the entire world consumed in 1990. The resulting releases of carbon dioxide would offset the best efforts of developed countries to reduce their releases to 1990 levels, as many governments committed to do at the Earth Summit in June 1992. As remote as the possibility may seem at first, the growth of China's economy along traditional lines of industrialization and fossil fuel use looms as a major contributor to global warming and sea-level rise, not to mention further deterioration of China's environment, including its coastal waters.

Although their contribution to carbon dioxide emissions is less significant, dozens of other developing countries are pursuing a path similar to China's and our own path of development. Until the Arab oil embargoes of the mid-1970s, economic growth in the industrialized countries also was closely linked to energy use. But the sudden rise in oil prices forced changes in energy use that government policy had encouraged but never achieved. Indeed, in the 1980s, improvements in efficiency allowed industrialized economies to grow without increased energy use.

Developed countries enjoyed a standard of living and national incomes that allowed them to invest in efficiency. By contrast, many developing countries have little surplus income for investment. Many developing countries already are very heavily in debt, and international lending institutions have devoted little funding for efficiency or renewable energy sources, particularly compared with the enormous levels of funding for dams and other large power-generating projects. The result is that the economic future of most developing countries will likely follow old patterns and require increased use of fossil fuels, with all of the attendant problems.

Surely there are alternatives, we might say. The Chinese must see that burning coal to speed economic growth is creating the worst urban air pollution conditions anywhere in the world, and is also adding to the risk of global warming and sea-level rise. But the conventional alternatives are hardly satisfying either. Consider the Three Gorges Dam, planned to be the world's largest. If built as designed, the dam will produce billions of kilowatts of electrical power without burning a single pound of coal. But the dam will require the relocation of more than one million people and will flood more than 100 miles of the Yangtze River. In doing so, it will wreak havoc with the chemistry of downstream and coastal waters and will threaten a number of endangered species, including Chinese sturgeon, finless porpoise, and the Yangtze River dolphin, the most endangered of all river dolphins.

If we find this alternative unacceptable, what then? Shall we in the industrial nations forget the dams we have raised, the coal and oil we continue to burn, the luxury of choice that we accept as if there were no other way? Is it too much for the developing world to ask that the Chinese be allowed to double their per capita use of energy, even if that means that they will remain poor beyond belief, and that in 2020, they will release more than three times as much carbon dioxide as they do today?

We have not confronted these larger questions of equity because it is much easier to regard the entire matter as technical. By focusing on scientific uncertainties and the difficulties involved in reforming the consumer way of life that we have fashioned, we can suspend any judgment about foreclosing choices for others by consuming as we do.

TRENDS IN CONSUMPTION

Thirty years ago, government leaders were well aware of the need to provide for growing numbers of people. At the time, when worldwide fish harvests were less than half their levels today, the leaders of the Free World spoke of feeding hundreds of millions of people with fish protein concentrate from untapped fishery resources. They little imagined the success in hunting down remaining fish stocks that followed in the next few decades. Nor did they envision that most of the increased harvests would enter international trade and move from developing countries, seemingly starved more for cash than for food, to developed countries whose affluence could support expending extraordinary amounts of fuel to capture, process, and ship fish and shellfish from around the world.

Between 1950 and 1989, the world's harvest of saltwater and freshwater fish grew from 24 tons to 110 million tons. By 1992, however, worldwide population growth and lower fish catches had decreased per capita seafood supplies from 43 pounds in 1989 to 39 pounds. For Americans, who consumed 50 percent more fish in 1992 than they did in 1950, the decline in fish catches often meant higher prices. In the last 40 years, U.S. seafood prices have risen 40 percent, as the nation's fishermen have deployed ever more sophisticated and expensive means of catching or raising fish, and importers have located foreign sources.

For many people in the developing world, the period has brought less seafood as fish populations have collapsed under relentless pursuit by increasing numbers of more and more sophisticated fishermen. Furthermore, demand for seafood in wealthier countries such as Japan and the United States has diverted increasing amounts of fish away from domestic markets in developing countries. The volume of seafood exports from developing to developed countries has grown by 75 percent just since 1981.

For Americans, who consume more beef and chicken than fish, the rise in prices caused by declines in the abundance of fish is an irritant. For many people in the developing world, however, it is a question of whether they will consume any animal protein at all. Worldwide, more fish is consumed than beef and chicken combined. In many developing countries, particularly in the tropics, seafood supplies 60 to 100 percent of the animal protein in people's diet.

The consequences of growing population and depleted or exported supplies of fish will aggravate the gap between need and supply. For instance, at about 90 pounds, annual per capita fish consumption in the Philippines is higher than in any other country in Southeast Asia. Already, the demand for fish has reduced groundfish populations 30 percent below their levels in 1947. By the year 2000, 83 million Filipinos will require more than 3 million tons of seafood, at least one million tons more than is caught now. By 2020, the population of the Philippines will have grown to 128 million people, whose traditional needs for fish will require more than 4 million tons, or more than twice the amount consumed by twice as many Americans in 1992.

The situation in the Philippines will be common among countries who enjoy very few alternatives for animal protein. Even if one accepts the optimistic assumption of the United Nations that world fish harvests, including aquaculture production, can consistently reach 110 million tons in the future, population growth between now and the year 2020 will reduce the per capita supply of seafood from 39 pounds to just 25 pounds. Put differently, to provide as much fish per person as in the early 1990s will require a harvest of 175 million tons of fish, not just 110 million tons.

Besides the direct losses caused by overfishing nearshore fisheries, gathering the necessities of life can indirectly damage coastal and ocean resources. In India and many other developing countries, where the muscles of humans and cattle are the principal sources of power, growing numbers of city residents have obtained fuel for cooking by felling trees in the surrounding countryside at rates well beyond the capacity of the forests to regenerate themselves. The area of forest around Bombay, for instance, declined by more than one-third between the mid-1970s and the mid-1980s alone. As in the case of so many overexploited populations of wildlife, wetlands, and other productive assets, this drastic decline occurred almost imperceptibly.

Worldwide, croplands have slowly increased sixfold in the last two centuries, at the expense of forests, wetlands, and grasslands. In many areas, this transformation of the countryside has dramatically shifted soil from land to rivers and the sea. According to one estimate, the rivers of Asia and Oceania now carry five times the amount of sediment they did before the felling of forests for fuel and farmland began centuries ago. In Vietnam, where wood serves as a common fuel for cooking, heating, and construction, deforestation has increased the amount of soil carried by the Red River into Haiphong Harbor so much that government authorities have considered moving the harbor altogether.

Continued population growth also will drive continued growth in the volume of water withdrawn from streams and rivers for agriculture, industry, and household uses. Nearly three-fourths of all water withdrawals worldwide are devoted to irrigating agricultural fields. Between 1900 and 1985, the amount of water withdrawn for irrigation alone increased fivefold. Three-fourths of this growth occurred in the last 30 years, as the amount of irrigated land more than doubled. The World Bank expects that by the year 2030 domestic water use in developing countries also will increase sixfold, primarily in crowded cities. This pattern of growing urban use of water will mirror similar growth in developed countries such as the United States, where cities are willing to pay higher prices to capture a greater share of water.

Around the world, demands for water set state against state, nation against nation, and region against region, as all people seek to maintain or increase their share of a shared resource. The health and viability of fish and wildlife, as well as of coastal eco-systems downstream, generally are lost from consideration in this competition for a scarce but undervalued resource.

Finally, whatever minor miracles may be achieved in feeding millions more, even greater miracles and investments will be required to deal with the wastes of even the simplest styles of life. Where sewage is treated before discharge, more and more money will have to be spent treating more and more sewage just to prevent further deterioration of coastal waters from pathogens and nutrients.

CARRYING CAPACITY

Nearly two centuries ago, in an environment of increasingly crowded cities and growing pollution, the English economist and minister Thomas Malthus wrote *An Essay on the Principle of Population As It Affects the Future Improvement of Society*. The Reverend Malthus's argument was simple in its basic elements: "Population, when unchecked, increases in geometrical ratio. Subsistence increases only in an arithmetical ratio. A slight acquaintance with numbers will show the immensity of the first power in comparison of the second."

From that observation flowed one of the principal schools of thought on population and the environment, for Malthus predicted that human numbers would soon overcome nature's ability to support them. (Curiously, Malthus opposed contraception of any kind.) Some of Malthus's contemporaries, including Benjamin Franklin, argued just as vigorously that human ingenuity would not only overcome nature's limitations but would usher in a period of unprecedented tranquility and wealth.

The argument whether humans will finally do themselves in by proliferating continues to this day. On the one side are those for whom free trade, economic growth, and the capacity of people to find substitutes for depleted resources offer not only hope but great opportunity. In this view, the pattern was established by the Industrial Revolution when, among other things, exhaustion of Europe's forests provoked not decline but innovation that ushered in a transition to coal and other fossil fuels and an unprecedented rise in social welfare.

Similarly, the industrialized countries overcame the rise in oil prices during the 1970s and 1980s through innovation that increased efficiency. Likewise, although Atlantic cod and haddock are no longer common items in the frozen-food case, new fishing gear and international trade have introduced deep-sea orange roughy from Australia, not to mention crab-flavored "Sea Legs" fashioned from the pulverized flesh of Alaskan groundfish.

Certainly, the technological advances of the last fifty years are impressive, from walking on the moon to eradicating smallpox, once the most deadly killer of all. For some apologists for growth, the prospect of more people simply promises more minds to solve the problems people create and to seize the riches the earth and human ingenuity together can produce.

These arguments are more easily made with a full stomach. Just as population and resources are unevenly distributed around the globe, so too is technology concentrated in a relatively few, developed countries. Generally, the industrial growth that is fueling economic advances in developing countries depends upon technology that often is outdated, if not outlawed in developed countries because of the harm it causes. Unfortunately, it is the developing countries that are most in need of technological advances that efficiently use resources such as energy. And if the past is any indication, they will pay a dear price and incur a large debt for the privilege. In the end, technology may well join other factors in masking the depletion of resources in developed countries, while diverting funding and other resources from carrying out the basics that can improve life in developing countries.

Finally, although the world economy has grown 20-fold in this century and population has merely tripled, wealth is not widespread. As Paul Hawken relates in *The Ecology of Commerce,* the phenomenal economic growth from 1960 to 1980 did not close the income gap between rich and poor nations. Rather, that period saw a doubling of the gap. By 1990, in comparison with the world's richest, the world's poorest had become twice as poor as they had been in 1960. Like prosperity, hardship has been unevenly distributed. Unlike prosperity, it has become a much more common condition during the explosive growth of the last two centuries.

In its 1992 report on world development, the World Bank did not predict dramatic breakthroughs in economic development and population stabilization in the next 40 years. Rather, the bank assumed that the future would be more or less like the past, with the economies of developing countries growing somewhat faster than the economies of developed countries. In their understated way, the bank's analysts concluded that without dramatic reductions in pollution, this increased economic activity will lead to "appalling environmental pollution and damage." Who loses what and how much will be determined by a race between generating wealth to correct environmental damage and damaging the environment in the process.

For those who share the calculated gloom of Reverend Malthus, technological innovation and free trade simply delay the day of final reckoning by masking the loss of resources and environmental quality that traditional business and governmental practices and policies inevitably cause. In this view, which relies heavily on ecology and physics, the earth is finite, and human activity—from filling wetlands for agriculture to discharging increasing amounts of sewage and industrial waste—is overwhelming the earth's carrying capacity.

Often, an analogy is drawn between the eutrophication of a pond and the consequences of exponential growth in human population and consumption. As related by ecologist D.T. Suzuki, a population of algae that doubled every 24 hours might seem to present no threat as it gradually covered a pond's surface. Indeed, most of us would notice the growth of the algae only the day before the plants completely covered the pond, at which point they would begin to die, decompose, and deplete it of its oxygen. Our failure to perceive the threat arises from the nature of exponential growth: The day before, the algae still covered only half the pond. In the final 24-hour doubling, they covered the other half. Suzuki points out that even if technology enabled the pond-stewards to double the oxygen in the pond, they would only postpone by 12 hours the inevitable end of oxygen in the pond.

When we in the developed world exhaust one pond, affluence enables us to move to the next pond. Reducing the Chesapeake Bay's once-abundant fishery for oysters to one percent of its size at the turn of the century has brought little outcry, partly because oyster-lovers have been able to continue buying oysters. Who would detect the difference among oysters from the Chesapeake Bay or from North Carolina or the panhandle of Florida or the bayous of Louisiana? And for those who bridle at the increasing cost of oysters from anywhere, alternatives abound, from chicken to analogue seafood products.

The next pond may not be nearby, but thousands of miles away. In 1992, there was less than a one in five chance that the shrimp you consumed was captured in U.S. waters. Much more likely, that shrimp came from ponds that were once mangrove forests or wetlands in Southeast Asia.

In earlier times, when the need to provide food and shelter was less acute in developing countries, the export of shrimp and other raw products to the developed world might not have been of much practical consequence. But times have changed. Exhausting someone else's pond affects far more people now.

10

≈≈≈≈

Future Seas

Have we fallen into a mesmerized state that
makes us accept as inevitable that which is
inferior or detrimental, as though having lost
the will or the vision to demand that which
is good?

RACHEL CARSON,
Silent Spring

As we approach the end of the 20th century, concern about the
abundance, diversity, and quality of life on earth mounts. Besides
the gloom that feeds on predictions of global warming, of future
losses in fisheries, wetlands, water quality, and jobs, people feel
less and less a part of broader communities and find division
rather than communion among themselves. Increasingly, people
seem cynical about the institutions that they press to improve their
lives. The gap between rich and poor has never been greater, nor
affected so many.

So complex a situation seems to demand an equally complex
response. Indeed, increasingly elaborate regulatory schemes, treaties, economic arrangements, and computerized models offer a
convenient haven for business-as-usual. But intricate solutions
generally are not as flexible and adaptable as the manifold uncertainty of the future demands. Furthermore, complex solutions
generated by centralized government generally preempt discussion
and agreement on the values and goals that motivate individuals
and communities. Centralized solutions also often ignore

important differences among regions, states, and communities that can help or hinder efforts to solve environmental problems. Narrow-interest politics and short-term gain regularly triumph.

In this concluding chapter, we propose a way of thinking about the future and developing the ability to make the most of what will likely be many challenging situations. Recognizing underlying trends and barriers to change can increase the odds of making a transition to sustainable ways of life in communities of people that no longer destroy but instead work to restore ocean and coastal resources.

In the long run, it is people's attitudes, prejudices, and perspectives that will influence the future of the oceans, and of all of us who depend upon them. Already, economists, conservationists, business owners, community leaders, villagers, and citizens are fashioning tools for fostering the kind of changes that address the challenges confronting us and for seizing the opportunities arising from a reassessment of our place on the planet. But all the technical fixes in the world will accomplish little without a fundamental transformation in attitudes—from thoughtlessly taking all we can get toward thoughtfully living with what we need.

THINKING ABOUT THE FUTURE

In his 1966 book *The Challenge of the Seven Seas,* Senator Claiborne Pell of Rhode Island described his vision of the oceans in the year 1996. Besides envisioning people swimming underwater with artificial gills and communicating with dolphins, Senator Pell foresaw enormous aquaculture operations offshore, nuclear-powered submarine tankers, and underwater resorts. In Senator Pell's view of the oceans in 1996, an International Sea Patrol enforced fisheries management measures and monitored the ocean environment, including the waters around a new nation called Sidonia, which had been built atop a submerged mountain on the high seas.

Like other predictions of the future, Senator Pell's vision for 1996 reflects the attitudes of the times, which viewed the oceans as a new frontier for development. Several years later, the report of the congressionally chartered Stratton Commission shared Senator Pell's optimism about the potential for technology to tap vast resources in the sea. Among other things, the commission predicted that total annual fish landings from the oceans could mount to more than 550 million tons, six times current best estimates. These riches, it was thought, could help meet the growing global demand for food.

In recent years, these visions of future riches from the seas have faded. In developing a long-term strategy for the Rosenstiel School of Marine and Atmospheric Science at the University of Miami, Bruce R. Rosendahl recently described his own vision of the oceans in the year 2043. Instead of harvesting enormous quantities of fish from the wild, people produce food fish entirely by aquaculture. Yellowfin tuna, raised in large offshore pens, no longer are canned but are consumed as sashimi or sushi by the wealthy. Near cities, bays are so crowded that boaters are allocated boating days based on their registration numbers. Enormous hurricanes repeatedly strike the Atlantic and Gulf coasts, as well as Caribbean islands, devastating state economies. Together with payments for hurricane damage, payments for a devastating earthquake in the San Francisco Bay area destroy the insurance industry.

At United Nations meetings on high seas fisheries in July 1993, the environmental newsletter *ECO* published a fantasy of the oceans in the year 2052 that reflects a rueful view that life in the oceans will give way completely to industrialization. In a fictional interview, a chief executive officer boasts that his multinational corporation, called Living Marine Resources International, holds complete rights to the management of entire ecosystems and produces jellyfish protein packaged as fish. Tapping the tourist market, the multinational also breeds docile whales that people pay money to watch as a way of retaining "the illusion that the seas are some vast, wild frontier." Traditional fishing has become a matter for museum exhibits, and the corporation refurbishes commercial fishing boats to take tourists to former fishing grounds such as Georges Bank off New England.

In the last two decades, creating scenarios for the oceans of the future has become a more deliberate activity, aimed at providing decision makers with assessments of the consequences of their decisions. You may recall the computerized modeling of the Chesapeake Bay described in chapter 1. Other regional coastal programs have also developed computerized models to guide decision making. For instance, state and federal agencies have developed a computerized model for Long Island Sound that describes the actions and costs involved in reducing the flow of nutrients into the sound. Among other things, this model shows that because of projected population growth and changes in land use and transportation, currently planned reductions in nutrient discharges from sewage treatment plants will not be enough. The modeling has allowed state legislators, federal agency officials, town council members, and citizens to assess how much they are willing to spend to clean up the sound.

On a grander scale, the Regional Seas Programme for the Mediterranean, sponsored by the United Nations Environment Programme since 1975, has developed an elaborate model of change in the Mediterranean Sea and its watershed to the years 2000 and 2025. *The Blue Plan*, as it is called, describes the interaction between the physical environment of the Mediterranean and agriculture, industry, energy use, tourism, transportation, and urbanization. The model projects three scenarios based on these interactions and on a range of assumptions about the world economy, growth and movement of the human population in the region, national economic development strategies, land management, and environmental programs. The model does not take into account social, political, and cultural trends, which will play an increasing role in this region. Prepared as a guide for government policy and investment, *The Blue Plan* warns that the quality of life and the environment in the Mediterranean will deteriorate rapidly by 2025, even if current trends do not worsen. As so often happens, funding that governments and multilateral banks are willing to devote to reversing these trends falls far short of the need.

No other scenario of the future has provoked as much interest and controversy as that generated by a computer model called World3 and described in the landmark study *The Limits to Growth*. Partly in response to heavy criticism of the initial report, the team of scientists at the Massachusetts Institute of Technology gathered new information, refined their computerized model, and published their results in *Beyond the Limits* just before the Earth Summit in 1992.

Unlike other computer models, which are linear, World3

includes mechanisms for adjusting a scenario in response to feed-back from interacting factors such as population growth, industri-alization, government responses, and technological developments. For instance, as the demand for food increases with growing num-bers of people, more money is diverted to transporting food at the expense of improving or maintaining infrastructure such as sew-age treatment plants and factories. In turn, public health and eco-nomic productivity may suffer, further undermining the quality of life, especially for the poor.

As in their earlier report, the authors of *Beyond the Limits* are decidedly pessimistic about the future if current trends continue. Already, renewable resources, from forests to fish, are declining, wastes and pollutants are accumulating, and greater amounts of money, labor, and energy must be devoted to exploiting ever rarer resources and trying to duplicate services such as flood control and sewage treatment that natural systems once supplied for free. The authors do offer hope for stabilizing a deteriorating environ-mental and social situation in the next century, provided that gov-ernments, businesses, and individuals take dramatic action soon.

Whether one agrees or disagrees with the specific findings of this or that model, thinking about the future in such a structured fashion fosters a careful and explicit examination of assumptions about the future, including key trends such as population growth and movement, and economic and technological development. Modeling exercises also can reveal the ways in which trends in one area, such as population or economic growth, can affect the demand for fish, for instance, and ultimately the long-term abun-dance of fish populations. Still, models may overlook important variables or exclude them because they are too expensive to mea-sure. For this and other reasons, models are valuable more for analyzing processes and relationships than for soothsaying about specifics.

Although computer-generated scenarios demand time, money and data, they and less intensive, systematic thinking about the future can help overcome one of the chief threats to the oceans now and in the future: the tyranny of small decisions. Borrowing a phrase that economist Alfred E. Kahn first applied to market economics in 1966, ecologist William E. Odum described the con-cept's application to the environment:

The insidious quality of small decision effects is probably best exemplified by water and air pollution problems. Few cases of cultural eutrophication of lakes are the result of intentional and rational choice. Instead, lakes gradually become more and more eutrophic through the cumulative effects of small decisions: the addition of increasing numbers of domestic sewage and industrial outfalls along with increasing run-off from more and more housing developments, highways, and agricultural fields.

Odum called upon policymakers and academic scientists to adopt a "holistic view of the world around us." The same recommendation applies to those most concerned about fisheries, or coastal environmental quality, or transportation, or community development, or teenage pregnancy, or national economic policy. Overcoming the tyranny of small decisions requires not only evaluating the cumulative effects of many small, similar decisions, but also taking a view much broader than any one of these issues.

Models also encourage developing testable theories about how the world works. These theories, which generally are not expressed, have a profound effect on day-to-day decisions by government officials and private citizens. Generally, our ways of viewing the world go unexamined and become embedded as common knowledge or prejudice. Time and monitoring of the variables in models based on our theories can reveal weaknesses and gaps in our view of the way the world works.

One need not be the head of a federal agency or a legislator to gain from even a little bit of structured thinking about daily life. Thinking how energy or water flows into and out of your house or relating your current and future use of gasoline to the release of carbon dioxide or nitrogen oxide that later fall on pavement or water bodies are just several examples of how to think holistically about the future at a personal level.

Similarly, we are all linked to other people in our own communities and to people in other communities. Examining your dependence upon communities upstream and downstream from your own community can reveal important relationships. Where is the sewage from your household discharged? Is your trash shipped to another community? How will converting your farmland to a residential subdivision affect the streams and coastal waters in your watershed? What food, energy, or services are produced in your community? What is currently imported from other communities, states, or countries?

Like other challenges to ocean conservation, thinking about the future and our relationships to those around us needs the attention of government agencies, businesses, and individual citizens. No one group has the answers or the tools to move us toward restoring the wealth of coastal and ocean resources. In the future, oceans and coasts will be more crowded, greater demands will be placed on marine waters and resources, and change will happen more quickly. We could afford to live on automatic pilot in the past. We must be more deliberate and thoughtful in the future.

KEY TRENDS FOR THE OCEANS

Setting the stage for future action can begin with describing trends or themes that are likely to shape future conditions and decisions. Some of these trends, such as population growth, already have gained momentum that we may slow but not reverse in the next several decades. Time itself and the mismatch between human institutions and natural processes form a second group of factors. A third group reflects common patterns of short-term thinking, which we can change. Likewise, we can acknowledge and try to compensate for our lack of knowledge about how the world works and our tendency to make only small changes when large changes are required.

Foremost among major trends is a continued growth in the number of people and their consumption of natural resources, from air and water to fish and forests. Even if birth rates fall much faster than they have in recent decades, the momentum from past population growth insures that the number of people will continue growing for decades to come. Supporting even the simplest of lifestyles will require converting more land from forests and wetlands into farmlands and cities, and will generate greater amounts of human, agricultural, and industrial wastes. Much of this waste will likely be discharged untreated into rivers and coastal waters. In coastal areas, population growth and related problems will intensify if the attractive life of cities continues to encourage people to move from inland communities to the coasts.

Like population growth, global warming and sea-level rise are trends already in motion. Even if the world's nations do reduce their carbon dioxide emissions to 1990 levels, as they committed to do at the Earth Summit in 1992, global warming has already begun. Most analysts believe that the only questions now are how much warmer the climate will get and what the secondary effects will be, such as sea-level rise in specific areas. These issues can seem abstract as long as you are not among the tens of millions of people living in low-lying coastal and delta areas.

The gap between consumption levels in developed and developing countries will tend to be a source of uncertainty and political anarchy around the world, reducing the ability for individuals, businesses, and governments to reverse wasteful use of resources and damage to the environment. During the last 40 years, the world economy expanded fivefold, while the number of people in absolute poverty and the gap between rich and poor doubled. Although they have fueled their own growth by relying on developing countries for expanding consumer markets and for raw materials such as shrimp and oil, most developed countries and multinational corporations have committed to only token efforts to reduce the gap.

Those of us who enjoy the benefits of cheap oil and consumer goods manufactured at low cost have not greatly changed our own consumption patterns. As long as these trends continue, the ranks of the poor and undernourished will continue to grow, and with their growth will come the familiar faces of war, crime, and political instability.

We assume that the industrialized countries will do little to close the gap—for example, by increasing direct funding for foreign assistance or by reducing barriers to the import of goods such as sugar cane and cloth from developing countries. Therefore, developing countries will continue to generate cash for meeting the needs of their people by selling off natural resources such as fish and offshore oil deposits or risking irreversible degradation of productive habitats such as wetlands and coral reefs through pollution.

FOSTERING SHORT-TERM THINKING

Other trends have to do with established patterns of thought and behavior that people and their institutions are unlikely to change, however desirable change might be. For instance, we expect that industrialized countries will continue to foster unsustainable use of coastal and ocean resources at home and abroad by promoting short-term thinking through foreign assistance programs, international trade rules, and bank lending.

Traditional foreign aid programs and lending by the World Bank and other multilateral banks reflect a model of economic and social development that measures welfare principally in short-term monetary values and assumes that a world of finite resources can support continued economic growth on a scale that will preserve the amenities that the industrialized countries enjoy while increasing the welfare of the developing world. Although recent administrations have embraced the theme of sustainable development that the 1992 Earth Summit sought to promote, they have held tenaciously to the goal of economic growth as the primary criterion of sound policy both domestically and abroad. As in the past, U.S. policy has assumed that we can grow our way toward a healthy future.

Among the consequences of this strategic error will be continued promotion and support for unsustainable use of natural resources and increasingly frequent collapses of fisheries and other coastal and ocean resources, including coral reefs, wetlands, and water quality. Pressed to rescue species whose depletion reflects the collapse of economically valuable resources and the resulting loss of jobs, government will find itself fighting rearguard actions and being blamed for the casualties of economic growth.

In economic terms alone, fish, wildlife, wetlands, coral reefs, mangrove forests, and other parts of the coastal mosaic will continue to decline in economic worth compared with other coastal economic activities, such as manufacturing and service industries. Partly as a result of this trend, traditional harvesting of coastal resources, especially fish and shellfish, will become even more economically marginal than it already is. However significant their role in building the economies of many communities and nations, fish, wetlands, reefs, and coastal forests together with the people who have depended upon them for their livelihood are likely to become the victims of new economic endeavors that are largely independent of natural resources.

This trend will be aggravated by the limitations of conventional methods of valuing natural resources. Quick breakthroughs are unlikely from new accounting methods that would make it possible to determine the full value of ocean and coastal resources rather than their current market value. Decades of research and experimentation have yet to yield methods that have practical meaning in the marketplace or are accepted by regulators. However technically correct future methods of determining nonmarket worth might be, their application will be fiercely resisted by those who have enjoyed benefits or avoided costs that current accounting methods do not recognize. Continued controversy among economists about how to assign nonmarket worth will aid those who oppose calculating environmental costs and benefits. Even measures such as individual transferable quotas in fisheries, which are widely recognized by economists and fisheries managers as being valuable tools in conserving resources, will meet resistance from fishermen and environmentalists who, for very different reasons, champion freedom of the seas.

Finally, new technology and schemes for exploiting fisheries and other living and nonliving resources will be adopted without meaningful evaluation of their long-term ecological, social, and economic effects. As Paul Gray, the president of the Massachusetts Institute of Technology, suggested in 1989, "New technology will be applied in ways that transcend the intentions and purposes of its creators, and new technology will reveal consequences that were not anticipated." Measuring success in terms of short-term benefits will obscure ways in which new technology may be used without undermining long-term benefits.

OTHER OBSTACLES

Of several other major hurdles for the future, time is the most formidable in several ways. First, detecting and analyzing environmental problems and fashioning effective responses normally lag well behind the actual loss of environmental quality. This delay in recognizing problems has many origins, ranging from denial to a general lack of environmental monitoring.

Where large governmental or private organizations become involved in problem solving, organizational inertia often delays action, as agencies or groups try to balance addressing environmental problems with maintaining a competitive edge against other agencies and organizations. Although the need to manage coastal land and water areas as a unit has been discussed for decades, integrating the management responsibilities and capabilities of different agencies has met with effective resistance within bureaucracies in administrative agencies, legislative bodies, and public interest groups.

Even when there is some agreement on how to address a problem, implementation of a proposed solution may consume many years. From large public works projects such as sewage treatment plants to satellite sensors and research vessels, planning and actual completion regularly take decades of work. Furthermore, the benefits of action may not be apparent for years. The moratorium on fishing for striped bass in Maryland waters did not lead to a recovery for five years. In the meantime, commercial fishermen had to move into other fisheries or leave fishing entirely. Other people who benefited from the fishery, including fish retailers and consumers, also did without.

Delays in implementing proposed solutions or in enjoying the benefits of change present easy targets for opponents. Instead of focusing upon how the negative effects of change might be managed while the transition to a healthier way of living and doing business is underway, short-term job loss or changes in business practices are used as reasons not to change. The costs of depleting fisheries or polluting rivers and bays are then diffused and forgotten, and no one is held accountable.

The gap between available funds and the costs of implementation presents another common obstacle to moving toward new ways of living and doing business. Already, government agencies, legislatures, businesses, and public interest groups have produced mountains of plans and strategies for changing the world. Generally, the projected costs of implementing these plans and strategies grossly exceed available funds. This is partly because identifying or developing means for securing funds generally receives much less attention and effort than does identifying or developing lists of things to spend funds on. Also, government and taxpayers have traditionally assumed the costs of environmental damage to habitats and wildlife that private interests have caused. These interests resist efforts to reduce the need for taxpayer funding of environmental programs by requiring that those who enjoy the benefits of using coastal waters for pollutant discharge or beaches for resort development also pay the costs.

Although we are very much a part of the natural world, our systems of values generally are quite independent of the natural world, focused instead upon the relations between people. In Western society, for instance, fairness is a widely accepted standard of behavior. Generally, we believe in splitting the difference between conflicting points of view. Although this approach maintains a kind of civil order, it also produces incremental measures when the situation may demand more dramatic action. The continued decline in most U.S. commercial fisheries is testimony to the phenomenon. Splitting the difference between preserving and developing a tract of wetlands when 90 percent of an area's wetlands have already been filled may seem fair, but ultimately must lead to exhaustion of that resource.

Although we have greatly improved our ability to make predictions, uncertainty will remain a common feature of decision making by individuals, businesses, and government agencies. Uses of natural resources that we had determined were sustainable often have proven unsustainable. Surprises such as the discovery of a hole in the ozone layer, the emergence of resistant strains of bacteria and viruses, the collapse of the Soviet Union, and emergence of new technology and products, from crack cocaine to cyberspace, will no doubt be followed by other surprises in the future.

Finally, as we transform entire watersheds, substituting the uniform for the diverse, and spend more time in artificial environments such as shopping malls, suburban subdivisions, automobiles, and computer simulations of the oceans, we transform ourselves. We learn to value convenience in place of the rich, unpredictable diversity of the natural world and of local products and customs.

POSITIVE TRENDS

Other trends offer hope that the trends just described will not dominate the future. Chief among these is the growth in public awareness and concern about the oceans that has marked the last several decades. Fed initially by dismay over the decline of great whales and dolphins, public concern about the oceans has gradually expanded to include the more visible forms of pollution, such as marine debris and oil spills, and most recently the exploitation of fish and shellfish. The principal challenge of the future will be to further expand awareness so that people become concerned with less visible but more pervasive forms of pollution, such as sewage, and the links between land activities and the oceans, including transportation and land use. This expansion will empower far more people to make a direct contribution to the future, both by altering their own activities and by participating in local decision making about the use of wetlands or the disposal of waste.

The explosive growth in telecommunications, from computerized networks to Cable News Network, has made it possible to identify and respond to disturbing trends or destructive activities sooner than in the past. Now, people around the world can learn about the violation of environmental standards in the construction of a major dam in India by reading on a computer network a report filed by an activist at the dam site. Thousands of letters may now pour into government offices in response to electronic bulletins that were unthinkable just five years ago.

Other technological developments promise to increase the ability of governments to ensure compliance with conservation measures even on the high seas. By requiring the installation of satellite transponders in the early 1990s, enforcement agencies in the United States were able to track drift-net vessels hundreds of miles at sea and to determine whether the vessels were complying with the United Nations resolution on phasing out the use of drift nets. Now, two consulting groups in Seattle are trying to develop the means for tracking outlaw vessels, which do not carry transponders, by using satellite-based instruments to monitor the plumes of exhaust from their engines.

As increasingly sophisticated satellite instruments become available, monitoring areas or features as large as entire continents, oceans, and layers in the atmosphere or as small as acres of coastal wetlands or submerged reefs will become more common and, in some cases, more affordable. Rather than having to develop their own monitoring programs, the governments of developing countries and local governments elsewhere will be able to rely upon satellite information for surveying their jurisdictions. Similar developments in computer technology, including the graphic display of different kinds of information, will increase the ability of scientists to study entire systems and of decisionmakers to assess the effects of their actions.

Government officials and others are increasingly aware of the benefits of managing activities on the basis of ecological principles and are beginning to realize that the complexity and unpredictability of human society and ecosystems demands conservative approaches to exploitation of habitats and living marine resources. Similarly, the new field of ecological economics has provoked a needed discussion of the limits to current accounting for ocean and coastal resources, and has reintroduced some of the broader philosophical considerations that animated early economic thought. Already, the World Bank has taken some steps to evaluate its projects from a broader perspective that includes impacts on ecological, social, and cultural values.

THE ROLE OF VALUES

In an article introducing a special issue of *Scientific American* devoted to "managing planet Earth," Harvard's William C. Clark argued that two key questions now confront us: What kind of planet do we want? What kind of planet can we get?

> What kind of planet we want is ultimately a question of values. How much species diversity should be maintained in the world? Should the size or the growth rate of the human population be curtailed to protect the global environment? How much climatic change is acceptable? How much poverty? Should the deep ocean be considered an option for hazardous-waste disposal?

> Science can illuminate these issues but cannot resolve them. The
> choice of answers is ours to make and our grandchildren's to live with.
> Because different people live in different circumstances and have differ-
> ent values, individual choices can be expected to vary enormously.

Rarely are the challenges confronting us put in such bare terms.
Generally, discussions of environmental and social issues avoid
exploring and assessing underlying values, and convert controversy about values into technical issues that presume technical
answers, often where none exist.

A renewal of discussions about what people want their future
to look like is one of the most promising steps toward reversing
the trends and overcoming the obstacles described above. Unlike
discussions of technical matters in which few are trained to participate, broad participation can help insure that community values
have practical meaning and can serve as a means for bringing
communities together around common goals. Furthermore, clear
statements of principles provide a guide for choosing a course of
action and for evaluating a course of action after it is taken.

Developing a broader view of ocean and coastal resources is
important for another very practical reason: As long as the only
widely accepted way to measure the worth of wetlands or fish is
the price they fetch in the marketplace, mangrove forests, fish,
reefs, clean waters, and other resources of the coasts and oceans
will be threatened, as will the well-being of the communities of
people who depend upon them. The transformation of wetlands,
reefs, and beaches and the decline in fisheries, from blue whales
to red snapper, all reflect the consequences of relying solely on
current market value. Without a deliberate recognition that we
are excluding values because we cannot measure them, we will
continue to lose much of what we treasure most. We cannot await
a revolution in accounting practices and in the behavior of capital
markets before better valuing the importance of natural areas
and resources.

As a final reason for seeking a broader discussion of values, the
intensity and diversity of people's demands places coastal areas at
tremendous risk of being nickled-and-dimed to no end. Even if
explicit decisions about priorities prove to be beyond reach, good
can come from increasing awareness among people that their uses

of these areas will affect other people's uses. Now, there is little such awareness.

In this regard, we should promote more comprehensive views over narrower ones. Now, government programs, environmental and business organizations, and scientific research emphasize specialization that fosters continued dissolution of links among communities and environments. The conservation of coastal areas will require not only treating land and sea as a unit but also appreciating the relationships among economic, demographic, and social trends in these areas.

In particular, we need to develop our moral imagination, our ability to put ourselves in another person's shoes, whether that is the CEO of a multinational corporation, or a Bangladeshi whose village could be flooded by the next monsoon or by a slowly rising sea level. We need to listen more than we speak, especially when we engage someone with whom we disagree. Without moral imagination, we cannot hope to carry on the kind of dialogue that will lead us back to a sense of common good, which is required if we are not to wander futilely.

We should seek and expect abundance and diversity, rather than merely trying to avoid endangerment. The prevailing pattern—that of slowing the exploitation of fisheries, wetlands, and other resources only when they become rare—continues to lead us toward a future of remnant populations and impoverished habitats. By maintaining or restoring abundant populations and productive habitats, we will gain opportunities for moving beyond crisis management.

Expanding our notions of fairness and equity is central to closing the consumption gap that threatens not only more than one billion poor people, but the future habitability of the planet and quality of life for all people. Our goal should be to promote fairness and equity across communities and across generations. As trendsetters for much of the world, which now can observe our lifestyles on television 24 hours a day, those of us in the industrialized countries bear a special responsibility and enjoy a special opportunity. Through even modest changes in lifestyle, we in the developed countries can demonstrate commitment to a wiser set of values, under which we derive enjoyment and meaning as much from how we spend our time as from how we spend our money.

With less emphasis on material consumption in our own lives, we can better encourage worldwide adoption of values that are environmentally sound.

We urge a greater emphasis on valuing and exploring the diversity of human cultures. Conservation of the diversity of life in the seas cannot be achieved without this emphasis. Continuing to separate people from the earth they inhabit and use is as futile as continuing to separate conservation of the land from conservation of the sea. The study of the diversity of life in the seas has yielded extraordinary insights into the ecological processes that produce abundance or decline. Developing a greater appreciation for the ecology of human societies will offer equally valuable insights.

Although restoration should not become an excuse for risking further damage, we must reverse decline wherever we can. In many instances, the means of restoration are fairly straightforward, although political controversy and social adjustment can be challenging. In the 1995 budget proposal for the U.S. Department of the Interior, Secretary Bruce Babbit proposed to begin dismantling two dams on Washington State's Elwha River, where tens of thousands of sturgeon, trout, and 100-pound salmon once spawned. Built earlier this century, these two dams provided cheap power to aluminum mills and pulp and paper mills. Now, there are other sources of electricity and the times of abundant water, money, and fisheries are long gone. Removal of the dams could help move the region toward a more sustainable way of doing business. According to a report for the Elwha S'Klallam tribe, any losses in jobs in the mills would be offset by the creation of nearly 500 jobs, including 160 full-time commercial fishing jobs.

PROMOTING CHANGE

Just as the problems, threats, and trends that make up the ocean challenge arise from decisions by individual people, businesses, and governments, so too does the challenge to change apply at many different levels. For too long, we have failed to ask ourselves the question: Who can best promote the changes that the future demands? The long-standing formula calls for policy debates, legislative hearings, legislative compromises, unfunded national and international standards, fundraising campaigns, and more meetings. This pattern results not simply because policy makers inside and outside of government pursue the well-worn path of seeking uniform solutions at the highest possible level. The pattern arises as well because individuals and communities prefer to remove local or regional controversy and problems to higher levels of government, thereby avoiding the difficult decisions that will actually affect people's lives.

There is no clearer example of this pattern than the collapse of many coastal fisheries and the decline of fishing fleets. Although the regional fishery management councils established by the Magnuson Fishery Conservation and Management Act arguably were meant to promote greater compliance with fishery regulations through involvement of regulated fishermen, they often have served as a means for fishermen to avoid managing themselves and, at the same time, for communities to continue marginalizing commercial fishermen by arguing that the health of the commercial fishing industry is a federal matter. It is as if the Magnuson Act prohibited fishermen themselves from taking steps to maintain and restore public fishery resources, which they benefit from using. Now, decisions affecting fishermen are taken up at levels farther and farther removed from the water, and a vicious cycle of avoiding responsibility and castigating government has set in.

One opportunity in this common situation is to redirect the time, money, and effort that continually fuels policy debates in Washington toward fostering a desire and capability for self-determination and cooperation among fishermen and coastal communities. At a minimum, federal and state governments should not mask the depletion of resources through subsidies or other mechanisms; national standards and management programs should insure that the interests of the general public in the conservation of fisheries are met.

These changes should not be confused with fostering stewardship and a sense of the common good among those who are the ultimate agents of conservation. Instead of thinking principally in terms of mandates, standards, and directives, national and state governments should perhaps think of themselves more as facilitators and supporters of change at the local level. This does not mean simply providing local governments with funds and advice.

Higher levels of government must also insure that the broader, long-term concerns of society are not sacrificed to the gain of private local interests. In the end, however, no one should harbor the illusion that government at any level can compel change in most situations. The task is subtler and demands the involvement of less formal measures such as education and community discussion.

We can greatly improve our ability to maintain and restore the productivity and diversity of marine and coastal areas also by insuring that, like the ecosystems that we depend upon, we change management measures in response to changed circumstance. Too often, laws are passed or decisions taken and forgotten until the problem they were meant to address or new, unanticipated problems reach crisis proportions. Most regulations, laws, programs, and actions that governments, businesses, and people take are based on a theory about how the world works. Paying attention to the way in which fish populations, water quality, or our communities respond to laws or actions can increase the effectiveness of what we do. Being able to track the effectiveness of our actions, however, will depend upon better and more thorough monitoring, not just of water quality and wildlife populations, but of the movement of people and changes in economic activity.

This continuing review and evaluation will be particularly important where uncertainty is great and the desire to await the results of further study jeopardizes taking any action at all. There is no contradiction between study and action, however much opponents of change may insist on the need for further study.

In evaluating adjustments to our ways of living and doing business, we should keep in mind that we can never do just one thing. Rather, our actions generally produce collateral benefits and costs. Thus, reducing gasoline consumption not only reduces dependence upon foreign sources of oil, but also reduces air pollution, the risk of oil spills, and runoff of oil and gasoline wastes into coastal waters. If removal of parking subsidies reduces gasoline consumption, taxpayers benefit as well. On the other hand, the transition to such a future would also generate some costs, from reduced revenues from gas taxes to temporary job loss in some industries.

Recognizing the limits of our capabilities, we should try to prevent pollution by reducing production of wastes to begin with. This applies to households and communities as well as to small businesses, government agencies, and multinational corporations. In most industrialized countries, the potential for such reductions is implicit in the high level of resource use and waste that our lifestyles and production processes encourage. Developing countries that are only now investing in manufacturing and municipal services, such as supplying electricity to industrial and domestic consumers, can leap over the inefficient technologies of most industrialized countries to more efficient technologies already available.

If ocean conservation emerges from its isolation, the opportunity for gaining strength through collaboration with other people and institutions will grow. Certainly, those interested in the conservation of coastal forests have much to offer those concerned with protecting coastal waters from runoff and anadromous fisheries from loss of spawning habitats. Similarly, the interests of those concerned about freshwater quality have much in common with those concerned with marine water quality. Learning to relate ocean concerns to the concerns of other interests will require broadening perspectives and valuing generalists more than has been the case in the past.

Similar opportunities exist among ocean professionals. Pooling the perspectives and interests of economists, community development specialists, anthropologists, fishery biologists, water quality specialists, and coastal planners, just to name a few, offers the potential for broadening the constituency for specific issues that now suffer from narrow support.

TOOLS FOR CHANGE

People around the world already have invested time and effort in developing principles and mechanisms for moving to a way of living and doing business that is friendlier to the world around us and to communities of people. For instance, a coalition of Asian nongovernmental organizations and others recently proposed that communities develop a balance sheet that shows their environmental and capital assets, as well as the flows of energy and material into and out of the community's households. This type of analysis can reveal the costs to a community from projects that deplete natural resources such as fisheries or forests for the benefit of a few, while undermining the long-term productivity of the community.

This type of analysis also can help communities identify ways in which they might redirect their time and money to more profitable and sustainable activities. Rather than using taxpayer money to attract large industry that does not use local resources, communities can enable local businesses to process raw materials into finished products that have greater value in the market than the community receives when it exports its resources to other communities for processing. Similarly, fostering the conservation of water and energy can lower the costs of households and businesses, enabling them to use their time and money on a variety of productive activities.

One last tool is regularly mentioned and regularly unfunded— education. Besides the widespread need to improve formal education, one of the most effective ways of encouraging discussion and assimilation of the values we mentioned above is through popular media. In the United States, the news media are the principal source of environmental information for three-quarters of the public. Elsewhere in the world, the potential offered by modern telecommunications is enormous: More than 450 million television sets and 55 million VCRs in developing countries offer means for reaching billions of people.

For more than a decade, Mexican television producer Miguel Sabido has been tapping the popularity of soap operas to promote public awareness about the benefits of family planning. Like Sabido, other TV producers around the world have been engaging large audiences with dramas that enliven otherwise abstract arguments about sex roles and fertility rates. Surveys have later found that these programs not only create interest and understanding, but also change behavior.

Moving from documentaries on natural history and environmental problems to the drama of people making decisions that affect oceans and coasts, as well as the people who depend upon them, may provoke the broad changes in attitudes and behavior that the future will demand. Until this human dimension of conservation is portrayed, the challenge of the future will remain abstract and impersonal and few people will draw any connection between their own lifestyle and the decline in quality of life that losses of fisheries, wetlands, and swimmable beaches impose.

Education should not stop with children or the general public. Elected officials, from U.S. senators and cabinet secretaries to town council members, often are responsible for a range of issues beyond their personal knowledge or experience. While expert advice about particular situations helps, continuing education has an equally important role to play. Seeing the big picture is as important as grasping the specifics of an immediate situation.

Other people whose decisions and activities affect coastal habitats and wildlife may assume they know more than they do. In recent years, the Old Woman Creek National Estuarine Research Reserve has sponsored workshops about wetlands for local realtors. These oversubscribed workshops have shown how many realtors were willing to learn about wetlands and to confront the many misperceptions about wetlands that they shared with the general public.

COASTAL COMMUNITIES

Just as watersheds define the physical relationship between land and sea, so too do communities define the relationship between people and the oceans. Learning to respect and support this relationship may be one of the most important contributions that national governments can make to the future of conservation. Already, communities are creating opportunities for this kind of partnership by recovering for themselves the responsibility and power that they had given to others.

Over a period of two years, more than 200 citizens in Puget Sound proposed, discussed, revised, and adopted 40 measures of the health of their community. In this intensely democratic process, citizens struggled to describe what future they would like to see in their region. Sustainable Seattle tried to capture the future as a whole rather than as a conglomeration of particular interests. For these citizens, a booming economy would not be enough, if the environment were being wasted, crime were rising, and infant birth weights continued to fall. They were convinced that one key to restoring their community was actively recognizing and probing the links among seemingly unrelated aspects of community life.

No measure of the community's future captured the imagination of these citizens more than the abundance of wild salmon in local streams. Revered by Native Americans as one link to the earth, Pacific salmon has been a source of pride for the people of the Northwest for many years. Unlike hatchery-raised salmon, wild salmon depend upon healthy streams for spawning and early growth. Degradation of water quality or the streambed, such as often is caused by development of surrounding lands, reduces successful salmon reproduction and eventually leads to a decline in the size of salmon runs.

Sustainable Seattle found that the salmon runs in the two local creeks they had chosen as indicators had declined steadily for at least the last 15 years. In their 1993 report to the community, Sustainable Seattle put the losses in a broader context. "Our careless stewardship of salmon—perhaps the most symbolically and economically important creature to share Puget Sound with us— is reflective of our attitude toward a variety of living systems, from neighborhoods to ecosystems."

Drawing support from national and international organizations as well as other local groups, Sustainable Seattle is just one of dozens of citizen groups that are not waiting for change to occur to them, but are launching themselves into an experiment with the future. In the end, they are attacking two of the gravest threats to oceans and coasts, to forests and wetlands, to children and healthy communities: indifference and isolation.

On the other side of the Pacific Ocean, in Bais Bay on the east coast of the Philippine island of Negros, residents in the village of Bindoy already have moved from studying to restoring their lands and waters. In the mid-1980s, collapsing fisheries and the obliteration of local mangrove forests and coral reefs convinced Wilson Vailoces to seek the help of Silliman University in reversing the decline. By 1993, after forming a voluntary group called Sea Watchers, Wilson and others from the village of Bindoy had planted more than 100,000 mangrove trees and had sunk more than 1,000 artificial reefs made of bamboo, tires, or concrete. The Sea Watchers did not stop with recreating habitat for fish, but convinced farmers to reduce their use of pesticides and to avoid tillage practices that send soil into coastal waters. Fifty members of Sea Watchers now patrol local waters to enforce restrictions on the use of dynamite, poison, and fine-mesh nets, leading to fines for hundreds and prison for a few.

No longer are the people of Bindoy simply exploiting their surroundings. They are rebuilding them. Their journey toward restoration of the environment that supports them began with the dream of Wilson Vailoces to build a future for his community.

It's a dream that can work again.

Further Reading

1: GREAT SHELLFISH BAY

Bay Journal, Vol. 1, No. 1, through Vol. 3, No. 10 (March 1991 to January–February 1994); published by Alliance for the Chesapeake Bay.

Capper, John, Garret Power, and Frank R. Shivers, Jr. *Chesapeake Waters: Pollution, Public Health, & Public Opinion, 1607–1972.* Tidewater Publishers, Centreville, Md., 1983, 201 pages.

Chesapeake Bay Program. *A Work in Progress: A Retrospective on the First Decade of the Chesapeake Bay Restoration.* Chesapeake Bay Program, Annapolis, Md., 1993, 44 pages.

Horton, Tom, and William M. Eichbaum. *Turning the Tide: Saving the Chesapeake Bay.* Island Press, Washington, D.C., 1991, 324 pages.

Lippson, Alice Jane, and Robert L. Lippson. *Life in the Chesapeake Bay.* The Johns Hopkins University Press, Baltimore, 1984, 229 pages.

Warner, William W. *Beautiful Swimmers: Watermen, Crabs, and the Chesapeake Bay.* Penguin Books, New York, 1976, 304 pages.

2: EXPLORATION

Acheson, James M. "Anthropology of Fishing." *Annual Review of Anthropology,* 1981, pages 275–316.

Drury, S.A. *A Guide to Remote Sensing: Interpreting Images of the Earth.* Oxford University Press, New York, 1990, 199 pages.

Holt, Sidney J., and Lee M. Talbot. *New Principles for the Conservation of Wild Living Resources.* The Wildlife Society, Washington, D.C., 1978, 33 pages.

Kaharl, Victoria A. *Water Baby: The Story of Alvin.* Oxford University Press, New York, 1990, 356 pages.

National Research Council. *Managing Troubled Waters: The Role of Marine Environmental Monitoring.* National Academy Press, Washington, D.C., 1990, 125 pages.

Schlee, Susan. *The Edge of an Unfamiliar World: A History of Oceanography.* E.P. Dutton, New York, 1973, 398 pages.

3: GLOBAL CHANGE

Edgerton, Lynne T. *The Rising Tide: Global Warming and World Sea Levels*. Island Press, Washington, D.C., 1991, 140 pages.

Firor, John. *The Changing Atmosphere: A Global Challenge*. Yale University Press, New Haven and London, 1990, 145 pages.

Glynn, P.W., Ed. *Global Ecological Consequences of the 1982–1983 El Niño-Southern Oscillation*. Elsevier, New York, 1990, 563 pages.

Houghton, Richard A., and George Woodwell. "Global Climatic Change." *Scientific American*, April 1989, pages 36–44.

Oceanus, Vol. 34, 1991 (Number 1: Marine Chemistry, Number 2: Physical Oceanography, Number 3: Biological Oceanography, Number 4: Marine Geology and Geophysics, Woods Hole Oceanographic Institution).

Schneider, Stephen H. *Global Warming: Are We Entering the Greenhouse Century?* Sierra Club Books, San Francisco, 1989, 317 pages.

4: LIFE IN THE SEAS

Elder, Danny, and John Pernetta, Eds. *The Random House Atlas of the Oceans*. Random House, New York, 1991, 200 pages.

Norse, Elliott A., Ed. *Global Marine Biological Diversity: A Strategy for Building Conservation into Decision Making*. Island Press, Washington, D.C., 1993, 383 pages.

Nybakken, James W. *Marine Biology: An Ecologist's Approach*. Harper and Row, 1988, 514 pages.

Thorne-Miller, Boyce, and Jon Catena. *The Living Ocean: Understanding and Protecting Marine Biodiversity*. Island Press, Washington, D.C., 1991, 180 pages.

Weber, Peter. "Reviving Coral Reefs," in *State of the World 1993*, Linda Starke, Ed. W.W. Norton, New York, 1993, pages 42–60.

5: ECONOMICS

Anderson, Terry L., and Donald R. Leal. *Free Market Environmentalism*. Westview Press, Boulder, Colo., 1991, 192 pages.

Clark, Colin W. "Bioeconomics of the Ocean." *BioScience*, Vol. 31, No. 3 (March 1981), pages 231–237.

Costanza, Robert, Ed. *Ecological Economics: The Science and Management of Sustainability*. Columbia University Press, New York, 1991, 525 pages.

Hodgson, Gregor, and John A. Dixon. *Logging Versus Fisheries and Tourism in Palawan: An Environmental and Economic Analysis*. East-West Policy Institute, Honolulu, 1988, 95 pages.

Meyer, Carrie A. "Environmental and Natural Resource Accounting:

Where to Begin?" *Issues in Development.* World Resources Institute, Washington, D.C., 1993, 20 pages.

Repetto, Robert. "Accounting for Environmental Assets." *Scientific American,* June 1992, pages 94–100.

6: COASTS

Culliton, Thomas J. *et al. 50 Years of Population Change Along the Nation's Coasts: 1960–2010.* National Oceanic and Atmospheric Administration, Rockville, Md., 1990, 41 pages.

Grenon, Michel, and Michel Batisse, Eds. *Futures for the Mediterranean Basin: The Blue Plan.* Oxford University Press, Cambridge, 1989, 279 pages.

Hinrichsen, Don. *Our Common Seas: Coasts in Crisis.* Earthscan Publications, London, 1990, 184 pages.

Stroud, Richard, Ed. *Stemming the Tide of Coastal Fish Habitat Loss.* National Coalition for Marine Conservation, Savannah, 1992, 258 pages.

United Nations Population Fund, World Conservation Union, and the International Planned Parenthood Federation. *People & the Planet. Life on the Margin.* Vol. 3, No. 1 (1994), 32 pages.

U.S. Department of the Interior. *The Impact of Federal Programs on Wetlands.* Vol. II, A Report to Congress by the Secretary of the Interior. Washington, D.C., March 1994, 397 pages.

7: POLLUTION

Joint Group of Experts on the Scientific Aspects of Marine Pollution. *The State of the Marine Environment.* UNEP Regional Seas Programme, 1990, 111 pages.

O'Connor, Thomas P. *Coastal Environmental Quality in the United States, 1990: Chemical Contamination in Sediment and Tissues.* National Oceanic and Atmospheric Administration, Rockville, Md. 1990, 34 pages.

Townsend, Richard, and Burr Heneman. *The Exxon Valdez Oil Spill: A Management Analysis.* Center for Marine Conservation, Washington, D.C., 1989, 239 pages with appendices.

U.S. Congress, Office of Technology Assessment. *Wastes in the Marine Environment,* OTA-O-334. U.S. Government Printing Office, Washington, D.C., April 1987, 312 pages.

Weber, Peter. *Abandoned Seas: Reversing the Decline of the Oceans.* Worldwatch Paper 116. Worldwatch Institute, Washington, D.C., 1993, 66 copies.

World Resources Institute. *World Resources: 1992–93.* World Resources Institute, Washington, 1992, 385 pages.

8: FISHERIES

Bartlett, Kim. *The Finest Kind: The Fishermen of Gloucester.* W.W. Norton, New York, 1977, 251 pages.

Bourne, Russell. *The View from Front Street.* W.W. Norton, New York, 1989, 282 pages.

Dewar, Margaret E. *Industry in Trouble: The Federal Government and the New England Fisheries.* Temple University Press, Philadelphia, 1983, 252 pages.

McGoodwin, James R. *Crisis in the World's Fisheries.* Stanford University Press, Stanford, Calif., 1990, 235 pages.

Ruddle, Kenneth, and R.E. Johannes, Eds. *The Traditional Knowledge and Management of Coastal Systems in Asia and the Pacific.* UNESCO, Jakarta, 1983, 311 pages.

U.N. Food and Agriculture Organization. *Marine Fisheries and the Law of the Sea: A Decade of Change.* FAO, Rome, 1993, 66 pages.

9: POPULATION

Brown, Lester R. "Analyzing the Demographic Trap," in *State of the World 1987.* Worldwatch Institute, Washington, D.C., 1987, pages 20–37.

Ehrlich, Paul, and Anne Ehrlich. *The Population Explosion.* Touchstone Books, New York, 1991, 320 pages.

Green, C.P. *The Environment and Population Growth: Decade for Action.* Population Reports, Series M, No. 10. Johns Hopkins University, Baltimore, 1992, 31 pages.

Hawken, Paul. *The Ecology of Commerce: A Declaration of Sustainability.* Harper Business, New York, 1993, 250 pages.

Kennedy, Paul. *Preparing for the Twenty-First Century.* Random House, New York, 1993, 428 pages.

Population Reference Bureau. *1994 World Population Data Sheet.* Population Reference Bureau, Washington, D.C. 1993.

United Nations Population Fund. *Population, Resources and the Environment: The Critical Challenges.* UNPFA, London, 1991, 154 pages.

10: FUTURE SEAS

Brown, Lester R. "A New Era Unfolds," in *State of the World 1993.* Linda Starke, Ed. W.W. Norton, New York, 1993, pages 3–21.

Clark, William C. "Managing Planet Earth." *Scientific American,* Vol. 261, No. 3 (September 1989), pages 47–54.

Silver, Cheryl Simon, and Ruth S. DeFries. *One Earth, One Future: Our Changing Global Environment.* National Academy Press, Washington, D.C., 1990, 196 pages.

Sustainable Seattle. *The Sustainable Seattle 1993 Indicators of Sustain-*

able Community. Sustainable Seattle, Seattle, Wash., 1993, 36 pages.

Van Dyke, Jon M., D. Zaelke, and G. Hewison. *Freedom for the Seas in the 21st Century.* Island Press, Washington, D.C., 1993, 504 pages.

Index

Page numbers in *italics* refer to captions.